LABYRINTH

An International Journal for Philosophy,
Value Theory and Sociocultural Hermeneutics

Printed ISSN 2410-4817
Online ISSN 1561-8927

Vol. 20, No. 1, Summer 2018

**METAPHYSICS, RELIGION, AND HERESY:
IN HONOR OF THE 80th ANNIVERSARY
OF FRANÇOIS LARUELLE (Part 2)**

Editor-in-Chief:
Prof. Dr. Yvanka B. Raynova

Managing Editor:
Dr. Susanne Moser

Advisory Board:

Prof. Dr. Seyla Benhabib (Boston), Prof. Dr. Debra Bergoffen (Fairfax), Prof. Dr. Peter Caws (Washington), Prof. Dr. Reinhold Esterbauer (Graz), Prof. Dr. Nancy Fraser (New York), Dr. Ludger Hagedorn (Vienna), Prof. Dr. Alison M. Jaggar (Boulder), Prof. Dr. Domenico Jervolino (Roma/Napoli), Prof. Dr. Andrzej M. Kaniowski (Łódź), Prof. Dr. François Laruelle (Paris), Prof. Dr. Hedwig Meyer Wilmes (Nijmegen), Prof. Dr. Herta Nagl-Docekal (Wien), Prof. Dr. Elit Nikolov (Sofia), Prof. Dr. Sonja Rinofner-Kreidl (Graz), Prof. Dr. Hans-Walter Ruckenbauer (Graz), Prof. Dr. Ronald E. Santoni (Granville), Prof. Dr. Anne-Françoise Schmid (Paris), Prof. Dr. Hans Rainer Sepp (Prague), Prof. Dr. Helmuth Vetter (Wien), Dr. Brigitte Weisshaupt (Zürich), Prof. Dr. Andrzej Wiercinski (Warsaw/Freiburg), Prof. Dr. Richard Wisser (Mainz)

Axia Academic Publishers

Bibliographische Information der Deutschen Nationalbibliothek:
Die Deutsche Nationalbibliothek verzeichnet diese Publikation in der Deutschen
Nationalbibliographie, detaillierte bibliographische Daten sind im Internet unter
http://dnb.dnb.de aufrufbar.

Die wissenschaftliche und redaktionelle Arbeit wurde von der Kulturabteilung
der Stadt Wien – Wissenschafts- und Forschungsförderung unterstützt.

*Labyrinth: An International Journal for Philosophy, Value Theory and
Sociocultural Hermeneutics* is a serial publication of the Institut für Axiologische
Forschungen / Institute for Axiological Research, Vienna – www.iaf.ac.at
For more information, please visit the Journal's homepage:
www.labyrinth.axiapublishers.com

© 2018 Axia Academic Publishers
Vienna
All Rights Reserved
Journal & Cover © 1999 Institut für Axiologische Forschungen
Printed in Germany

ISSN 2410-4817 / ISBN 978-3-903068-25-4

www.axiapublishers.com

METAPHYSICS, RELIGION, AND HERESY
In Honor of the 80th Anniversary of François Laruelle (Part 2)

Table of Contents

METAPHYSICS, RELIGION AND HERESY

Vincent Le (Burwood, VIC)
The Origins of Laruelle's Non-Philosophy in Ravaisson's Understanding
of Metaphysics ... 5

John M. Allison (Pittsburgh, PA)
Religious Pluralism within the Limits of Thought ... 23

Eleni Lorandou (Lancaster)
Non-philosophical mystique and the rehabilitation of heresis ... 51

Stanimir Panayotov (Sofia)
Non-Theurgy: Iamblichus and Laruelle ... 64

Ameen Mettawa (Madrid)
Non-Philosophy and the uninterpretable axiom ... 78

David Bremner (Paris)
Non-Standard Stainless: Laruelle, Inconsistency and Sense-impressions ... 89

Yvanka B. Raynova (Sofia/Vienne)
"L'âge de la non-philosophie": Martin Heidegger et François Laruelle ... 108

DISCUSSION

Karel Hlaváček (Prag)
Adorno und Habermas im Vergleich: Vom Säkularismus zum Postsäkularismus? ... 143

Susanne Moser (Vienna)
A personalist versus a rationalist theory of virtues ... 169

METAPHYSICS, RELIGION, AND HERESY

VINCENT LE (Burwood, VIC)

The Origins of Laruelle's Non-Philosophy in Ravaisson's Understanding of Metaphysics

---

Abstract

Laruelle's first book Phenomenon and Difference: An Essay on Ravaisson's Ontology *(1971) is unanimously overlooked as having little relevance to his later non-philosophy. On the contrary, this paper analyses Laruelle's dissertation and Ravaisson's writings to show how Ravaisson enables Laruelle to develop non-philosophy's three central ideas of decision, radical immanence, and cloning. Firstly, Laruelle inherits Ravaisson's critique of Platonism and anti-Platonism as dividing the unity of being between two terms, of which one alone is conflated with being to the detriment of the other as non-being. Moreover, Laruelle follows Ravaisson's third way of envisioning being as a radical immanence, which philosophy presupposes to constitute its dualisms by dividing being into opposed terms. Finally, Laruelle's cloning adheres to Ravaisson's eclectic method of expressing being's true immanence through his cohering of all philosophies, as well as disciplines like art and religion, into a single narrative of one and the same being's self-unfolding.*

Keywords: Laruelle, Ravaisson, non-philosophy, metaphysics, ontology

---

More than any other aspect of his oeuvre, Laruelle's untranslated dissertation and first published book, *Phenomenon and Difference: An Essay on Ravaisson's Ontology* (1971), is unanimously overlooked in Laruellian scholarship. This lack of attention is partly due to the fact that Laruelle's work on Ravaisson has yet to be translated into English. However, the fact that it has not been translated speaks to the implicit consensus that it is an idiosyncratic exception, which has little to do with Laruelle's subsequent development of a mature non-philosophy. Laruelle himself tacitly encourages this reading of his dissertation insofar as he never mentions Ravaisson again, and retroactively characterizes his non-philosophy as emerging out of his subsequent critiques of the philosophies of difference.

Finally, the dissertation is not only overlooked because of its perceived irrelevance to Laruelle's mature non-philosophical thought, but also because of its subject matter of Ravaisson. Whereas translations of Laruelle's writings on Badiou, Derrida, Deleuze, Nietzsche and Heidegger have either been published or are forthcoming due to the immense interest in these other thinkers, there is relatively little interest in Ravaisson. Ravaisson's whole corpus has yet to even be published in French, and his selected writings have only recently been translated into English (Ravaisson 2016). Where Ravaisson is mentioned, it is almost always as a historical footnote to Bergson's theory of habit.[1] So, what ultimately emerges out of the secondary scholarship on Laruelle is the absence of any detailed discussion of his first work on Ravaisson, which is due to its perceived irrelevance for comprehending his non-philosophical science of philosophy that interests most commentators.

Contrary to this dominant (non-)reading of his first work, this paper shall analyse both Laruelle's dissertation and Ravaisson's own writings to show how Ravaisson first enables Laruelle to develop non-philosophy's three central ideas of philosophy as decision, the Real as radical immanence, and cloning as the staging of a vision-in-One. Firstly, Laruelle inherits Ravaisson's critique of both Platonism and various anti-Platonisms as dividing the unity of being between two terms, of which one alone is conflated with all of being to the detriment of the other as mere appearance or non-being. Moreover, Laruelle follows Ravaisson's third way of envisioning being or the Real as an originary radical immanence, which all philosophies presuppose to constitute their various dualisms by dividing being into two opposed terms. Finally, Laruelle's ideas of cloning and modelisation adheres to Ravaisson's eclectic method of expressing being's true immanence through his cohering of the diversity of philosophies, as well as other disciplines like art and religion, into a single historical narrative of one and the same being's self-unfolding. By tracing how Laruelle discovers the notions of decision, radical immanence and cloning in Ravaisson's ontology, we will see how non-philosophy is still providing an answer to philosophy's own fundamental question of being conceived as the Real, even as it rejects all historical philosophies' ideas of being understood as decisions.

1. Non-Philosophy in a Nutshell: Decision, Immanence, Cloning

Over the course of the works composing what he terms the Philosophy II and III periods of his corpus, Laruelle argues that all philosophy is constituted by a "decision" that

---

[1] The almost exclusive reception of Ravaisson's thought through Bergson has led to a focus on the former's concept of habit. See Bergson 2017. As we shall see, Laruelle goes against this grain by focusing on Ravaisson's more metaphysical writings.

divides the unity of the Real by arbitrarily privileging a mere part of it as exhausting all of the Real to the detriment of the opposite term as mere non-being or illusion. In what we will see is an appropriation of Ravaisson's critique of Platonism, Laruelle gives as an example of philosophical decision Plato's "Greek" gesture of identifying being with an ideal unity to the detriment of the sensible world of becoming as mere appearance:

> Philosophy is a manner of thinking that reduces all phenomena to the combination of two parameters relative to each other: Unity and Scission, or Identity and Difference. The Greeks, our contemporaries, could never surpass this mixture, and it is this invariant that forms our tradition through its innumerable variations (Laruelle 1991, 249).[2]

Although this decision is arbitrary in the sense that it is not based on what the Real is actually like in its totality, but merely on what the philosopher decides reality to be, it gains its aura of validity from the philosopher's own sense of its self-sufficiency, what Laruelle calls "the principle of sufficient philosophy" (Laruelle 1989, 17).

Of course, Laruelle is not the first to critique Plato; the philosophers of difference like Nietzsche and Deleuze also attempted to overcome Platonism. If Laruelle's critique of Platonism still holds for these anti-Platonists, however, it is because their attempt to surpass Plato simply makes the inverse mistake of deciding that the sensible world of becoming, multiplicity and difference is alone real to the detriment of the ideal, representation and unity as mere illusions of thought. So, although the anti-Platonists are able to bestow a reality to the sensible world where Plato saw only appearance, they still fall into the same trap of *deciding* that it alone is real. Laruelle continues: "difference does not give us the One but rather the Dyad, which is an ontological concept or peripheral to ontology [where ontology denotes philosophical decision]" (Laruelle 1991, 23). Whether philosophers decide that the Real is an ideal unity or sensible difference, for Laruelle, both rest on an arbitrary decision that fails to account for the opposite term that they denigrate as non-being.

Laruelle's own non-philosophy is designed to avoid making such decisions by exposing how all philosophies presuppose a greater Real which is indifferent to the dualisms that philosophical decisions create. For Laruelle, all decisions presuppose a "radical immanence" or "One-in-person" that philosophy cuts up into two falsely opposed terms, of which only one is granted an ontological stature. In reality, however, both terms are equally real in that they are immanent to the Real as a One anterior to all oppositions. It is crucial to delimit Laruelle's notion of the One, what he also calls "unary," from the Neo-Platonic concept of the One, or what Laruelle distinguishes as the "greco-unitary": *"the One is especially not the Unity with which Greco-Western thought regularly confounded it.* I insist: from the

---

[2] All citations to French texts are my own translations unless otherwise stated.

Greeks to the thinkers of difference, one has put the One at the service of the synthesis of opposites. (...) This confusion is the foundation of unitary or authoritarian thought" (Laruelle 1989, 25). On the one hand, the Neo-Platonic One is predicated as an ideal unity which thereby excludes sensible becoming from its ontological midst. Conversely, the Laruellian One is simply the name for the immanence of *both* the falsely opposed ideal and sensible terms, which the Neo-Platonic One presupposes in order to separate itself as the ideal from the sensible in the first place.

Since all philosophical decisions rest on attributing certain predicates to the Real to the exclusion of other terms not covered by those privileged predicates, it is not possible to positively think the Real in its radical immanence. To think the Real would be to describe it in terms of predicates. To attribute predicates to the Real, however, would be to exclude their opposite predicates, and thereby create an opposition between the Real and its contrary predicates. To grasp the Real *qua* the One is to instead think it as encompassing all predicates we can ever conceive, but without any one or number of them exhausting it. As Laruelle succinctly puts it, "the One is the immanent paradigm of the term and its specificity irreducible to all ideality or rapport" (Laruelle 1985, 52). Given that we can never directly describe the One, grasping it becomes a matter of indirectly alluding to it by showing how philosophy always presupposes an anterior immanence that it slices up to decide that which *is* and is not. Laruelle terms "cloning" this process of showing how philosophical decisions that constitute reality, or what Laruelle also calls the "world," presupposes the Real as a radical immanence: "because it is foreclosed to all knowledge, the vision-in-One can only clone its identity from the material of the mixed with which the capital-world furnishes it" (Laruelle 2000, 54). Termed differently, cloning stages a vision-in-One through the non-philosophical procedure of taking a philosophical decision as one's material, and revealing how it implies an original radical immanence to generate its world by separating it from the rest of the Real as an incompossible term.

Already in the later works of Philosophy III and evermore so in Philosophies IV and V, Laruelle develops the similar notion of "modelisation." Like cloning, modelisation amounts to a staging of a vision-in-One, albeit beyond philosophy in other practices, such as art, religion and science: "we can use diverse models, philosophical, theological, scientific, to interpret, and not to illustrate, this formalism" (Laruelle 2007, 23). While Laruelle had already been modelling other practices such as ethics and political theory before 2004, it is with that year's publication of *La Lutte et l'utopie à la fin des temps philosophiques* that he formalizes this procedure of modelling. There, Laruelle explains that not only philosophy, but all practices rest on certain decisions that split the immanence of their respective objects of study into contraries: "we pose that each practice, ordinarily called 'regional,' possesses a specific quasi-ontology, an original conception of the real and procedures for appropriating it for itself" (Laruelle 2004, 101). Since all practices make philosophical decisions, non-philosophy is not limited to cloning philosophy, but every practice by identifying their decision, subtracting it, and thereby making way for the vision-in-One. Here, Laruelle is quick to specify that non-philosophy does not decide the true essence of the objects of other practices, which remain autonomous. On the contrary, non-philosophy precisely bestows these practices their autonomy by extracting philosophy's infiltration of their methods and objects of inquiry: "non-philosophy only affects the sciences and arts as much as the philosophizable has infiltrated their meta-language, it has no effects on the practices themselves" (Laruelle 2004, 111-2). Laruelle envisions this subtraction of philosophical decisions from regional practices as the vocation of an "international non-philosophical organisation," or "ONPHI." The work of ONPHI consists in applying non-philosophy's conceptual tools to local practices by re-modelling those practices on a radical immanence to locally materialize a vision-in-One: "an ONPHI must be a manner of *modelling by way of the operatory practice of communicating the philosophizable and its appearance*" (Laruelle 2004, 141). The bulk of Laruellian scholarship that applies non-philosophical concepts to disciplinary fields like psychoanalysis, feminist theory, ecology, political theory and media studies can thus be seen as modelling the One's regional apparition in the world of decisions and predicative thought (see, for instance, Moulinier 1999; Smith 2013; Kolozova 2014 and 2015; Galloway 2014; Gangle, Rocco and Greve 2017).

Such are the essentials of Laruelle's non-philosophy: the critique of Platonism and anti-Platonisms for deciding the Real by dividing it into two opposed terms; the re-envisioning of the Real as the One of radical immanence; and the materialization of a vision-in-One by cloning or modelling philosophical materials and regional practices as diverse as art, science and religion.

2. Laruelle's Approach to Ravaisson: Phenomenon, Difference, Ontology

The best entry-point into Laruelle's *Phenomenon and Difference: An Essay on Ravaisson's Ontology* is by looking at the three keywords of its title: phenomenon, difference, and ontology. The subtitle clearly indicates that Laruelle is specifically interested in Ravaisson's writings on the history of metaphysics rather than the much more frequent interest in his theory of habit. The fact that Laruelle uses the word ontology instead of metaphysics as Ravaisson does also betrays Laruelle's intention to constantly update older conceptual paradigms with new terms. In this case, the change from metaphysics to ontology can be read in light of Heidegger's critique of metaphysics as distinct from a fundamental ontology (which Laruelle repeatedly links to Ravaisson's ontology). By referring to Ravaisson's metaphysics as ontology, then, Laruelle is positioning Ravaisson's thought as something to be advocated rather than abandoned as per the metaphysics of presence.

Laruelle opens the book by explaining that, although he will discuss difference, he is not seeking to rehabilitate difference against identity: "difference is only this essay's theme, not its thesis or concept" (Laruelle 1971, 9). It is crucial to avoid lopping in Laruelle's work with Deleuze's *Difference and Repetition*, Derrida's *Writing and Difference*, and other celebrations of difference in late 1960s France. Against this grain, Laruelle proposes to *critique* difference by drawing on Ravaisson's critique of anti-Platonic philosophies. While Ravaisson does not describe such anti-Platonic, pluralistic philosophies as "philosophies of difference" as Laruelle does, his target is nonetheless the same in that he takes aim at philosophers who cut up the unity of being in favour of a multiplicity of irremediably particular, individuated things. Here as with the term ontology, Laruelle updates Ravaisson's critique of anti-Platonism so as to transform it into a critique of the philosophies of difference that were all the rage in late 1960s and early 1970s Paris.

Finally, the first term of the title is phenomenon. This refers to the way that Laruelle uses Ravaisson to precisely save that which is precisely condemned as phenomenon or appearance from both Platonism and anti-Platonism's stripping it of all reality. On the one hand, Platonism cuts up being by deciding that only the ideal is real to the denigration of the sensible part of being as mere epiphenomena. On the other hand, philosophies of difference do link difference to what Plato called appearance, and thus seek to ontologize it. However, they then oppose this to unity, ideality and representation as a new phantasmic phenomenon. For Laruelle as for Ravaisson, any concept of being conceived as the Real has to include everything that there *is*, including even phenomena, be it the ideal *or* the sensible, if it is to seize the radical unity of all things without remainder.

3. Ravaisson's History of Metaphysics: Materialism, Idealism, Being

On Laruelle's reading, Ravaisson conceives of philosophy as *first* philosophy, ontology or metaphysics, which he in turn understands to be the study of the unity of being cohering the multiplicity of seemingly different things. It is by looking at Ravaisson's two-volume work on the historical reception of Aristotle's *Metaphysics* that we can best grasp his own concept of being.[3] Ravaisson begins by arguing that the first pre-Socratic philosophers affirmed that the sensible world is what is real (water, air, fire, etc.). More precisely,

---

[3] Apart from Laruelle's monograph, the best overview of Ravaisson's thought is Boutroux 1900.

Ravaisson focuses on Heraclites' idea of being as a fire of becoming. According to Ravaisson, the idea that being is a constant flux of becoming paved the way for the sophists' belief that there is a multiplicity of different and even contradictory truths without any overarching unity to cohere them all:

> *Everything flows*; such is the formula where Heraclites, perhaps without realizing it, creates the germ of scepticism. (…) If the principles are opposites that exist together and mixed one with the other, everything is at once white and black; (…) the contradictory can be affirmed at once of the same thing; the true is confounded with the false. (…) Individual sensation is the only possible science: *man is the measure of all things* (Ravaisson 1963a, 274).[4]

On Ravaisson's reading, both the pre-Socratics and the sophists split being into infinite differences upon differences. What Socrates then did was to introduce the idea of a conceptual unity underlying the multiplicity of sensible things: "abandoning the search for a general explication of natural phenomena, Socrates attached himself to ethics, and he discovered therein the true object of science, independent of sensation, the universal" (Ravaisson 1963a, 276). Socrates' dialectical method thus involves moving from different and even contradictory ideas of what is good, virtuous, just or beautiful, to one unified Idea beyond all particular sensible instances: "the goal that he proposes for himself is to rediscover in particular existences an element of generality, and to bring the sensible diversity to the intelligible unity of the universal" (Ravaisson 1963a, 282). By seeking to cohere the sensible manifold around a unified Idea, Socrates tentatively grasped philosophy's true mission, a mission that Aristotle would later formalize, as the study of the unity of all things.

For Ravaisson, Plato marked a regression from Socrates' thought of the unity of being when he affirmed that the ideal unity was *alone* real, and hence transcendent and separate from particular, sensible things: "in itself, consequently, the idea, which gives particular things the unity of a general form, the idea is a thing apart, singular and individual" (Ravaisson 1963a, 292). The problem with Plato is that by conflating the ideal with all of reality, he thereby reduced the sensible world to a mere non-being, privation, or appearance: "there is thus a *non-being*, to which all participates, or rather which is mixed and scattered in everything" (Ravaisson 1963a, 312). By identifying the very sensible phenomena that we experience as non-being, Plato's concept of being as an *ideal* unity does not really capture all of being insofar as it excludes our very own experience. On the contrary, Plato divides the unity of being between two opposed terms of ideal unity and sensible

---

[4] I shall leave aside the question as to whether Ravaisson's readings of other philosophers are entirely accurate, since my present goal is to see how Ravaisson's understanding of the history of metaphysics informs Laruelle's non-philosophical thought.

multiplicity: "if the One, in a general manner, is the opposite of multiplicity, the first principle, God has his opposite, immortal, eternal like him" (Ravaisson 1963a, 342-3). Being thus loses the sense that it is supposed to be everything in favour of being only the ideal *part* of a greater Being, which is also sensible:

> All this occurs to the Platonists, because they (…) take opposites for principles, because they make of the One a principle, because they make numbers and ideas the first essences, and because they attribute to them an independent and separated existence. To these radical errors, from which derive all the absurd consequences that overwhelm Platonism, there is still a common root: it is the confusion of the logical order with the order of being (Ravaisson 1963a, 340-1).

Clearly, Ravaisson's critique of Platonism anticipates Laruelle's idea that Plato identifies the real with the unitary ideal to the detriment of sensible differences in a way which divides the unary One between two opposed terms.

For Ravaisson as for Laruelle, Platonism is wrong to conflate the ideal term with the totality of that which *is*. Instead, both the ideal unity and sensible diversity must be somehow united in a single structure, law, principle, cause or being. Ravaisson ultimately finds such a synthesis of these two terms through his reading of Aristotle. Contrary to Plato, Aristotle grants a certain reality to individual sensible things. Affirming the irremediable difference of all things alone, however, would merely recapitulate the sophists' philosophy of difference. Instead, Aristotle argues that all individuated things are so many actualisations to different degrees of a pure act or absolute potentiality, which they presuppose in order to differentiate themselves by moving from potency to act. For Ravaisson, Aristotle's idea of the pure act or prime mover thus grants a reality to individuated things while also maintaining their absolute unity as so many acceptations of one and the same being:

> The universe thus forms a continuous system of ascending progressions, ordered by one and the same term. It is not an assemblage of independent and detached principles, (…) it is a chain of successive potencies subordinated one to the other, (…) according to their common rapports with a same principle (Ravaisson 1963a, 59).

With Aristotle, Ravaisson holds that metaphysics found its proper ground in the idea of the unity of all things, a unity that does not disavow the brute fact of sensible becoming, but rather subsumes it into a larger whole.

In the second volume of his *Essay on Aristotle's Metaphysics*, however, Ravaisson argues that the stoics and epicureans mistook Aristotle for a pure empiricist without the idea of an overarching pure act. Consequently, they returned to an essentially pre-Socratic philosophy of sensible becoming and infinity diversity without any universalising principle: "from Aristotle's first successors to the first century of the Christian era, it is a common character to all the sects that dispute each other (…) to not suppose anything beyond nature" (Ravaisson 1963b 64-5). Ravaisson sees what Laruelle calls the "anti-Platonists" as equally problematic as Plato insofar as they simply assert the opposite of Plato by holding that only sensible diversity is real to the detriment of the ideal unity of thought. While Ravaisson holds that the exclusion of the sensible from being was where Plato fell afoul, to oppose the sensible as alone real as the stoics and epicureans did equally strips the ideal of any reality. The anti-Platonists thus maintain Platonism's essential dualism that cuts up the unity of being by merely inverting what counts as real (now the sensible) and what is merely phenomenal (the ideal). As Laruelle reformulates Ravaisson's critique of anti-Platonism, "to think difference *in opposition* to identity, *in opposition* to the concept, to think *the simulacrum in opposition* to the model and to the Idea, this is to reintroduce in the act of thinking negativity that one endeavoured to dissociate from difference" (Laruelle 1971, 71). Although Ravaisson prefers to use proper names like stoicism and epicureanism, Laruelle generalises his critique of these philosophies as a critique of "anti-Platonisms" or "philosophies of post-factum difference" (Laruelle 1971, 37-8, 39). Here, Laruelle updates Ravaisson's critique of the stoics and epicureans to take aim at Deleuze, Derrida, Nietzsche and other more contemporary anti-Platonic philosophers of difference. We can thus see how Ravaisson's critique of Ancient Greek philosophies of difference first enables Laruelle to see the problem with the reigning anti-Platonism of his own time. It is not merely that Ravaisson's critique of anti-Platonism coincides with Laruelle's own critique of philosophies of difference; rather, Laruelle goes so far as to say it is *only* through Ravaisson that we can understand how philosophies of difference make the same, albeit inverted mistake as Platonism of dividing the unity of being: "it is only from the ravaissonian perspective that a thought of difference as transcendental principle falls into the abstraction equal to that of the Platonism that it pretends to overcome" (Laruelle 1971, 99). Clearly, Laruelle is deeply indebted to Ravaisson's critique of anti-Platonism, and of Platonism, as so many productions of oppositions, which tear a real unity asunder.

In his other works on the history of philosophy, Ravaisson traces how philosophy continues to be anchored in this battle between the Platonic ideal unity and anti-Platonic sensible becoming. In his *Philosophy in France in the 19th Century,* for instance, Ravaisson argues that 19th century French philosophy can be seen as a long civil war between Auguste Comte and the positivists' idea that there is nothing beyond the empirical world, and the spiritualists' notion of spirit as transcending the material body. While each favour the opposite term, both positivists and spiritualists share a mutual mind-body dualism that splits the world between supposedly incompossible terms of subject and object, spirit and nature (Ravaisson 1885, 258). Much as Aristotle had developed an armistice for the ancient battle between the Platonists and anti-Platonists, however, so does Ravaisson see Schelling as a 19th century foil for the excesses of both positivism and spiritualism.[5] On Ravaisson's account, Schelling provides another way to unify nature and spirit in one self-identical absolute, which is indifferent to all dualisms. In short, Schelling's whole project centred on uniting the I and the non-I, nature and subject, which had been falsely opposed by both Fichte's privileging of the ideal over the object on the one hand, and Spinoza's reduction of spirit to nature on the other (Schelling 1994, 111-2). To this end, Schelling argues that the I can only be itself *qua* self-consciousness by externalizing itself as an other or object of its own thought. Nature or the non-I is thus the absolute spirit's alienation of itself to paradoxically affirm its self-identity by coming to think itself. In Schelling's terms, "the self cannot intuit the real activity as identical with itself, without at once finding the *negative element* therein, which makes it nonideal, as something alien to itself"; and: "it is with it in order to have an Other through which it would be able to contemplate itself" (Schelling 2001, 53; and 2000, xxxvi). The paradox of self-consciousness is that it has to negate itself by becoming an other of itself to affirm itself as the thinking of itself. At times, Ravaisson characterizes his own concept of being in these Schellingian terms of an absolute that thinks itself via its alienation in nature in a way that unites the subject and object from the false opposition that had been set up between them in 19th century French philosophy: "in all the different degrees of the immense scale of things, there is everywhere one and the same thought, divided in some way from itself, dispersed in all directions into material multiplicity, but which, gradually retrieving itself, re-acknowledges itself" (Ravaisson 2016, 87). By combining Aristotle and Schelling, Ravaisson is able to show both how unity presupposes sensible diversity, and how sensible differences presuppose an ideal unity. On the one hand, unity needs difference insofar as it can only affirm its self-identity by becoming an object of itself as Schelling explains. On the other hand, difference only emerges as individuations of a unified, pure act as Aristotle has shown. As Laruelle reformulates it, "unity can only affirm itself by differences, movement, and differences can only suffer the Same in grace, which is thus the final ontological synthesis" (Laruelle 1971, 94-5).

We can see from Ravaisson's history of metaphysics that the fundamental failure of philosophers to achieve a properly unified concept of being is due to the way they set up oppositions between two terms, of which only one is purportedly real. On the one hand, Platonism and its spiritualist variants affirm the ideal as alone real contra the sensible multiplicity of things. On the other hand, anti-Platonisms, from the stoics to the positivists, affirm that sensible diversity is alone real against the fantasies of thought and representa-

---

[5] For accounts of Schelling's influence on Ravaisson, see Courtine 1994; and Guibert 2007.

tion. In both cases, we are confronted with the problem of how being can be said to be the unity of all things given that there is a second term that exceeds its grasp. As Laruelle encapsulates Ravaisson's critique of philosophy, "Ravaisson searches Being in the falling short of metaphysical oppositions. All the oppositions are metaphysical, and in all opposition or scission, the excluded term continues to impregnate and govern the affirmed term" (Laruelle 1971, 37). Even if the excluded term is said to be merely appearance, phenomenon, or non-being, it nonetheless forcefully impresses itself on the affirmed term as its presupposition in a way, which shows the philosophical concept of being to be purely arbitrary, partial, and unitary rather than unary.

Drawing on Aristotle and Schelling, Ravaisson's positive project consists in reconciling these philosophical oppositions between sensible difference and "alterity," and identity and "assimilation," by developing a concept of being that is able to encompass both without relegating one to the realm of non-being. As Laruelle explains, "[Ravaisson's novelty] is, rather than creation, the experience of creation, the experience which is neither founded on radical alterity, nor on identification and assimilation – two symmetrical and twin hypotheses that Ravaisson will refuse –, the fusion in movement of subject and object" (Laruelle 1971, 33). Of course, Ravaisson's unified theory of being cannot be the One of the Platonists, which opposes itself to the difference of the outside. Instead, Ravaisson's being becomes an identity that is indifferent to oppositions insofar as it sees no oppositions between them, but only a unity, a reconciliation, or an immanence. Laruelle goes on: "the concept of *identity* must be modified. Identity interpreted as indifference of the opposed" (Laruelle 1971, 175). Notably, Laruelle first uses the term "radical immanence" that later denotes his own concept of the Real when describing Ravaisson's ontological concept of being as an absolute unity indifferent to all the opposites that it subsumes: "the problematic of ontologies of identity and radical immanence is only, more generally, the development of this post-Kantian principle: every opposition, whatever the content of its terms, must be founded on a synthetic substrate that is the presupposed identity of the two terms" (Laruelle 1971, 191). Although Laruelle later abandons the notion that radical immanence is the project of *philosophy*, we can see that it first emerges as a possible conception of being that is adequate to meet the demands of ontology understood as the study of the single structure, law, principle, or cause that unifies all things. While still a philosopher, Ravaisson's goal, and even his solution of radical immanence, is thus the same as that of Laruelle's non-philosophy: to develop a new, post-Platonic concept of the One that is able to incorporate that which Plato declared to be the difference of non-being in a radical unity without remainder.

4. From Eclecticism to Modelisation:
The Philosophy of Art and the Art of Philosophy

Throughout his dissertation, Laruelle not only upholds the content but also the form of Ravaisson's writings as proffering a method for synthesizing opposed terms. Given that Ravaisson wants to unite the ideal and the sensible, syntax and being itself, it is crucial that his philosophical writing not be a thought *of* being that is distinct from being. Instead, his writing must somehow become one with being as its immanent self-expression. This is what Laruelle is getting at when he describes Ravaisson's method as "expressive" and "ambiguous" in the sense that it shows how ostensibly opposed or "paradoxical" terms are actually equivocal, blurred, and even one and the same: "what Ravaisson will propose is to renounce the scission of the concept and the sensed. (…) He substitutes *ambiguity* and *expression* for paradox, and aesthetic grace to the transcendental exercise of thought. Difference as ambiguity is more apt than paradox to operate representation's effective 'overcoming'" (Laruelle 1971, 75). Laruelle contends that Ravaisson's ambiguous or expressive method betrays the influence of both late Neo-Platonism and Victor Cousin's eclecticism. On Ravaisson and Laruelle's readings, both spiritualists and late Neo-Platonists attempted to encapsulate different philosophies and fields of culture by showing how they are all partial expressions of one and same unified reality. According to Laruelle, Ravaisson's own method adheres to this eclectic method of tracing how the diversity of different cultural practices and disciplines presuppose a universal object of inquiry: "like Neo-Platonism and Alexandrianism, he attempts a reconciliation of thoughts, philosophies and religions in all the dimensions of history and in a unique principle: the reading is inseparable from an attempt at unification" (Laruelle 1971, 45). Simply put, Ravaisson's eclectic method attempts to cohere the diversity of all particular objects of regional fields of inquiry as variations on a general theme. In this way, Ravaisson's hermeneutics should not be seen as thinking being from outside itself, but rather as being's immanent self-expression.

To see what Laruelle is getting at in more detail, we can classify Ravaisson's writings into two categories: the long book-length histories of philosophy, and the shorter essays on art, religion and particular philosophies in isolation from their larger historical context. Apropos the first class of writings, Ravaisson's studies of the history of philosophy seek to show that there is one, universal truth of being, which different philosophies "actualise" to varying degrees of success. Rather than see the history of philosophy as a plurality of discontinuous theoretical frameworks, Ravaisson unifies them as expressive to different levels of participation of one, monist reality. Although Ravaisson critiques Plato and favours Aristotle, this ought not therefore suggest that Platonic philosophy is completely false or illusory. To oppose Platonism as outside the true thought of being as expressed in Aristotle would only set up a dualism at the heart of philosophical thought. While Platonism is therefore included in the history of true philosophical thinking, it only captures the ideal fragment of being's radical immanence while overlooking its sensible dimension. As Laruelle puts it:

> The history of philosophy is not of a dialectical nature. (…) All philosophy already manifests on condition of its own difference the final sense of philosophy, which is to say the expression of Being. The distribution operated between two methods, one that goes into the sense of the decomposition of the all into its elements—all philosophies that arise from the first method already participate in the manifestation of Being and the two between them can only be separated by a difference of degree in the expression of Being (Laruelle 1971, 53-4).

We can thus see how Ravaisson's very approach to developing his own metaphysics of radical immanence by tracing a history of other philosophies is crucial to revealing that radical immanence by cohering all philosophies around it as so many instantiations, whose differing degrees of emanation constitute their principle of individuation. Given that Laruelle appropriates Ravaisson's concept of being or the Real as a radical immanence, it is unsurprising that he also takes up Ravaisson's eclectic method when he proposes that the vision-in-One be staged by cloning philosophical decisions throughout the history of philosophy to show how they all presuppose the One.

The rest of Ravaisson's works are small, even fragmentary essays on "regional" subjects such as art and religion. If Ravaisson cannot simply privilege one field as the foci of his entire inquiry, it is because his concept of being as a radical immanence demands that he do otherwise. To focus on one field would amount to upholding it as the privileged discourse of being, thereby opposing it to other possible syntaxes. Instead, Ravaisson's understanding of being requires that he be a renaissance man and cohere the multiplicity of disciplines and their various objects of inquiry into one radical immanence without outlier. In Laruelle's terms: "rather than attribute to them too precise functions in a system of logical possibilities, (…) he searches, like true Neo-Platonism did, to derive them from a unique principle of which they reveal themselves to be historically finalised expressions and manifestations: this principle, this will be Being" (Laruelle 1971, 47). By demonstrating how a diversity of fields ultimately presuppose the same concept of one, all-encompassing essence, Laruelle contends that Ravaisson's eclectic method becomes one with his ontology of being as the pure act that all regions of reality more or less actualise: "the determination of the method thus drives to the heart of ontology, (…) for the method is only the being in movement or the process of Being manifesting itself" (Laruelle 1971, 30). Much as Ravaisson expresses this immanence in other extra-philosophical disciplines such as art and religion, so, too, does the later Laruelle materialise the vision-in-One by subtracting decisions in other local practices, such as religion and art as well, but also politics, ethics, science, and especially quantum physics.[6] In what recalls his own characterization of Ravaisson's fragmentary, eclectic style of analysing many regional disciplines, the Laruelle of Philosophy V even goes so far as to say that to properly understand a figure or subject, we should not delve too deep into the details for fear of losing the sense of the whole of which they are a part: "to seize a doctrine's fundamental or ideal enunciations, it is even recommended to sometimes cease to read a too admired author" (Laruelle 2011, 29). In Laruelle's understanding of how Ravaisson expresses his concept of being through the very eclectic form of his thought, we can thus see in embryonic form Laruelle's mature idea of cloning and modelisation as the staging of a vision-in-One through philosophical, aesthetic, scientific, political and religious materials.

To give just one more concrete example, we shall look at Ravaisson's idea of the art of drawing.[7] For Ravaisson, there are two approaches drawing can take when representing figures. On the one hand, drawing can model itself on geometry by cutting figures up into their smaller parts and particular differences. On the other hand, drawing can take Ravaisson's preferred artistic approach and model itself on the naked eye's spontaneous intuition of how the parts of a figure cooperate together for the sake of the whole's greater harmony. So, whereas the geometrical approach divides figures into their parts, the artistic approach grasps the unity that the parts serve (Ravaisson 2016, 145).[8] As Laruelle explains Ravaisson's point here, "sight is not the object of a construction and is not discovered element by element, to which a mechanical juxtaposition would assure a factitious unity. Its coherence gives itself straightaway as such" (Laruelle 1971, 31). Ravaisson gives the specific example of how architects design buildings' particular rooms, doors and windows with an eye to serving the larger function of the whole: "a building, whatever it is exactly, should, like an animate being, be a whole whose parts cooperate, with the whole ensemble, in the pursuit of the same goal, and contribute to the expression of one and the same thought" (Ravaisson 2016, 147). By linking parts to a greater whole, a multiplicity to a unity, architecture, drawing and art more generally capture the harmony underlying all things beyond their individu-

---

[6] Laruelle stages the vision-in-One through many more disciplines than Ravaisson, such as science broadly speaking (1992; 2008); quantum physics (2010); ethics (2013; 2003; 2012); Marxist politics (2000); religion (2002; 2007; 2014); and photography (1996; 2014).
[7] For Ravaisson's writings on religion, see "Greek Funerary Monuments" and "Mysteries: Fragment of a Study of the History of Religions," *Ravaisson* 2016.
[8] See also "On the Teaching of Drawing," *Ravaisson* 2016.

ated particularities. Ravaisson affirms: "art (…) condenses what accidents have separated and what the spirit of nature gathers together" (Ravaisson 2016, 148). To the extent that art expresses the unity of being, it is not a separate mediation or discourse *of* being; rather, it immanently expresses being's self-manifestation. As Laruelle reformulates how art seizes the unity of radical immanence "in person": "aesthetics in Ravaisson's works is not mediating, art is not a derived expression of Being. (…) *The flowing movement is even grace or the 'in person'*" (Laruelle 1971, 32). Here, Laruelle makes his first use of the term "in person" to describe the way Ravaisson's eclectic method unveils a radical immanence behind all differences. While Laruelle will abandon much of the terminology he uses in his dissertation, he maintains this term (as well as radical immanence), both of which he initially uses to characterize Ravaisson's idea of being as a unity enveloping all things, a being that therefore closely resembles Laruelle's own idea of the Real as precisely a radical immanence, or the One-in-person.

5. Laruelle, a philosopher?

I began by outlining non-philosophy's key concepts of philosophical decision, radical immanence, and cloning or modelisation. I then turned to Laruelle's first work to trace how he initially derived each of these concepts through his reading of Ravaisson's ontology. The critique of both Platonism and anti-Platonism as scissions of the Real, the need to synthesise them through a single concept of being as radical immanence, and the means of materialising the One-in-person through different regional practices, the germ of all of this can already be found in Laruelle's reading of Ravaisson.

What is most strikingly different in this early Laruelle compared to the later Laruelle is not that he lacks a concept of radical immanence that he clearly already possesses, but rather that he characterizes radical immanence as the object of study of *philosophy* or *ontology*. For the early Laruelle, the philosophies that divide the unity of the Real between two opposed terms do not mark the failure of philosophy *as such*, but merely that of all hitherto *historical* philosophies to achieve what remains philosophy's own mission to achieve a unified concept of all things, which radical immanence can alone provide. In his first book, then, Laruelle still holds that being and ontology have two significations: on the one hand, they denote a radical immanence at the root of all things whose study is the object of philosophy; on the other hand, they name only a part of immanence that all historical philosophies have separated off from the whole and falsely opposed to the rest of it *qua* mere phenomena: "being itself can thus be interpreted in two opposed manners, of which the opposition explains the duality of methods: either as being of a synthetic nature or as reduced to given phenomena" (Laruelle 1971, 237). At this early stage, Laruelle is content to say that we can conceive of being as an opposition *or* as radical immanence where the later Laruelle will only associate being (and ontology) with the former.

By Philosophy II, Laruelle resolutely rejects that radical immanence is an answer to the question of being. Instead, being solely denotes Plato's Greco-unitary one rather than the unary One, which becomes the object of study for a *non*-philosophy or "science": "the One is not convertible with Being and must be described by itself outside of all functional requisition" (Laruelle 1991, 19). At the same time, Laruelle's notion in the dissertation that radical immanence is an answer to philosophy's project to uncover a unity of all things continues to betray itself whenever he repeatedly insists that non-philosophy, or what he has recently and tellingly referred to as "non-*standard* philosophy" is not the negation of philosophy, but its expansion (beyond decisional oppositions): "non-philosophy is not the absence or negation of philosophy, it is on the contrary its generalisation or its opening as correlate of the One rather than of Being" (Laruelle 1991, 20). What changes between Philosophy II and the dissertation on Ravaisson is thus not the fundamental concepts, but the semantics: Laruelle conflates being with the Greco-One as distinct from his unary One, as well as ontology and philosophy with their historical decisions about being as distinct from non-philosophy and science as a cloning and modelisation of the Real.[9] Ravaisson's critique of Platonic and anti-Platonic philosophies thus becomes Laruelle's critique of philosophy *tout court* as decisional. Ravaisson's post-Platonic ontology of the unity of being is translated as Laruelle's non-philosophical concept of radical immanence or the One-in-person. And Ravaisson's eclectic method reappears in the guise of Laruelle's notions of cloning and modelisation.

By looking at Laruelle's reading of Ravaisson, we can see that Laruelle's own project has the same goal as that of first philosophy: the study of being *qua* being or the Real understood as the radical immanence of all things. Given that at the very least Ravaisson would have to be excluded from Laruelle's critique of philosophy in Laruelle's own account of his ontology as expressing a radical immanence, it would seem that Ray Brassier is right to argue that Laruelle conflates *a certain kind* of philosophizing (by decisions) with philosophy *as such*: "Laruelle conflated the critique of a certain kind of philosophy with the critique of philosophy *tout court*" (Brassier 2007, 121). Along these lines, we can very well imagine philosophers objecting that Laruelle is wrong to distinguish philosophy from his

---

[9] Even here, a historical philosophical precedent connected to Ravaisson can be found when Schelling makes a distinction between other philosophies and his own, which is more of a "science," and even a "non-philosophy" in that it alone captures the absolute unifying all things (see Schelling 1980, 40; and 2010, 8).

own project, since he is committed to philosophy's basic mission of seizing the unity of all things, even as he departs from the historical solutions offered by philosophers hitherto as remaining too decisional.

Ultimately, whether Laruelle is justified in distinguishing his non-philosophy from philosophy *tout court*, on the grounds that it differs in its solution if not its aim, is a matter of semantics. What is really of interest is how not only ecologists, feminists, and media, political and art theorists, but also philosophers and metaphysicians can take up Laruelle's (and indeed Ravaisson's all too overlooked) critique of our own tradition, so as to immanently reform philosophy rather than oppose it from the outside.

Vincent Le, Faculty of Arts and Education, Deakin University,
v.le[at]deakin.edu.au

References

Bergson, Henri. "Notice sur la vie et les oeuvres de Felix Ravaisson-Mollien." L'Académie des Sciences morales et politiques. 2011. Web. 8 February 2017.
    <https://www.asmp.fr/travaux/notices/ravaisson_bergson.htm>.
Boutroux, Emile. "Philosophie de Ravaisson." *Revue de métaphysique de morale*. Vol. 8, Nr. 6 (1900): 699-716.
Brassier, Ray. *Nihil Unbound: Enlightenment and Extinction*. New York: Palgrave Macmillan, 2007.
Courtine, Jean-François. "Les Relations de Ravaisson et de Schelling." *La réception de la philosophie allemande en France au xixe et au xxe siècles*. Ed. Jean Quillien. Lille: Presses Universitaires du Septentrion, 1994, 111-134.
Gangle, Rocco and Julius Greve (eds.). *Superpositions: Laruelle and the Humanities*. Lanham: Rowman and Littlefield International, 2017. Ebook.
Galloway, Alexander R. *Laruelle against the Digital*. London: University of Minnesota Press, 2014.
Guibert, Gaëll. *Félix Ravaisson: d'une philosophie première à la philosophie de la révélation de Schelling*. Paris: L'Harmattan, 2007.
Kolozova, Katerina. *Cut of the Real: Subjectivity in Poststructuralist Philosophy*. New York: Columbia University Press, 2014.
Kolozova, Katerina. *Toward a Radical Metaphysics of Socialism: Marx and Laruelle*. Brooklyn: Punctum Books, 2015.
Laruelle, François. *Anti-Badiou: sur l'introduction du maoïsme dans la philosophie*. Paris: Éditions Kimé, 2011.
Laruelle, François. *Christo-fiction*. Paris: Fayard, 2014.

Laruelle, François. *En tant qu'un: la non-philosophie expliquée aux philosophes*. Paris: Aubier Montaigne, 1991.
Laruelle, François. *Éthique de l'Étranger. Du crime contre l'humanité*. Paris: Éditions Kimé, 2000.
Laruelle, François. *L'ultime honneur des intellectuels*. Paris: Textuel, 2003.
Laruelle, François. *Introduction au non-marxisme*. Paris: Presses universitaires de France, 2000.
Laruelle, François. *Introduction aux sciences génériques*. Paris: Pétra, 2008.
Laruelle, François. *La Lutte et l'utopie à la fin des temps philosophiques*. Paris: Éditions Kimé, 2004.
Laruelle, François. *Le Christ futur, une leçon d'hérésie*. Paris: Exils, 2002.
Laruelle, François. *Mystique non-philosophique à l'usage des contemporains*. Paris: L'Harmattan, 2007.
Laruelle, François. *Non-Photographie—Photo-Fiction*. Paris: Merve, 2014.
Laruelle, François. *Phénomène et différence: essai sur l'ontologie de Ravaisson*. Paris: Éditions Klincksieck, 1971.
Laruelle, François. *Philosophie et non-philosophie*. Mardaga: Liege Pierre, 1989.
Laruelle, François. *Philosophie non-standard: générique, quantique, philo-fiction*. Paris: Kimé, 2010.
Laruelle, François. *Principes de la non-photographie*. Paris: PUF, 1996.
Laruelle, François. *Théorie générale des victimes*. Paris: Mille et une nuits, 2012.
Laruelle, François. *Théorie des identités: fractalité généralisée et philosophie artificielle*. Paris: PUF, 1992.
Laruelle, François. *Une biographie de l'homme ordinaire: des autorités et des minorités*. Paris: Éditions Aubier Montagne, 1985.
Moulinier, Didier. *De la psychanalyse à la non-philosophie*. Paris: Éditions Kimé, 1999.
Ravaisson, Félix. *Essai de la métaphysique d'Aristote tome 1*. Hildesheim: Georg Olms Verlagsbuchhandlung, 1963.
Ravaisson, Félix. *Essai de la métaphysique d'Aristote tome 2*. Hildesheim: Georg Olms Verlagsbuchhandlung, 1963.
Ravaisson, Félix. *La philosophie en France au xixe siecle*. Paris: Librairie Hachette, 1885.
Ravaisson, Félix. *Ravaisson: Selected Essays*. Ed. Mark Sinclair. London: Bloomsbury, 2016. Ebook.
Schelling, F.W.J. *On the History of Modern Philosophy*. Trans. Andrew Bowie. Melbourne: Cambridge University Press, 1994.
Schelling, F.W.J. *Philosophy and Religion*. Trans. Klaus Ottmann. New York: Spring Publications, 2010.
Schelling, F.W.J. *System of Transcendental Idealism*. Trans. Peter Heath. Charlottesville: University of Virginia, 2001.
Schelling, F.W.J. *The Ages of the World*. Albany: State University of New York Press, 2000. Print.
Schelling, F.W.J. *The Unconditional in Human Knowledge*. Trans. Fritz Marti. London: Associated University Presses, 1980.
Smith, Anthony Paul. *A Non-Philosophical Theory of Nature: Ecologies of Thought*. New York: Palgrave MacMillan, 2013.

JOHN M. ALLISON (Pittsburgh, PA)

Religious Pluralism within the Limits of Thought[1]

Abstract

There is an aporia *to finitude: if I am limited as a finite being, I cannot know what the limits of my finitude are, because if I knew what those limits are, then I would have transcended them. I refer to this* aporia *as the "hard problem of finitude," interpreted through Graham Priest's work on inclosure paradoxes. Here I offer an interpretation of François Laruelle's theory of the Philosophical Decision in terms of his attempt to resolve this* aporia *through his suspension of standard philosophy's form of ontological dualism. Next, I apply non-standard philosophy to the problem of religious pluralism, presenting a novel theory of "standard religion" and the "Hierophanic Decision" through a non-standard reading of Mircea Eliade's philosophy of religion, and end by pointing towards what a consistently performative and finite form of religious pluralism might look like from within the "democracy-of-thought," here rendered as the "parliament of religions."*

Keywords: François Laruelle, Mircea Eliade, Graham Priest, religious pluralism, finitude

---

"Whereof one cannot speak thereof one must be silent" (Wittgenstein 2018, §7)
"Whereof one cannot speak, thereof one has just contradicted oneself" (Priest 2002, 233)
"[The language of the One] speaks what we cannot say, or speaks
the identity-in-the-last-instance of saying and silence" (Laruelle 2013b, 227)

There is an *aporia* to finitude: if I am limited as a finite being, I cannot know what the limits of my finitude are, because if I knew what those limits are, then I would have transcended them.[2] With apologies to David Chalmers (Chalmers 1995), we may refer to this *aporia* as "the hard problem of finitude." As understood here, the hard problem of

---

[1] Many thanks to Sally Brown, Nathan Jumper, Bryan Rennie, and Richard Young – all of whom offered comments and conversation on earlier drafts of this paper. Very special thanks goes out in particular to Jon Cogburn, whose commentary on the inclosure schema was invaluable.
[2] Both Hegel (1997, §60) and Wittgenstein (2018, §1) have offered formulations of this *aporia*.

finitude arises due to the transcendental fact that we always already presuppose something (let us call it "reality") prior to our conceptual determination of it. We find ourselves in the midst of the fact that anything is at all. But we do not even know what being "inside" of reality means since we do not have access to it as a whole as finite beings or, by definition, to anything *outside* of it. Our finitude therefore not only underdetermines our ability to conceptualize reality in a well-defined way, but it also underdetermines a complete account of finitude itself. In this sense, we might say that the limits of thought are boundaries that cannot be crossed, but we do not even know what they are.

This *aporia* also haunts religious pluralism. We may define religious pluralism as the idea that all religions are so many parts of a whole, whether in terms of reality, sacrality, and/or truth. In other words, religious pluralism amounts to the idea that all religions are equally real, equally true, and/or equally valuable parts of some whole. Religious pluralism is aporetic because, if I claim equality with others due to our shared finitude, then I cannot determine in terms of what we are equal to each other exactly, for such a knowledge would put me in a position of epistemic predominance over them. It would put me in a "meta-exclusive" position *outside* of the plane of finitude, thus rendering my religious pluralism logically inconsistent. This charge of inconsistency is, in a nutshell, Gavin D'Costa's critique of John Hick's pluralistic hypothesis (Hick 2004), which makes religious pluralism an apparent "impossibility" (D'Costa 1996).

Here we may remember the parable of the blind men and the elephant. In one version of the story, four blind men are wandering in the forest when they unexpectedly come across an elephant, which none of them has encountered before. Each of the four describe the elephant variously as being like a snake (one holds the trunk), a pillar (one grasps the leg), a smooth wall (one touches the side), and smooth, thin stone (one grips the tusk). After quarreling, the blind men conclude they must have each been touching different animals ff because their descriptions mismatch each other. Of course, we the readers know how misguided this conclusion is. In certain retellings of the story, this epistemic benefit is shared with a king who, in order to make a point to his court advisors about pointless bickering, asks the blind men to his court to describe an elephant. Here both us readers and the king benefit from an optic advantage over the blind men – a transcendent, royal knowledge.

Hick operates from this royal knowledge insofar as he uses the parable of the blind men and the elephant (Hick 1973, 37) to suggest religious exclusivism and inclusivism are false, and that all religions are really phenomenal conceptualizations of one noumenal reality that transcends us all. But how can Hick claim both to be "blind" like everyone else and also to have an optic advantage? This is inconsistent.

There are two other ways to imagine this *aporia*. The first comes from William Irwin Thompson, who likens the human condition to being that of a fly crawling across the ceiling of Sistine Chapel – a fly that cannot comprehend the images of angels and gods under its own feet (Thompson quoted in Kripal 2010, 159). The second comes from William James, who invites us to wonder whether we are not as cats or dogs in a library, surrounded by books we are unable to comprehend (James 1977, 140). Both scenes present us with a difficulty as finite beings, for how could a finite being know the nature of its finitude or how it is finite? Neither the fly nor the cats and dogs could conceptualize their lack of comprehension, for then they would cease being flies, cats. And dogs. The *aporia*, then, is that we cannot know how we are finite precisely because we are finite. Any demand made that all knowledge is finite *inconsistently* contravenes those same posited limits of finitude. Every attempt to determine one's own position in finitude violates the very assertion of one's position therein. To determine one's immanence to finitude requires a transcendental perch, an "outside" of immanence, by which to determine as much.

We may understand this *aporia* by applying Graham Priest's work on "inclosure paradoxes." Let us posit Ω, the totality of what is knowable, and x, religious knowledge, which is taken as a subset of Ω (just in case all of the propositions in x are knowable). Next, let us apply an operator, δ, to x, which is the contention that all religious knowledge is correctly construed pluralistically because all religious knowers are finite. However, if we say that the pluralist's contention belongs to the set of religious knowledge, then this demand should itself be understood pluralistically – as in $\delta\{\delta(x)\}$ – which is a self-defeating proposition. So, in order to avoid this situation, an operation of Transcendence is required, which tells us that $\delta(x)$ transcends x. In other words, the demand that religious knowledge be construed pluralistically is not contained within the set of religious knowledge itself. However, this demand still belongs to Ω (as described by an operation of Closure). An inclosure paradox arises, however, insofar as we apply $\delta(x)$ to Ω itself, for then $\delta(x)$ *both* is contained within (Closure) *and* transcendent of (Transcendence) the totality of what is knowable. Said differently, if religious knowledge is finite and a subset of the totality of what is knowable, then the demand that religious knowable be construed pluralistically transcends the set of religious knowledge while nonetheless being an element of Ω. And yet, insofar as Ω is understood to be itself finite, then Ω is subject to the demand of pluralization, dictating that such a demand is both within and beyond the limits of Ω. This is, I claim, the inclosure paradox at the heart of standard forms of religious pluralism.[3]

As is well known, Priest himself *affirms* such inconsistency, declaring "the limits of thought are boundaries which cannot be crossed, but yet which are crossed" (Priest 2002, 3). Priest is a "dialetheist," that is, he affirms the existence of some true contradictions. However, if we are indeed like the blind men who, in the first telling of the parable, are wandering in the forest when they bump into an elephant, then we might say we do not even know what an elephant is in the first place. This means that both Ω are x are undetermined variables. What an elephant is, is precisely what is under question, because here there is no king to tell us how it is we are blind or what we are all touching. In what follows, I offer a model of religious pluralism that operates from an axiomatic assumption that we do not have access to royal knowledge, which dictates that we must think like blind men in the forest, a fly on the ceiling, a cat or dog in the library.[4] I thus attempt to formulate a consistently incomplete (that is, finite) model of religious pluralism, which does not devolve into *aporia*.[5]

Given that some proponents of "polydoxy" present a theory of religious pluralism through Whiteheadian and/or Deleuzian models of formalized incompleteness (Keller and Schneider 2011), Elliot Wolfson's comment on polydoxy is relevant here. "Polydoxy is not superior to orthodoxy," he observes, "if the beliefs promulgated under the pretext of plurality regurgitate erroneous claims, as in the case of envisioning immanence from the standpoint of transcendence" (Wolfson 2014, 231). Wolfson here points to the constitutive inability of many religious pluralists, despite the posited consistent finitude of their theories, to theorize pluralism in a consistent manner. For even if they treat the elephant as ontologically pluralistic or immanent in constitution, reflexive knowledge of this circumstance is still an inconsistent exception to finitude. For to have made finitude transparent to conceptualization, to a transcendental knowledge of immanence, is a performa-

---

[3] See appendix A, §1, for a visual representation of Priest's Inclosure Schema. I am indebted to Jon Cogburn for helping me formulate this presentation of religious pluralism's inclosure paradox.
[4] I do not employ the blind men as an ableiest trope, nor the limitations of flies and cats or dogs in a speciesist way, but rather as figures emblematic of the universality of finitude.
[5] The term "consistent incompleteness," and its opposite, "inconsistent incompleteness," come from the work of Paul Livingston, and refer to the two options available to post-Gödelian thought insofar as Gödel demonstrated the impossibility of both a consistent and complete system of thought (see Livingston 2012).

tive contradiction. In this light, we may assert that regardless of whether a pluralist believes that the religions are so many blind men touching different parts of the same elephant, as for Hick (Hick 2004) or various forms of perennialism (see Ferrer 2002:71-114), or that there are many elephants (Cobb 1999; Ferrer 2008; Griffin 2005; Heim 2001), the pluralist nonetheless maintains a position of royal transcendence: the king who can see and so tells the blind men what is really going. So is religious pluralism a logical impossibility? My claim is that it is impossible to maintain from within a conceptual idiom of thought, but not from within a *performative* (or non-conceptual) idiom of thought. My goal, therefore, is to develop a model of religious pluralism in a consistently performative, pluralistic, and finite way.

A Kantian Interlude

To think from within finitude: this is, essentially, a Kantian imperative, deriving from both a Kantian problem and a Kantian solution. The problem is that trying to determine the nature of reality as a whole leads to an antinomy. The solution to this problem is to be *empirical* about reality – to think from the *inside* of it. Kant himself proposes such a "empirical directive" (see Braver 2007, 53). He writes: the "I or he or it (the thing) which thinks… is known only through the thoughts which are its predicates, and of it, apart from them, we cannot have any concept whatsoever" (Kant 1965, A346/B404).[6] Kant, however, cannot apply this directive to external reality, but only to the subject since the subject is transcendental for him. Reality is transcendentally correlated to the subject, dictating that all experience is phenomenal and never experience of the noumenal thing-in-itself. This, of course, made Kantianism vulnerable to the Berkleyan/Fichtean argument against transcendence that it is impossible to think the unthinkable, and since the noumenal is unthinkable, we are not justified in positing it (see Cogburn 2017,7). This kind of argument ushered in German idealism, anti-realism, and then the supremacy of socio-linguistic constructivism in the 20th century. However, what if we were able to bypass the Berkleyan/Fichtean argument? Then we would be free to apply Kant's empiri-

---

[6] As Wilfrid Sellars describes it, "our concept of an I is the concept of *that which thinks*, in the various modes of thinking. The idea that concepts pertaining to thinking are essentially *functional* in character raises the question: What non-functional characterization can be given of the processes, which embody these functions. . . . We don't know these processes save as *processes which embody these functions*" (Sellars quoted in Braver 2007:55).

cal directive not only to the subject, but to external reality itself. And then we could, moreover, revise the empirical directive and assert: *reality, whatever it is, is known only through its effects, and of it, apart from them, we cannot have any concept of reality whatsoever.*[7]

Arguably, it is precisely this kind of imperative that energizes the work of François Laruelle, which, as I reconstruct it, offers us the means by which to bypass the master argument and operate from within finitude in a performatively consistent manner.

Non-Standard Philosophy

Laruelle himself does not describe his brand of "non-standard" philosophy specifically in terms of "the hard problem of finitude." But this is arguably one of the motivating conundrums underlying his project. For Laruelle takes as axiomatic that thought presupposes and is transcendentally immanent to reality ("the Real"), prior to any determination of its essence from within a thought-world.[8] And this dictates that thought is immanent to the Real, and so the Real is underdetermined. In Priestian terms, Laruelle operates from a *presupposed* Domain (Ω: the generic immanence of the Real) and Closure (thought's immanence to the Real), but rejects any operation of Transcendence by which one could make the Real a well-defined object of conceptualization.[9] To clarify, the term "Domain" is *not* here an ontological referent. The Real is not the "One-All," to borrow a term from Badiou's philosophy (Badiou 1988), and so is neither the totality of how everything is logically ("the One") nor the totality of what everything is ontologically ("the All"). The Realis underdetermined . Laruelle's ambition is thus to humble any attempt to treat the Real as an ultimate reality or totality, thus staging a "de-ultimatization" or "de-ontologization" of reality. Here Jon Cogburn's musings on metaphysics is illuminating. He comments:

---

[7] Cf. Rocco Gangle who asserts that immanence, "roughly, names then any metaphysical position or method rejecting the notion that the ultimate structure of reality may be investigated independently of its real content in the way that Kant's, for example, does" (Gangle 2016, 3).

[8] "The Real," like "the One," is just what Laruelle calls one of the "first names" of generic immanence, referring to that which resists signification in order "to evoke what is already-manifest for philosophy to even act" (Smith 2016, 43).

[9] See appendix A, §2, for more details.

Metaphysics tries to give us explanations of what reality must be like such that what we know about it is true. But suppose for argument that part of what we know about reality is the impossibility of providing an explanation of what reality must be like such that what we know about it is true. Then the metaphysician would have to provide an account of what reality is like such that metaphysics is impossible. (Cogburn 2017, 60)

To provide an account of what reality is like such that metaphysics is impossible: this is a useful starting point for understanding Laruelle, because he precisely attempts to offer an account of what immanence (Domain) is like from within finitude (Closure) such that a transcendental determination of what finite immanence is (Transcendence) is impossible. Of course, Laruelle is certainly not alone in such an effort.[10] However, what marks his project as qualitatively different than standard forms of philosophy is that he does not operate from a conceptual, but rather a performative idiom of thought, treating the Real aesthetically. This is precisely why his philosophy may be said to be "non-standard" or, as I put it, "non-dualistic."

Admittedly, Laruelle does not (as far I as know) use the term "ontological dualism" in his work, but this is just the sort of thing he describes in terms of the Principle of Sufficient Philosophy: that thought, in principle, is able to have knowledge of the Real as a conceptual object. Laruelle refers to this Principle as the "Parmenidean" heart of standard philosophy, since Parmenides assumes a pre-established harmony, or isomorphism, between ideality and the Real. For standard philosophy, there is a "cookie cutter" shape of, or "perforated lines" around, reality. Or as Raimon Panikkar puts it in his own diagnosis of Parmenides, the Real "is Thinking, that is, Intelligibility—not certainly for an individual mind, but as such" (Panikkar 2008, 119). In this way, standard philosophy functions in terms of what Laruelle refers to – riffing on René Girard – as "mimetic rivalry" (Laruelle 2015c, 29). Here, thoughts are treated as so many competing representations or approximations of the Real.

Of course, this Principle alone does not determine what the Real is. A Philosophical Decision is required, which may be understood as the *operationalization* of the Principle of Sufficient Philosophy. For if the latter tells us that the Real is, in principle, given to thought, then the Decision tells us *what* the Real specifically is given as conceptually in terms of F, and *how* it is given as much. "Givenness" is a phenomenological term,

---

[10] Cf. Cogburn on "object-oriented-ontology" (OOO) as operating from a suspension of the operation of Transcendence (Cogburn 2017, 60-90).

which points to the basic assumption of standard philosophy, namely, the Real appears. Specifically, the Real appears ontologically: as either being or its negation, non-being (Laruelle refers to this second term as "alterity"). Here "being" is synonymous with the conceptual object of what Heidegger refers to as "ontotheology" whereas non-being or alterity is the conceptual object of what Conor Cunningham refers to as "meontotheology" (Cunningham 2002). Ontotheology operates upon a determination of the Real as something (*a* being), while meontotheology operates upon a determination of the Real as nothing (non-being). We might also refer to this dualism in terms of "identity and difference," for whereas ontotheology operates upon the presupposition of a *univocal* identity between thought and the Real (qua *a* being), meontotheology operates upon the presupposition of an *equivocal* difference between thought and the Real (qua non-being).

Standard philosophers thus assume their sufficiency to determine what the Real is conceptually, in terms of univocity or equivocity, and how they are able to do so epistemologically. This combination of "what" and "how" constitutes a dualistic conditioning/conditioned schema. For instance, in realist philosophy, the Real (the object of knowledge: *ontos*) conditions how thought (the means of knowledge: *logos*) has access to the Real; whereas in anti-realist philosophy, thought becomes both its own object and means of knowledge without reference to a knowable external reality, thus overdetermining the Real and reducing it effectively to non-being. (Anti-realism is, remember, the upshot of the Berkleyan/Fichtean argument against the noumenal.) Regardless, then, whether one treats the Real as being or non-being, either way, one assumes thought can obtain dualistic distance by which to determine the Real and so turn it into an object of knowledge. Here, thoughts are treated as so many competing representations or approximations of the Real, as either being or non-being (see Laruelle 2013b, 1999, 2003; cf. Smith 2016, 13-34).[11]

Standard philosophers assume a dualistic, bilateral relationship between thought and reality: both that reality determines thought and that thought is able to determine an assumed previously existing, knowable reality back conceptually. In Priestian terms, thought is able to effect an operation of Transcendence by which to turn around, as it

---

[11] Both John Milbank and Ray Brassier have critiqued the theory of the Philosophical Decision as only applicable to post-Kantian thought (Brassier 2007, 118-149; Milbank 2011; 2014, 101-2). Laruelle's schema is, indeed, not universal. However, Laruelle's significance is that he identifies the operational structure of philosophy *insofar as it is conceptually dualistic* – a structure that applies across many times and systems of thought.

were, and objectify the Real. As Laruelle puts it, philosophy "is always a *decision* or a transcendence" (Laruelle quoted in Smith 2016, 180; emphasis original). Or as he describes it elsewhere, "philosophy projects a reality in itself, which is to say, one that has been constructed in the realm of operational transcendence, within which it claims to intervene, and in terms of which it gauges all possible intervention" (Laruelle 2003, 183-4; emphasis original). However, such an operation of Transcendence is *inconsistent*, according to Laruelle. He protests:

The philosopher, legislating for reason, the life of the mind or social life, makes an exception even of the fact that he does not do what he says or does not say what he does, but, speaking the law, he makes an exception and enjoys the privilege of speaking about it and imposing it with his authority. (Laruelle 2012a, 230)

In other words, when thought makes a Philosophical Decision (that the Real is best approximated by thought-world x), this constitutes an inconsistent operation of Transcendence by which thought both is and is not contained within the Real. For insofar as a Philosophical Decision determines that some posited thought-world accurately approximates the Real, this Decision inconsistently both belongs to and transcends the generic immanence of the Real. Laruelle rejects any and all determinations of this kind.

Laruelle is a non-Parmenidean, which means that the Real cannot be treated as ultimate reality. This is because the attempt to objectify the Real as an ultimate reality presupposes a dualistic difference between thought and the Real, and he denies such a possibility. We may therefore justifiably refer to Laruelle's position as a form of *generic non-dualism*. For Laruelle, thought and the Real constitute a non-duality (what he calls a "unilateral duality"), dictating that every attempt to determine the Real in terms of some distinguishable property is but a pipedream. Every Philosophical Decision, admittedly, creates the appearance of a conceptual duality between a thought-world and the Real, subject and object, but it is just that – an appearance. Raimon Panikkar, in his own writings, describes the problem of non-duality this way: "to ask about the 'meaning' of a thing is different when asking about reality because we cannot make reality an object that would leave the (asking) subject outside it" (Panikkar 2008, 3). Laruelle himself describes this kind of non-dual problematic in terms of thought's *radical immanence* to the Real.

We may understand radical immanence in terms of a phrase appropriated from Maurice Blondel's theology: the Real is "the beyond *of* thought" (Blondel quoted in Cunningham 2002, xvii-iii; emphasis original).[12] This does not mean that thought has conceptual knowledge of what is *beyond* conceptualization – such a proposition would generate an inclosure paradox. How could thought conceptualization that which is beyond conceptualization? Rather, that the Real is the beyond of thought means that it is the transcendental *a priori* from which thought necessarily thinks. The Real is given to thought "prior-to-the-first" determination of what the Real is ontologically. Laruelle defines it as "given-without-givenness" (*don sans donation*). Said differently, the Real is given to thought without being given as being or non-being. It is presupposed without being conceptually posited since it is "*the* presupposed, *the* condition" of all thought-worlds (Laruelle 2015c, 38; emphasis original). The Real is, therefore, strictly non-phenomenological. It does not appear within the confines of a thought-world, and so every attempt to determine the Real *as* world *x* comes too late because the Real is "the strictly unreflected upon form of truth" without any definable form or content, the generic truth prior to conceptualization (Laruelle 2010d, 20). Inverting Cusanus' idea of "learned ignorance" (*docta ignorantia*), Laruelle therefore asserts that the Real is a kind of "unlearned knowledge" (*savoir indocte*). This sounds as though the Real operates like Kant's transcendental synthetic *a priori* categories of the mind, but the Real is non-thetic. Indeed, Laruelle may be said to take the road abandoned by Kant insofar as the Real may be understood as the transcendental analytical *a priori* of thought, that is, the necessary condition of thought, which not does not add to our knowledge in any way but is the generic tautology ($A = A$) from which thought thinks (see Galloway 2014).[13] In this sense, the Real is a strictly non-conceptual form of knowledge. The implication of this is that one can articulate the transcendental *a priori* of thought without making recourse to empirical experience, pace Wilfrid Sellars (see Sellars 1997). The Real is non-inferential, immediate, and transcendentally prior to any determination of what it is: the bare fact *that* there is anything at all.

---

[12] As Anthony Paul Smith comments, non-standard philosophy "is formally similar to theology. . . . Theology thinks from God and not of God in the same way that philosophy would think of God," although the critical difference is that the Real is foreclosed to authority (Smith 2013, 95, 102). This formal similarity is unsurprising given that non-standard philosophy operates from a post-Cantorian model of consistent incompleteness, and thus shares with ontotheology, despite their divergences, the axiom that "some truth is beyond language" (Livingston 2012, 59).

[13] The proposition that "the Real = Real" is, of course, an iteration of the "Law of Identity." But unlike the Aristotlelian version of this idea, which states that a thing is *what* it is, a non-standard Law of Identity generically states that *a thing is that it is*.

Ray Brassier, the fiercest Anglophone critic of Laruelle, dismisses non-standard philosophy precisely at this point, rejecting any appeal to intuition as unintelligible (Brassier 2012). I am sympathetic to Brassier insofar as Laruelle ties intuition specifically to the *experience* of the "human-in-person," though to what extent this identification is performative rather than decisional remains an open question. However, insofar as Brassier simply denies the very possibility of non-conceptual knowledge as but a manifestation of Wilfrid Sellars' "myth of the given" – thereby endorsing that an experience of something is a function of the *concept* of that thing – this is but dogmatic assertion. The demand that non-conceptual knowledge must be justified is incoherent, since if there is indeed such a thing as non-conceptual knowledge, it is unjustifiable, by definition, within the confines of conceptuality.

Specifically, we may understand this as a "digital" dogma. As Alexander Galloway defines it in his work on Laruelle, "the digital is the basic distinction that makes it possible to make any distinction at all" (Galloway 2014, xxix). This is another way to describe the assumption of conceptual dualism – that the Real (s) has some property (F) that makes it distinguishable from all other things, and that F is what allows s to be an object of ultimate knowledge. A digital representation of s bears the information that s is F, and no other information but this information (not including whatever is entailed by s being F). By contrast, an analog representation, besides the information that s is F, bears *additional* information with it that resists digital determination or systematic recombinability (Dretske 1981). We might say, then, that what makes non-standard philosophy "non-standard" is what makes it *analog*, which Galloway defines in terms of "the two coming together as one" (Galloway 2014, xxix). In this sense, every conceptual determination of the Real in terms of some property bears additional information – the transcendental, non-conceptual knowledge of generic immanence – which is precisely what underdetermines the stability of every digital, conceptual duality. Every determination of s in terms of F is in "excess of itself" (Laruelle 2013b, 4). The Real is thus non-conceptual knowledge, which resists recombinability to representation. However, it is not perceptual, computational, or even ontological knowledge. It is, rather, *real* knowledge of the noumenal thing-in-itself transcendentally given prior-to-the-first determination of the thing-in-itself. Playing with a Derridean term, we might say that the unlearned knowledge of the Real is a *real trace*. And as a real trace, it describes precisely that which is the *relation*, which itself not relational or conceptualizable, between every-thing and its objectification as F. As "a subject for the relation of two signifiers" (Laruelle 2015c, 32), the

Real determines every conceptual dualism as immanent to itself "in-the-last-instance" (which is simply another way to refer to a thing's immanence to the Real).

The real trace stands in opposition to how conceptual dualism operates, which operates from the assumption that a reflexive procedure is possible whereby thought is able to obtain a transcendental viewpoint (Transcendence) by which it can conceptually determine the Real, and how it can know as much. Every dualism thus operates upon a model of conditioned datum (the domain of experience posited through an operation of Closure) and its conditioning faktum (the *a priori* of experience posited through an operation of Transcendence), which are together posited as being the givenness of the Real as a whole: a synthetic unity of datum and faktum (as posited through an operation of Domain). Standard philosophy thus treats the Real as a "relative-absolute whole" (Laruelle 2013b, 232), that is, the conceptual synthesis of s and F, transcendence and immanence, faktum and datum, ontology and epistemology. But how is such an appearance possible if thought is radically immanent to the Real? As the transcendental analytical *a priori* of thought, the Real is the *necessary* but *insufficient* condition of knowledge. What is therefore needed is a Philosophical Decision, which is the *occasional* cause that creates a thought-world. In other words, the Real is first given-without-givenness, from which then a "cut" is made. And it is this decisional cut – the *positing* of the Real as world x – that projects a reality, a thought-world, which then appears to stand in separation from the Real. It is a Decision that causes the Real to appear as a potential object of knowledge that has some property F that distinguishes it from other things. In this sense, the very distinguishability of the Real only appears in and through a Decision, that is, a Priestian operation of Transcendence.

This appearance is made possible by what Laruelle refers to as the "unilateral duality" of the Real, or what I refer to as the "non-duality" between the Real and thought. As the transcendental analytic *a priori* of thought from which thought thinks, the Real determines thought unilaterally. Unilaterality dictates that every thought-world is determined by the generic immanence of the Real without it being able to determinate the Real in return conceptually back. This one-way determination is why thought always comes "too late." Using a mixture of Laruellian and Priestian terms, we might say that from the "vision-in-One," that is, the purview of generic immanence, every Decision to determine the Real (an operation of Transcendence) is immanent to the Real in-the-last-instance (Closure). A Decision cannot objectify the Real successfully because the Real is precisely that which is transcendentally operational prior-to-the-first positing of the Real as anything whatsoever.[14]

Non-duality thus signifies if the equation of the Real is the transcendental, generic tautology of thought (a = a), then a Decision does not add anything to the Real at all (a fact that be transcribed as $1 + 1 = 1$).[15] From within the purview of the vision-in-One, then, the appearance of duality is explicable precisely as just that – an appearance. As Brassier puts it, this duality has "only one side" (Brassier 2007, 142). Compare this to Raimon Panikkar's observation that the appearance of duality "is the so-called *relation vel distinction rationis* (distinction of our mind, but not objective or real). It was the opinion of Śankara, Thomas Aquinas, and others that the link is only real from our side" (Panikkar 2008, 215). In this light, we may assert that standard philosophy's conceptual dualism is an operation of paradoxical "auto-entrapment." For every attempt to trap (to determine) the Real within any given thought-world only ends up trapping philosophers themselves in an inclosure paradox. This includes those who would posit the Real as incomplete and immanent, for this very positing constitutes thinking of "*immanence in the mode of transcendence*" (Laruelle 2010b, 31; emphasis original).[16] Inhabitants of a thought-world, insofar as they operate from the Principle of Sufficient Philosophy, trap themselves in inconsistency. And in this sense, we might go so far as to say that inclosure paradoxicality is the very essence of standard philosophy. Herein lies "the endless confusion" of thought insofar as it treats the Real as an object (Laruelle in Barber, et al 2013, 103).

Here we come full circle to the *aporia* of finitude. Insofar as we are like blind men in the forest who have never met an elephant, we truly do not know what an elephant is. Insofar as are like a fly, we cannot know we are on the Sistine Chapel ceiling. Insofar as

---

[14] I take this argument to be representative of what I call the "Openness Schema" (see appendix A, §2).
[15] This might sound like Laruelle is a monist of some indeterminate kind. This is, for instance, how John Milbank misreads him (Milbank 2011). However, insofar as Laruelle adheres to a kind of generic actualism, he is able to treat the plurality of thought-worlds as irreducibly pluralistic because since thought-worlds have been stripped of their representational sufficiency, and so bivalence no longer applies. Thoughts-worlds are not competing approximations of the Real, but differential spheres of performative *actualization*.
[16] This is why we may refer to models of the Real, even those that determine the Real *as* immanence, as models of transcendence (see appendix A).

we like a cat or dog, we cannot know the contents of the books around us. Otherwise we would cease to be finite. We would have taken an exit from immanence.

Performance

Unlike ontological dualism, non-standard philosophy operates from a position of non-conceptual performance. Specifically, it operates from the presupposed, non-conceptual knowledge of the Real (Domain) and Closure (thought's radical immanence), while denying Transcendence (the sufficiency of thought to determine Ω). Laruelle is a *consistently* finite thinker who operates from an aesthetic rather than conceptual idiom of thought. Non-standard theory's consistency, is however, not logical in kind, but rigorously aesthetic and performative (cf. Ó Maoilearca 2015a, 97-140). Laruelle does what he says and says what he does in an open-ended performance without representing anything whatsoever. As performative, non-standard philosophy "exhausts itself as an immanent practice rather than as a programme," as he puts it (Laruelle 2003, 177). And this is because non-standard philosophy is theory that is inseparable from praxis, its content inseparable from form: all thoughts, as determined in-the-last-instance, are "art-thoughts" (Laruelle 2012b, 2).

We may refer to non-standard aesthetics in terms of the artificialization of thought. Laruelle has any number of terms for referring to thought-world's artificiality, foremost among them, "philo-fiction" (see Laruelle 2010c), which is a term used to designate the operations of a thought-world separated from its representational sufficiency. Specifically, we may define a thought-world, aesthetically, as *a differential sphere of performance*. For from within the "Non-Parmenidean Equation: Practice = Thought," performance "and thought are identical in-the-last-instance" (Laruelle 2012c, 114-15). A thought-world *is* its performance, it is as it does, and its "what" is its "how." We might say therefore that insofar as all thought-worlds are comprised of philo-fictions, every thought-world may be understood as a kind of "art-world." For since the Real is without appearance or presentation, there can be no "re-presenting" it; and since there is no way to re-present the Real, every philo-fiction is a kind of originary presentation of the Real (or what Laruelle sometimes refers to as a "clone"). Of course, the fictional status of philo-fictions does not mean they are somehow unreal. Indeed, given that Laruelle is an actualist (meaning that everything that is, is actual), this tells us that all philo-fictions are determined as real or actual in-the-last-instance (Del Bufalo 2003). They are real constructions. And what else is a "real construction" but a synonym for *techné*? – a technology, a craft, an organon, an artifice. So we may say that the artificialization of thought dictates its operationalization – that thoughts are to be *used* to perform, think, and create in new ways.[17] The Real is not an apophatic abyss, and non-standard philosophers do not take it as their highest vocation to stare senselessly into the opacity of immanence. Rather, non-standard philosophy is more like a cataphatic engine, that is, a means of innovation by which to create new art-worlds. As Laruelle himself declares, "Invent Philosophy!" (Laruelle quoted in Mullarkey 2012, 143).

Here we may think of another elephant other than the one we met earlier in the parable of the blind men. This elephant comes from the Buddhist Yogācārin philosopher Vasubandhu (c. 4th-5th). In *The Twenty Verses*, Vasubandhu asks us to imagine that we are seated at a magic show where a magician appears to make an elephant appear on stage. He tells us that insofar as we are unenlightened – that is, insofar as we have not realized the emptiness (*śūnya*) of the conceptual duality (*Dvaya*) of subject and object (*grāhyaṃ grāhakaṃ ca*) – we naively believe that world is as it appears to us. In other words, we believe that the magician has actually conjured up an elephant. Yet through training and practice, we can understand how the illusion works, and enlightenment is nothing else but knowing that the elephant is an illusion. However, and this is the key point, despite our enlightenment, it still *appears* as if there is an elephant on stage. Even after enlightenment, the appearance of conceptual duality persists – it is just that one now apprehends it in a non-conceptual way (see Gold 2015, 244-8). In the same way, we might say that insofar as art-worlds are apprehended from within the Principle of Sufficient Philosophy, one believes that the elephant projected as x is the elephant in-itself. When one understands the hard problem of finitude, however, one suspends this Principle and is able to think non-dualistically, that is, according to the Real in-the-last-instance. Nevertheless, even after this suspension has been enacted, the appearance of a duality between thought and the Real, between one's projected elephant and the elephant in-itself persists. But this is not a problem for non-standard philosophy because it is precisely in and through such illusory elephants that we think, experiment, and perform the Real in-the-last-instance. So the goal is not to transcend the apprehension of duality, but specifically to transcend thought's supposed *sufficiency* to objectify the Real conceptually. In

---

[17] Cf. this to Cogburn's reconstruction of OOO as a form of art, that is, "a way to make sense of things in new ways" (Cogburn 2017, 75).

this regard, the "blindness" of out finitude does not put us at distance from the Real but is precisely the transcendental condition for superpositioning and performing it. Here the "what" of reality is identical with "how" thought conceptualizes it in-the-last-instance.

In contrast to the conceptual idiom of thought, there is no onto-logical distance between the noumenal elephant (the Real) and the phenomenal elephant (philo-fiction). Every art-world is a kind of "phenoumenal" performance of the Real (if one will excuse the neologism). Such a proposition stands in a repudiation of the Berkleyan/Fichtean prohibition upon thinking the unthinkable noumenal. As Laruelle declared in his well-known debate with Jacques Derrida, non-standard theory operates *"from the thing itself"* (Derrida and Laruelle 2005; emphasis original). Fittingly, it was Derrida who proclaimed "there is nothing outside the text" (Derrida 1976, 158-9), which amounts to a reiteration of the Berkleyan/Fichtean argument that we cannot get "behind" the phenomenal to the noumenal. However, if we suspend ontological duality, then what becomes clear is that we always already think from the thing-in-itself because every thought is a thing-in-*itself*. It is phenoumenal. In this sense, we can separate the Real from ideality (logocentrism) while still recognizing the reality of all thoughts in-the-last-instance. We might even say *the text is always already outside of itself*. Non-standard philosophy is "not so much a question of breaking out of the circle," as Brassier put it in his earlier work, "as realizing that you were never inside it [the text] in the first place" (Brassier 2007, 129). Said differently, from within the vision-in-One, there is no way to distinguish the text (the finite, phenomenal projected elephant) and what is outside the text (the noumenal elephant of the Real) conceptually. We may there assert that the "problem" of an external noumenal reality is not truly a problem at all. It is an illusory *aporia* created by the procedures of standard philosophy, which creates the appearance of distance from the Real through an operation of Transcendence. One here could conceivably speak of non-standard philosophy as "externalizing" the phenomenal or "internalizing" the noumenal. But both descriptions still operate from a kind of conceptual dualism that is inappropriate, not because the difference is sublated, which is the route Hegel and German Idealism took, but rather because the phenomenal and the noumenal are held together in quantum "superposition" (see Laruelle 2010c). Superpositioning, in a basic sense, is another way to think of art-worlds not as approximations of the Real but as so many immanent performances of the Real. For the Real is indifferent to how it is superpositioned, performed, or cloned through philo-fictions. It is a "weak force" (see Laruelle 2015b). And non-standard philosophy is an alchemical means, as it were, by which to incubate and execute an endless proliferation of artistic performances. As an underdetermined weak force, the Real bears an illimitable series of determinations and superpositions. Here, then, it is noumenals materialized "all the way down," so to speak.

We may here reinvoke our adaptation of Kant's empirical directive ("reality, whatever it is, is known only through its effects, and of it, apart from them, we cannot have any concept of reality whatsoever"). For non-standard philosophy, the question is no longer, "What is the Real?" but "What can the Real do?" This points toward the generically empirical attitude of non-standard theory, which motivates its users to create and inhabit new art-worlds, new philo-fictions, new imagined elephants by which to superposition, perform, and explore in endlessly creative ways. For if we take this empirical directive as axiomatic, then – to play upon Spinoza's famous dictum about the body – we might say *we do not even know what the Real is capable of*. If the Real is only knowable in and through its effects, then we are in the position of blind men in a forest, a fly on the ceiling, a cat or dog in the library who cannot determine their lack of comprehension and so do not even know aprioristically what the Real can do .

This is, in so many words, what Laruelle points to as the "democracy-of-thought" (Laruelle 2012a), that is, an open-ended, performative conjunction and aesthetic exchange of art-worlds with no one in a position of royal transcendence. Here, philosophy, science, politics, and art converge as one, unable to be disentangled from each other in-the-last-instance. And this is because all art-worlds are forms of *rationality, experimentation, relationality,* and *creativity* all at once.

Non-Standard Religion

What would it look like to run religion through the organon of non-standard philosophy? Of course, Laruelle has already undertaken a number of religious experiments in terms of heresy, messianism, Gnosticism, and mysticism (Laruelle 2010a, 2015a, 2015d; cf. Dubilet 2015); and others have taken up theology (Smith 2013, 2011) and Buddhism in their own non-standard work (Wallis, Pepper, Steingass 2013). However, in what follows, I offer a theory of what we may call "non-standard religion" in general, which runs parallel to Laruelle's account of standard philosophy.

Let "the Sacred" be one of the first names of the Real (see n. 6). In this light, the axiom of non-standard religion is that all performance is transcendentally preceded by and presupposes an underdetermined domain of value: "the Sacred."[18] This dictates that all performance is immanent *to* the Sacred, and so is unable to determine what the Sacred is or how this is so. In Priestian terms, non-standard religion operates from the presupposition of Domain (the generic immanence of the Sacred) and Closure (performance's immanence to the Sacred), but is foreclosed from any operation of Transcendence by which thought could determine the Sacred as an ultimate end. Our project is, therefore, to provide an account of what the Sacred (Domain) is like from within finitude (Closure) such that transcendental determination of what the Sacred is (Transcendence) is explicated as both impossible and inconsistent. This would humble any attempt to treat the Sacred as an ultimate *telos*. Such would stage usher in a "de-ultimatization" or "de-teleologization" of sacrality, for the Sacred is precisely that which is prior-to-the-first determination of itself as a goal. Or, said differently, it is the real trace anterior to every determination of the Sacred.

"Standard religion," if we may use the term, is classifiable as a species of conceptual dualism, specifically, a type of *teleological dualism*. Teleological dualism operates from the following assumption: that the Sacred (s) has some property (F) that makes it distinguishable from all other ends, and that F determines s as an object of ultimate achievement. The assumption here is that performance can realize the Sacred as an end (*telos*) through practice (*pragma*). We may describe this idea in terms of "the Principle of Sufficient Hierophany" (as derived from Eliade's term, "hierophany": an appearance of something sacred). This Principle states that both that the Sacred is a goal and that performance is able to realize that goal through some posited way of life. The implication of this principle is that thought is able to obtain a dualistic distance by which to represent the Sacred as an object of realization for performance. We may refer to this as the "Pla-

---

[18] The term, "the Sacred," derives from combination of the work of Mircea Eliade and Ann Taves. Specifically, the Sacred is an *intentional* (and therefore not necessarily existent) object of ultimate value correlated to human consciousness, both apprehended through, and ascribed to, various things (Eliade 1969, i; Taves 2009, 16-55; cf. Rennie 2017). Here I offer a *non-phenomenological* and *non-ascriptive* reinterpretation of this term through a non-standard mutation of Eliade's philosophy of religion. I am of one accord with Bryan Rennie's sentiment that if Eliade "expressed a coherent understanding of religion which allows for sacrality to be identified with the ascription of reality without involving the assumption of autonomy, without defining sacrality in terms of a supernatural and independent ontology, he has surely made a contribution to the history of religions" (Rennie 2017:9).

tonic" heart of standard religion. Here Nietzsche's reconstruction of Plato is illuminating: "The real world, attainable to the wise, the pious, the virtuous man – he dwells in it, *he is it*. (Oldest form of the idea, relatively sensible, simple, convincing. Transcription of the proposition 'I, Plato, *am* the truth.')" (Nietzsche 2003, 50; emphasis original). The assumption here is that there is a pre-established harmony, or isomorphism, between teleology and sacrality, which dictates that the Sacred is the realizable goal of performance.

In order to put the Principle of Sufficient Hierophany into action, a "Hierophanic Decision" is required. The Principle states that, in principle, the Sacred is given as a goal whereas a Decision states *what* that goal (the *telos*) is specifically given as and *how* that goal is realizable (the *pragma*) in order to achieve what we may generically refer to as a "maximally beneficial" way of life, such as enlightenment, salvation, etc. Givenness, as we have already seen, is a phenomenological term, which signifies that the operative assumption of standard religion is that the Sacred appears, that is, that the Sacred gives itself as hierophany X, Y, or Z. Specifically, the Sacred appears teleologically: either as *the* purpose of life (as in ontotheology) or the purposelessness of life (as in meontotheology, that is, nihilism). In this sense, standard religion – as well as its mirror, "standard secularism" – operates from a model of teleological rivalry, for regardless of whether one treats the Sacred as an ultimate purpose (ontotheology) or ultimate purposelessness (meontotheology), one operates from the assumption that the Sacred is given as a goal, or the negation thereof. Teleological rivalry is the constitutive structure of both standard religion and secularism in that they both operate from the assumption that religions are so many spheres of representation and performance competing to conceptualize and achieve the one true maximally beneficial form of life.

As opposed to standard religion, let us explore a non-Platonic model of the Sacred. Here the Sacred would not be determined as an ultimate end. This is because the attempt to objectify the Sacred as an ultimate end presupposes a dualistic difference between performance and the Sacred, which is inconsistent. Why? Let us take the Sacred as the *generic immanence* that is transcendentally prior to its objectification as an ultimate end. We may define the Sacred, then as the transcendental analytic *a priori* of performance, that is, the generic tautology ($a = a$) from which we think and performs. In this sense, the Sacred, strictly speaking, is a form of non-conceptual knowledge, which we can articulate as a transcendental *a priori* of performance without making recourse to any experience, including even religious or mystical experience. Specifically, the Sacred is given-without-givenness, that is, given to thought and performance prior-to-the-first objectification of the Sacred as an ultimate end (that is, as the ultimate purpose or purposelessness of life). From the within the vision-in-One, therefore, *the Sacred does not appear*. It is not a hierophany. It is, rather, the non-inferential, immediate given that transcendentally draws performance into action prior-to-the-first-determination of goal-making. The Sacred is that which always already lures thought into a performative aim, whether that aim is spontaneous or sustained, near or far, great or small. Prior to any conceptual determination, we may describe the Sacred precisely as the transcendental analytic *a priori* of performance.[19]

As the transcendental analytical *a priori* of performance, the Sacred may be defined as the necessary but insufficient condition for goal-making. The Sacred is transcendentally given-without-givenness, and only thereafter posited as goal X, Y, or Z. For in order to make a goal, a Hierophanic Decision is required. A Hierophanic Decision may be defined as the *occasional* cause that makes a teleological formation, a differential sphere of performance, possible. Every differential sphere of performance constitutes a kind of cut from the generic immanence of the Sacred, which *conceptualizes* the apparent separation of "what is" from "what should be." Mutating Eliadean terms, teleological dualism operates in terms of a conditioning/conditioned schema whereby the conditioned datum (the profane plane of experience as posited through an operation of Closure) and its conditioning faktum (the Sacred as posited through an operation of Transcendence) are posited together as the givenness of the Sacred as a whole: the synthetic unity of the Sacred and the profane (the Domain). Here the Sacred and profane, problem and solution, diagnosis, etiology, prognosis, and treatment plan are all posited *simultaneously*. The Sacred and its opposite, the profane, are a single package deal (cf. Eliade 1959, 10). In Priestian terms, standard religion may be said to operate from the assumption that an operation of Transcendence, whether brought about by human or superhuman autonomy (or some combination thereof), can be effected by which to reveal the Sacred as an ultimate goal realizable through religious performance. In other words, the assumption is that either adherents of standard religion can obtain a transcendental viewpoint (Transcendence) by which they can determine the teleology of the Sacred (Ω) or that the Sacred (God, Being, Brahman, etc.) reveals and determines *itself* through a hierophanic operation of Transcendence. Either way, the knowledge and realization of the Sacred as

---

[19] In the language of Jorge Ferrer's participatory approach to transpersonal phenomena, we refer to the Sacred as *the undetermined mystery of reality* (see Ferrer 2017). One might helpfully contextualize my project here within the "participatory turn" (see Ferrer 2008; cf. Allison 2017)

ultimate end is made possible. Here we may mimic Laruelle and propose that adherents of standard religion may be said to project an ultimate end for themselves, which is to say, one that has been constructed in the realm of operational transcendence, within which they claim to intervene, and in terms of which they gauge all possible interventions.

This operation of Transcendence is inconsistent, however, given that the Sacred is precisely that which unilaterally determines performance in-the-last-instance. This dictates that thought is unable to determine the Sacred as an ultimate end of performance. Because from within the vision-in-One, every attempt to turn the Sacred into a realizable end of performance overlooks the fact that the Sacred is transcendentally prior to every teleological determination. Mutating Laruelle, Priest, and Eliade together, we can say that from the vision-in-One, every conceptualization of the Sacred (the operation of Transcendence) is in fact transcendentally immanent to the Sacred (the presupposed Domain) in-the-last-instance (Closure). In other words, thought is unable to determine the Sacred as an object of realization, because every performance is immanent to the Sacred to begin with. This we can understand that every Hierophanic Decision, every posited end, is only apparent and relative to the differential sphere of performance itself created through that Decision.[20] This appearance is possible due to the non-dualistic relationship between the Sacred and performance, whereby the Sacred unilaterally determines every performance as sacred in-the-last-instance. And this fact dictates that every determination of the Sacred as an ultimate end is one-sided, nothing but another occasion of the *relation vel distinction rationis* (distinction of our mind, but not ultimate in-the-last-instance). We may now assert, then, that since all religious worlds are immanent to the Sacred, we are all unable to objectify the Sacred from the outside. We are always already performing it prior to our conceptualization of it, and so are unable to determinate what it is. Performance is suspended in an axiological openness whose boundaries it is unable to demarcate, and any attempt to determine them reinstates the basic *aporia* of finitude. For insofar as thought posits the Sacred as religious world *x* to which it is supposedly immanent, this very positing constitutes an inconsistent operation of Transcendence by which thought both is and is not contained within world *x* conceptually.

---

[20] Every Decision serves a *differential* function existentially and politically. As Eliade puts it, we formulate hierarchies of values in order to make sense of, or "cosmicize" the Real, into the religious worlds we then inhabit (Eliade 1982, 201).

However, if we go way of non-standard religion, then we are free to bypass this *aporia* through the suspension of both the Principles of Sufficient Philosophy and Hierophany and their decisional operations.[21] Insofar as we recognize the unilateral determination of performance by the Sacred, we are free to treat every Hierophanic Decision in a religiously pluralistic way. Religions are so many "hiero-fictions" – a proposition that signifies the artificialization of religion.[22] Here, therefore, we may invoke Eliade, who declares, "no 'form' [of the Sacred] is exempt from degradation and decay, no 'history' is final" (Eliade 2004, xxiv). Mutated through non-standard religion, this declaration not only undermines any standard form of exclusivism, inclusivism, or pluralism, it also dictates that there can be no such thing, definitionally, as an ultimate end. Moreover, and as Eliade writes, "we cannot be sure that there is anything… that has not at some time in human history been somewhere transformed into a hierophany" (Eliade 1996, 11); or as he put it elsewhere, "the Sacred is manifest in an infinity of forms" (Eliade 1960, 353). In other words, because there can be no such thing as an ultimate end, the Sacred is precisely that which allows for an infinite proliferation of hiero-fictions, none of which is sufficient to determine it in-the-last-instance. The Sacred is infinitely performable. The Sacred allows for an illimitable number of axioms.

If we begin from the axiom that all of us are like blind men in a forest, flies on a ceiling, or cats and dogs in a library, then we do not and *cannot* know what the Sacred is, or even what it would mean for something to be the "ultimate" end of existence. Because from within non-standard forms of religion, we no longer ask "what is the Sacred?" or "Which religion is true?" We rather ask, "What can the Sacred do?" To adapt our revised empirical directive to religion, we might say that the Sacred, whatever it is, is known through its effects, and of it, apart from them, we cannot have any concept of sacrality. What constitutes a maximally beneficial form of life is no longer a dogmatic given, but an *open* and *empirical* question.

To think the Sacred from within finitude: such would usher in a democracy-of-thought, a democracy-of-religions, or, even better, a "parliament of religions" (with a nod

---

[21] A certain history of philosophy and religion would be possible through narrating the relationship between these two principles in terms of their dual-operationalization (ontotheology), the suspension of religion's sufficiency in favor of philosophy's sufficiency (secularism, atheism, materialism), or vice versa (as in various forms of Christian orthodoxy (see Adams 2014; Hart 2004); or their *dual-suspension*. The history of such dual-suspensions has yet to be written.

[22] As Peter Sloterdijk suggests, religions are "anthropotechnics," that is, technologies of the human being (Sloterdijk 2013).

to the 1893 Chicago World's Fair). For the formation of such a parliament of religions would initiate a true *scientia sacra*, as if for the first time. And such a science would be pluralistic, open-ended, empirical, performative, and democratic (cf. Blake 2016).

Conclusion

It is one of the great ironies of post-metaphysical thinking that in attempting to reject a transcendental viewpoint, it so often ends up with royal knowledge anyway. This is because to know the boundaries of immanence, one would have to know where immanence ends and transcendence begins. But how could one ever determine the boundaries of immanence from within the vision-in-One? We thus find ourselves suspended in this indeterminate, open interval between the finite and a limit we cannot comprehend, caught up in the creation of art-worlds from which we design and enact an endless supplementation of non-dualistic thought and performance without finality. Of course, this does not mean that we cannot make, or have not made, progress in knowledge. Relative, finite progress is always possible empirically and ethically. It is rather the idea of *ultimate* progress that has been rendered unintelligible.[23] We might again say that the limits of thought are boundaries that cannot be crossed, but we do not even know what they are. And since we do not know the limits of the thought, *we do not even know what the Sacred is capable of*. Organized research programs into the Sacred are needed.

It therefore becomes imperative to think pluralistically and non-dualistically, that is, to think *generically*. For it is, finally, only a rigorously generic thought of the infinite, which would be able to approach the infinite freed from the authority of both philosophy and religion – an infinity that we could never conquer through conceptualization or achievement, but requires open-ended experimentation. And such a thought of the infinite that dictates the incompleteness of the finite.[24] We never find closure on the Real or the Sacred. And why would we want to? If indeed our goal is not to transcend the apprehension of duality, but specifically to transcend the apparent sufficiency of thought to conceptualize infinity, then non-standard religion may be understood as an apparatus of the

---

[23] In order to account for *how* such progress from within non-standard theory, the relationship between *art* and *truth* would need to be explicated (see Graham 1996).

[24] A generic infinity is closest to Cusanus' model of the infinite in that, unlike the Scotist-Cartesian lineage's treatment of infinity as a "clear and distinct idea," it is a rigorously finite and purely *negative* concept.

impossible: the site of unending production for thought and performance. As Vasubandhu insists, after enlightenment, the appearance of duality persists. Conceptuality is not the enemy, but a conventional tool to be *understood*.

We always already finds ourselves within the finite, unable to determine the infinite. However, this should not drive us to overcome this indeterminancy and so fall into an inclosure paradox, but rather to embrace endless art-making: an "open *doxa*" of performance that is more "musical" than it is dialectical. We may understand this process of art-making as a kind of *empirical mysticism*, a mysticism that cannot be separated from philosophy, science, politics, or art. For *sacrality* cannot be separated from the designing of art-worlds, and every art-world is a site of rationality, experimentation, relationality, and creation In this sense, we might say such empirical mysticism is the very means of our own self-creation and becoming. For in the end, a non-standard procedure is nothing else but an *asceticism* – a "divinely artificial art" (Nietzsche 2010, 37). And so we offer a closing imperative: invent future religion!

John Matthew Allison, M.Div, Princeton Theological Seminary,
allisojm[at]gmail.com

References

Adams, Marilyn McCord. "What's Wrong with the Ontotheological Error?" *Journal of Analytic Theology*, Vol. 2 (2014): 1-12.
Allison, Matthew John. "Participation and the MysteryTranspersonal Essays in Psychology, Education, and Religion," Reading Religion: A Publication of the American Academy of Religion (October 23, 2017). <http://readingreligion.org/books/participation-and-mystery>
Badiou, Alain. *Being and Event*. Oliver Feltham (trans.). New York and London: Bloomsbury, 2013.
Blake, Terence. "FEYERABEND'S ONTOLOGY: pluralist, diachronic, apophatic, empirical, and democratic." Agent Swarm (2016). Web. 8 September 2017. <https://terenceblake.wordpress.com/2016/02/02/feyerabends-ontology-pluralist-diachronic-apophatic-empirical-and-democratic/>
Barber, Daniel Colucciello, Alexander Galloway, Nicola Masciandaro,and Eugene Thacker. *Dark Nights of the Universe*. Miami: [NAME] Publications, 2013.
Brassier, Ray. "Laruelle and the Reality of Abstraction." in John Mullarkey and Anthony Paul Smith (eds.). *Laruelle and Non-Philosophy*. Edinburgh: Edinburgh University Press, 2012: 100-21.
Brassier, Ray. *Nihil Unbound: Enlightenment and Extinction*. Basingstoke: Palgrave Macmillan, 2007.

Braver, Lee. *A Thing of This World: A History of Continental Anti-Realism*. Evanston, IL: Northwestern University Press, 2007.
Chalmers, David. "Facing Up to the Problem of Consciousness." *Journal of Consciousness Studies*, Vol. 2, Nr. 3 (1995): 200-19.
Cobb, John. *Transforming Christianity and the World: A Way Beyond Absolutism and Relativism*. Orbis: Maryknoll, NY, 2002.
Cogburn, Jon. *Garcian Meditations: the Dialectics of Persistence in* Form and Object. Edinburgh: University Press, 2017.
Cunningham, Conor. *A Genealogy of Nihilism*. London: Routledge, 2002.
D'Costa, Gavin. "The Impossibility of a Pluralist View of Religions." *Religious Studies*, Vol. 32, Nr. 2 (June 1996): 223-32.
Del Bufalo, Erik. *Deleuze et Laruelle: de la schizo-analyse à la non-philosophie*. Paris: Kimé, 2003.
Derrida, Jacques. *Of Grammatology*. Gayatri Chakravorty Spivak (trans.). Baltimore, MD and London: Johns Hopkins University Press, 1976.
Derrida, Jacques and Laruelle, François. "Controversy Over the Possibility of a Science of Philosophy." Robin Mackay (trans.). *La Decision Philosophique* No. 5 (April 1988): 62-76, Accessed 09/06/2017: http://pervegalit.files.wordpress.com/2008/06/laruelle-derrida.pdf.
Dretske, Fred. *Knowledge and the Flow of Information*. Cambridge MA. MIT Press, 1981.
Dubilet, Alex. "'Neither God, nor World': on the One foreclosed to transcendence." Palgrave Communications (2015). Web. 8 September 2017. <www.palgrave-journals.com/articles/palcomms201527>
Eliade, Mircea. *Imagination and Meaning: The Scholarly and Literary Works of Mircea Eliade*. Norman J. Girardot and Mac Linscott (eds.). Ricketts. New York: Seabury Press, 1982.
Eliade, Mircea. *The Quest: History and Meaning in Religion*. Chicago: University of Chicago, 1969.
Eliade, Mircea. *Patterns in Comparative Religion*. Rosemary Sheed (trans.). Chicago: Chicago University Press, 1996.
Eliade, Mircea. *The Sacred and the Profane: The Nature of Religion*. Willard R. Trask. (trans.). New York: Harcourt, Brace & World, Inc., 1959.
Eliade, Mircea. *Shamanism: Archaic Techniques of Ecstasy*. Princeton: Princeton University Press, 2004.
Eliade, Mircea. "Structures and Changes in the History of Religion," in *City Invincible—A Symposium of Urbanisation and Cultural Development in the Ancient Near East*. C. Kraeling and R. Adams (eds.), 1960. Chicago: Chicago University Press:11-14.
Ferrer, Jorge N. "Spiritual Knowing as Participatory Enaction: An Answer to the Question of Religious Pluralism." in Jorge N. Ferrer and Jacob H. Sherman (eds.). *The Participatory Turn: Spirituality, Mysticism, Religious Studies*. New York: SUNY, 2008.
Ferrer, Jorge. *Revisioning Transpersonal Theory: A Participatory Vision of Human Spirituality*. Albany, NY: SUNY, 2002.
Galloway, Alexander. *Laruelle: Against the Digital*. Minneapolis: University of Minnesota, 2014.
Gangle, Rocco. *Diagrammatic Immanence: Category Theory and Philosophy*. Edinburgh: Edinburgh University Press, 2016.
Gangle, Rocco. 2014. "The Theoretical Pragmatics of Non-philosophy." Angelaki, Vol. 19, Nr. 2 (April 2014): 45-57.
Graham, Gordon. "'Aesthetic Cognitivism and the Literary Arts." *Journal of Aesthetic Education*, Vol. 30 (1996): 1-17.

Gold, Jonathan. *Paving the Great Way: Vasubandhu's Unifying Buddhist Philosophy*. New York: Columbia University Press, 2015.
Hart, David B. *Beauty of the Infinite: The Aesthetics of Christian Truth*. Grand Rapids: Eerdmans, 2004.
Hegel, J.G.W. *Encyclopaedia of the Philosophical Sciences. Part One: The Shorter Logic* digital transcr. by Andy Blunden, 1997 <https://www.marxists.org/reference/archive/hegel/works/sl/>
Heim, S. Mark. 2001. *The Depth of the Riches: A Trinitarian Theology of Religious Ends* (Grand
Hick, John. *An Interpretation of Religion: Human Responses to the Transcendent*. New Haven and London: Yale University Press, 2004.
Hick, John. *God and the Universe of Faiths*. London: Macmillan, 1973.
James, William. *A Pluralistic Universe*. Cambridge, Massachusetts and London, 1977.
Kant, Immanuel. *Critique of Pure Reason*. Norman Kemp Smith (trans.). New York, NY: St. Martin's Press, 1965.
Keller, Catherine and Laurel C. Schneider (eds.). *Polydoxy: Theology of Multiplicity and Relation*. London and New York: Routledge, 2011.
Kierkegaard, Søren. *Concluding Unscientific Postscript*. D. Swenson and W. Lawrie (trans.). Princeton: Princeton University Press, 1968.
Kripal, Jeffrey J. *Authors of the Impossible: The Paranormal and the Sacred*. Chicago: University of Chicago Press, 2010.
Laruelle, François. "A Summary of Non-Philosophy." *Pli* 8 (1999): 138-48.
Laruelle, François. *Christo-Fiction: The Ruins of Athens and Jerusalem*. Robin Mackay (trans.). New York: Columbia University Press, 2015a.
Laruelle, François. *Future Christ: A Lesson in Heresy*. Anthony Paul Smith (trans.). New York, Continuum, 2010a.
Laruelle, François. *General Theory of Victims*. Jessie Hock and Alex Dubilet (trans.). Malden, MA. Polity Press, 2015b.
Laruelle, François. *Intellectuals and Power: the Insurrection of the Victim*. Anthony Paul Smith (trans.). Malden, MA: Polity Press, 2015c.
Laruelle, François. *Mystique non-philosophique à l"usage des contemporains*. Paris, France: L'Harmattan, 2015d.
Laruelle, François. "Is Thinking Democratic? Or, How to Introduce Theory into Democracy." in John Mullarkey and Anthony Paul Smith (eds.). *Laruelle and Non-Philosophy*. Edinburgh: Edinburgh University Press, 2012a: 227-237.
Laruelle, François. *Photo-Fiction, a Non-Standard Aesthetics*. Drew S. Burk (trans.). Minneapolis: Univocal Publishing, 2012b.
Laruelle, François. *Philosophies of Difference: A Critical Introduction to Non-Philosophy*. Rocco Gangle (trans.). New York: Continuum, 2010b.
Laruelle, François. *Philosophie non-standard : générique, quantique, philo-fiction*. Paris, Kimé, 2010c.
Laruelle, François. *Principles of Non-Philosophy*. Nicola Rubczak and Anthony Paul Smith (trans.). New York, Bloomsbury, 2013b.
Laruelle, François. *Struggle and Utopia at the End Times of Philosophy*. Drew S. Burke and Anthony Paul Smith (trans.). Minneapolis: Univocal, 2012c.
Laruelle, François. "The Truth According to Hermes: Theorems on the Secret and Communication." *Parrahesia* Vol. 9 (2010d): 18-22.

Laruelle, François. "What Can Non-Philosophy Do?" trans. Ray Brassier. *Angelaki*, Vol. 8 Nr. 2 (August 2003).

Livingston, Paul. *The Politics of Logic: Badiou, Wittgenstein, and the Consequences of Formalism*. New York: Routledge, 2012.

Ó Maoilearca, John. *All Thoughts Are Equal: Laruelle and Nonhuman Philosophy*. Minneapolis: University of Minnesota Press, 2015.

Milbank, John. "The Habit of Reason." Stanton Lecture. University of Cambridge, Cambridge (February 23, 2011). Lecture.

Milbank, John. *The Suspended Middle: Henri de Lubac and the Renewed Split in Modern Catholic Theology*. Grand Rapids, MI: Eerdmans Publishing, 2014.

Mullarkey, John. "1 + 1 = 1: The Non-Consistency of Non-Philosophical Practice (Photo: Quantum: Fractal)." in John Mullarkey and Anthony Paul Smith (eds.). *Laruelle and Non-Philosophy*. Edinburgh: Edinburgh University Press, 2012: 143-168.

Panikkar, Raimundo. *The Rhythm of Being: the Gifford Lecture*. Maryknoll, NY: Orbis Books, 2008.

Priest, Graham. *Beyond the Limits of Thought*. Oxford: Clarendon Press, 2002.

Rennie, Bryan S. *Reconstructing Eliade: Making Sense of Religion*. Albany, NY: SUNY, 1996.

Rennie, Bryan S. "The sacred and sacrality: from Eliade to evolutionary ethology." *Religion* Vol. 4, Nr. 4 (2017): 1-25

Sloterdijk, Peter. *You Must Change Your Life: On Anthropotechnics*. W. Hoban (trans.). Malden, MA: Polity Press, 2013.

Smith, Anthony, Paul. *A Non-Philosophical Theory of Nature: Ecologies of Thought*. New York: Palgrave Macmillan, 2013.

Smith, Anthony Paul. "A Stumbling Block to the Jews and Folly to the Greeks: Non-Philosophy and Philosophy's Absolutes." *Analecta Hermeneutica* 3 (2011).

Smith, Anthony Paul. *Laruelle: A Stranger Thought*. Malden, MA: Polity Press, 2016.

Wallis, Glenn, Tom Pepper, Matthias Steingass. *Cruel Theory - Sublime Practice: Toward a Revaluation of Buddhism*. Denmark: EyeCorner Press, 2013.

Wittgenstein, L. *Tractatus Logico-Philosophicus*. Side-by-side-by-side edition, version 0.53 (5 February 2018), containing the original German, alongside both the Ogden/Ramsey, and Pears/McGuinness English translations. < http://people.umass.edu/klement/tlp/tlp.html>

Wolfson, Eliot R. *Giving Beyond the Gift: Apophasis and Overcoming Theomania*. New York: Fordham University Press, 2014.

Appendix A: Inclosure and Openness Schemas

1. Inclosure Schema (see Priest 2002, 156):

(1) $\Omega = \{y; \varphi(y)\}$ exists and $\psi(\Omega)$ Existence
(2) if $x \subset \Omega$ and $\psi(x)$ (a) $\delta(x)$ not-$\in$ x   Transcendence
                                (b) $\delta(x) \in \Omega$ Closure

Figure 1. Inclosure Schema

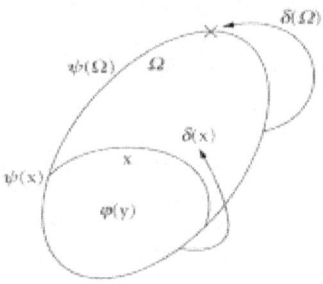

2. Non-standard Philosophy's Openness Schema[25]

The Real (Ω) is immanence (y) given-without-givenness (φ), as in $\varphi(y)$. Non-standard philosophers think according-to the Real, meaning the Ω is non-conceptual and thus undetermined, as in $\psi(\Omega)$. Let us posit x, the domain of thought, which is taken as a subset of Ω, and that $\psi(x)$. Together, $\psi(\Omega)$ and $\psi(x)$ make up the axiomatic basis of non-standard philosophy. Next, let us apply an operator, δ (a Philosophical Decision) to x, which conceptualize Ω specifically in terms of F. However, insofar as $x \subseteq \Omega$, then $\delta(x)$ is immanent to the undetermined limits of both x and Ω in-the-last-instance. Thus non-standard philosophy is constituted by an "open doxa" of performance that is *aesthetically* consistent and incomplete.

(1) $\Omega = \{y \mid \varphi(y)\}$ is given and $\psi(\Omega)$ Domain
(2) if $x \subseteq \Omega$ and $\psi(x)$ (a) $\delta(x) \in \Omega$ Closure
                                    (b) $\delta(\Omega) \in \Omega$ Closure

Figure 2. Openness Schema

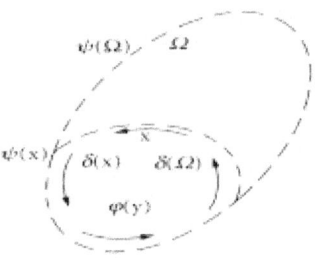

---

[25] Cf. Gangle 2014. Elsewhere Gangle proposes that "diagrams are the appropriate method for investigating immanence immanently" (Gangle 2016, 2).

ELENI LORANDOU (Lancaster)

Non-philosophical mystique and the rehabilitation of heresis

Abstract

In the second part of the Triptych, Mystique non-philosophique à l'usage des contemporains, *François Laruelle puts to the test of "non-philosophy" the field of phenomena that are termed as "religious" whether Christian, Judaic or Gnostic. Non-philosophical mystique is born in the spirit of heresy rather than sanctity. It springs from the effort to join Man with himself rather than with God founding the radical cause of the new Logos in the One-in-One. Man is emptied from his identity, becomes a Christ-subject who comes to fight for the World. Future mystique ends as the amorous knowledge, an erotic a priori constitutive of the mystical subject: it is not an illusory transformation of Man or a revision of his relation to God or the World. The final aim – as I will try to show – is to transfigure the heretical experience, mystical as well as erotic of the human such as it becomes capable of a form of unison with itself as unique Other.*

Keywords: Non-philosophical mystique, One-without-God, Man-in-Man, Christ subject, Heretical fight

A non-philosophical mystique?

In the Triptych, that has been inaugurated with *Future Christ: a lesson in heresy* (2002), Laruelle does not invite us to a historical wandering to the limits of Christianity. Rather, he attempts to sketch the outline of an organon that would render the Christian phenomenon theoretically intelligible and allow it to be experienced in a human way. The second part[1] entitled *Mystique non-philosophique à l'usage des contemporains* (2007) makes this even more evident as it refrains from redesigning Christian mysticism and renewing it on a philosophical basis or from composing literary fiction on the basis of a body of traditional texts. Rather than doing a theoretical exercise, Laruelle attempts to put to the test of "non-philosophy" the field of phenomena that are termed as "religious" whether

---

[1] The third part has yet to be published.

Christian, Judaic or Gnostic because, as he says, "the problem concerns the plurality of universals and a capacity (*puissance*) of thought that would admit their plurality, at the conflicting origin, without relativising them by a relationship of one to the other, but rather extracting them from their warfare." (Laruelle 2011, 32) The idea is of "unloosing the original nucleus" by initiating a mystic experience that is devoid of any trace of onto-theological transcendence. Already, in the pages of the *Principles of Non-Philosophy*, Laruelle defines the "mystical" (*le mystique*) strictly in terms of a radical immanence,

> We distinguish mysticism and mystique [*la mystique et le mystique*][2]. Mysticism is an experience of the soul's identity with transcendence. It therefore entails transcendence *within* certain immanence, a mix of the two; it does not separate the soul from transcendence through a real mode but rather ties it to transcendence; finally it makes immanence a property or attribute of the relation of the soul and of God rather than a subject-essence as such. On the other hand, we call the mystic a real and actual essence, an already-performed-without-performance as we will call it, an absolutely autonomous instance rather than an attribute, property, event or relation. This essence therefore no longer involves transcendence, rather it excludes it absolutely. (Laruelle 1996, 55)

As it is, the whole difficulty seems to lie in understanding that the simplicity of non-philosophical mystique is not something new but lies profoundly hidden in the depths of traditional mystical quests.[3] More specifically, it attempts to unify on the radical basis of the Real[4] three modes of religious experience that have ignored or even critically challenged each other: the legacy of Christian and Neo-Platonic mysticism through Eckhart and the Russian Hesychasm (with primacy to the Real as Man-in-Man rather than to God or to the Deity), the heretical thought, burdened by centuries of persecution and an eschatological/messianic sort of inspiration put in the service of a certain philosophic and religious practice of the "Last Days" (Laruelle 2007, 8). Moreover, the non-mystical project takes the form of a tentative non-Christian heresy since as Laruelle puts it, "heresy, more so than Judaism, can be the opportunity to pose this problem, the chance of freeing the universals from their competition." (2002, 32) Ancient mysticism has always been close to heresy: it

---

[2] Revised translation of the English translation by the author.
[3] "But the real difficulty in understanding the simplicity of non-philosophy is profoundly hidden in the depths of philosophy itself" (Laruelle 2012, 3).
[4] Real (One-in-One, Vision-in-One): Instance defined by its radical immanence under all possible conditions of thought: thus by its being-given (of) itself, yet called Vision-in-One or One-in-One, and by its being-foreclosed thought (Laruelle 1998, 61).

places man at the center of its device of salvation and God in its infernal periphery. Speculative and simple, it pretends to exceed philosophy and onto-theology at the same time that it uses their conditions to address all humble souls. Laruelle describes heretical thought as,

> The combination of speculation and "poverty of mind", the erasure of the hierarchy between the simple and the learned, the collusion of humility and transcendence by *epekeina*, the bracketing of the meta, here is an intolerable short circuit, a heresy. (Laruelle 2007, 86)

Inspired, hence, by the spirit of heresy, we are called to posit the hypothesis of an identity that is more than speculative or dialectical, a radical identity of poverty of mind and of theory as thought by those who are devoid of any thought or doctrine. This is the unified theory of mysticism and heresy which, in its radical simplicity, is not meant to receive an ontologico-theological meaning even after conceptual explanation, "Future mystique must be born in the spirit of heresy and manifest itself as the posture of the ordinary man or the Subject-existent-Stranger (Sujet-existant-Étranger)" (Laruelle 2007, 86). The heretical subject, a stranger to the World constituted by mystical and philosophical decisions does not hold the keys for unlocking the hidden secrets of the Real; extricating himself from all dogmatic belief according to the Vision-in-One, he is an ordinary subject, an anonymous stranger, indifferent to the philosophical categories pretending to the Real.

Old-mysticism and fiction-mysticism

> *"Mysticism is less a heresy or a liberation from religion than an instrument for the work of unveiling, within religion itself, a truth that would first be formulated in the mode of a margin inexpressible in relation to orthodox texts and institutions, and which would then be able to be exhumed from beliefs. The study of mysticism thus makes a nonreligious exegesis of religion possible. It also gives rise, in the historical relation of the West to itself, to a reintegration that eradicates the past without losing its meaning"* (Kearney 2010, 9).

The heretical feeling is in fact one of urgency, urgency to break with the market of salvation, the sufficiency of religions, God too. What non-philosophy calls "future" or "non-religious" mystique is opposed in its Christian references, its sources and its material to the "religious" or "old" mysticism. It is also called 'Fiction-mystique' (mystique-fiction) or even 'Christo-fiction' as opposed to 'World-mysticism' (mystique-monde), religious or corrupted by the spirit of the World (Laruelle 2007, 58). The aim here is to challenge the philosophico-religious sufficiency, the dogmatic consistency of the old form of mysticism and place the mystical experience free from the traces of unclaimed, dogmatic transcendence within the reach of Man-in-Man.

Laruelle calls World-mysticism (*mystique monde*) the old mysticism of philosophical and Christian style that has been accumulated in history and culture as to give a new form of World that is more of a mixture of philosophical experiences and theological dogma. The guiding definitions of the old mysticism such as "God and Man", "alone with God" program a communication of types of reality, a type of conversion and often of convertibility that makes the mystical union a philosophical servitude for man. More precisely, "'they transform into insoluble questions and into a simple infinite desire for realization the performative-immanent act which is that of the Vision-in-One or the Man-in-Man"(Laruelle 2007,36). That is why an operation is required, other than the classic union of God and man, an operation which, by treating the religious relationships according to a practice of *dualization* (unilateral duality), sets at play the cloning of the subject by Man.

The purpose of a non-philosophical mystique bereft of transcendence and constitutive of human reality is to maintain an experimental science of thoughts and affects and to invent new statements that have God and the world as objects. It is not a question of rejecting all previous notions but instead of trying to conserve some of them in new functions by 'modeling' the construction through their unification-without-synthesis. The conditions for this modeling "must be acquired inside of a radical setting between parenthesis of every philosophical sufficiency of faith and Gnostic knowledge, lest their materiality will be destroyed" (Laruelle 2002, 128). Since the new mystique is one of fiction, to be invented in the way of an experimental science, it requires an object of experimentation, which, in this case, is the old mysticism. This latter, offers its conceptual and experiential material, which the fiction mystique is willing to appropriate first by removing its sufficiency, then its structure and meaning. In what concerns this appropriation, Laruelle explains:

> It requires an impoverishment in transcendence from which we will remove not only its particular philosophical postulates but philosophy itself, as mediation presupposed necessary to the unification between a creature and God. A mystique without constitutive theology that is born in the spirit of humility rather than that of the capital-world will proceed by suspense of these axioms. (Laruelle 2007, 57)

Axiomatisation of philosophico-religious symptoms

The old mysticism was characterized by the sufficiency of the religious belief in God as the hyper-philosophical Real or the One with all its alienating effects. Instead of dividing man according to metaphysical clivages such as the soul and the body, non-philosophy will *dualize* him *unilaterally* advancing through axioms, and formulating theorems of fiction-mystique. Is it then a question of returning to man what religion snatched from him? Return the mystical experience to its holder? If the old mysticism is conversion of man to God, the fiction mystique will not merely repeat it in the reverse order. Instead, "it must experience and consume it for the sake of a Man-without-God, who is always capable of an innermost experience" (Laruelle 2007, 37). Then, the call is for a mysticism that must be revised according to a new apparatus, theoretical as well as pragmatic, rather than turning itself into the object of a dialectical re-appropriation that invokes man only to re-appropriate him to God. In Laruelle's own words:

> We did not come to fulfil the ancient mystique but universalize it under non-religious conditions, according to a universal sense of humanity whose messianity (messianeté), the religions, *always particular*, have never suspected. (Laruelle 2007, 38)

It is the method of ultimation that distinguishes the two mysticisms, by inserting them in a difference so radical that is not even a "difference". To achieve this, non-mystique needs a material of symptoms to practice, to dualize according to the Vision-in-One, which is to be found in the omissions of ancient mysticism. The old transcendental terms of philosophy, generalized and formalized, obliged to part with their ontological anonymity, are emptied from their content and religious meaning only to be reborn as non-philosophical axioms and theorems. From the structure of Christian mysticism and from the onto-theo-logical realm in general, we get first names such as "Christ", "World", "son of God", etc., that are subjected to certain rules and procedures required by the Vision-in-One. They are *first names*[5] because they designate the "persons" – in the non-conceptual sense of the term – of the Man-in-Person, of individuals who have the form of the One-in-One in-the-last-instance. Through its operation, the non-philosophical mystique addresses and transforms three fundamental problems of traditional philosophical mysticism:

- The problem of the *One* that is the cause of all mystic thesis which is no more God but the Vision-in-One or the Man-in-Person, with God being only its symptom. See-in-One, that is, in-man, ceasing to want to unite with a transcendental being.
- The problem of the *subject* properly mystical -no more the religious or philosophical creature but the "Son of Man-in-Man" or the "Future Christ". Union as a subject to the world by uniting to the Man-in-Man through the Christ-subject.

---

[5] *First name*: Symbolic element of the transcendental axiomatic, formed on the basis of a philosophical concept and entering into the constitution of the axioms that describe the One (*Laruelle* 1998, 18).

- Finally the problem of the *World,* no more theological or metaphysical but the World of their mixture as *melange* [6], viewed also as Hell (*enfer*).

As God is reduced to a simple theological model, the first axiom of "Vision-in-One", which is necessarily more than an axiom, becomes the very cause of mystique. The radical identity of the One is bound to be heretical because it is indefinable, indemonstrable not only in philosophy and theology, but intrinsically so.

One-without-God

> "In contradistinction to mysticism, here we postulate an absolute autonomy, the Real itself, of the mystical experience in the sense whereby it is the mystical that is the core-in-the-last-instance of all possible experience". (Laruelle 2007, 56)

To free oneself from the infernal sufficiency of united philosophy and theology, is to redefine the One no longer as God but, by the first name of "One-in-One" or "in person", which in fact corresponds to the last essence of Man. In practice, non-philosophical mystique starts with the non-positional position (of) oneself of the One rather than from a supposed desire of the Other, "the mystical is not in front of us, far from us, or close behind, virtual or potential, demanding reversal, conversion, return or turn. It is in-us or rather it is us who are actually in it, in-mystique or in-One as the One itself" (Laruelle 1998, 56). More specifically, the Vision-in-One means that the One is not supported by anything - even not by itself and at the difference of the One-God or the One-in-One is without-essence, non-unitive or non-unitional.

Neither does it pretend to bring the One by the intermediary of the Other or the Same, figures of extreme transcendence. The Vision-in-One is Given-before-all-givenness, radically unreflected experience-(of)-itself, deprived by the support of the being and never constituting a mystic dimension for the flux and return of beings.

As non-intellectual, "unlearned knowledge" (*savoir indocte*) that however determines a theory, the Vision-in-One enables the concept of a heretical mysticism that is not itself a heresy.

---

[6] Other first name for the philosophical Decision insofar as it is founded on reversibility as structure or limit-tendency of the mélange, fold, relation, correlation, synthesis, convertibility, etc. –characteristic of specifically philosophical unitary syntaxes. (Laruelle 1998, 33)

Heresy is then the intrinsic character of the Real, the fact for one to be without essence rather than a solitude of situation, that a doctrinal and institutional separation. (Laruelle 2007, 88)

Future mystique is closer to psychoanalysis than philosophy in its refusal of the supposed enjoyment of God through the medium of philosophy. It installs itself in the heart of the One, "distinguishing it from the classic *(impossible) enjoyment of the Other* as *Enjoyed-without-enjoyment* but also from the enjoyment that is now possible and determined by the Enjoyed which is foreclosed to enjoyment" (Laruelle 2007,71). This distinction is quite important because the absence of a possible enjoyment *of* and unison *in* the One are the conditions for a new determination of the unison *for* the subject. The non-consistence of the *separate-without-separation*, which is not to be confused with nothingness (*le néant*), is not a mode of ecstatic *epekeina* but the phenomenal content of it.

The non-consistency of Man-in-Man

The One-without-God can alone renew our idea of man as being heretical or separated *par excellence*. Is future mystique the simple inversion of the philosophical, the exchange of roles between God and man? The first ultimation of man can always appear, from the philosophical point of view, as a substitution of man for the divine and a rebellion, "however vision-in-One is more than a rebellion, it is the real presupposition of any rebellion" (Laruelle 2007, 68). It is not man who is substituted for God by a kind of inversion of the fundamental relation. Taking the position of One-Man as pre-supposed radical, it is Man (calling himself the last-identity of the existing Christ subject) who is substituted for the convertibility of God and human. Instead of joining the human to God and God to philosophy, it is a move towards joining the human to itself or to leave mysticism to its non-human destiny.[7]

Traditionally, man is found separated by the world by an act of divine creation. Nevertheless, this is not exactly a sign of separation but more one of his inclusion in an enlarged world-form. In a non-mystical context, man is separated from the world not in the ordinary sense but in an immanent manner untainted by an act of separation. Heresy in not the result of a detachment from the world and a union with God, rather it coincides perfectly with the *being-performed* of the One. Humans have no more essence than to be or exist-

---

[7] In The "Call and the Phenomenon" (2013:11), F. Laruelle, referring to Jean-Luc Marion, says, "He joins the human to God and God to philosophy, instead of joining the human to itself or of leaving philosophy to its non-human destiny."

ence, they have a being-giving-in Man. Their non-consistency renders them Man-in-Man, independent of God and the World, Being and the Other, but capable on the other hand of determining a certain experimental knowledge of these things Laruelle talks about the "void" of the non-mystical human figure:

> Only Man is this empty identity where nothing other than him is found, except man. It is this non-consistency of Identity-without-unity where one does not even find God. Human "abandonment" means "man is abandoned (to) Man and he can only abandon God with the world and abandon Him to the World" (Laruelle 2007, 83).

Future mystique is born from the being-separated (of) the Man and his primacy over God in the spirit of the heresy rather than the sanctity. The true spirit of heresy is that God and man do not redouble each other in the worldly human order nor redouble themselves in the in-human order of God. If heretics claim mysticism, it is without transcendence first, de-deified. It is the One-without-God alone that can renew our idea of man such as a heretic characterized by, "the radical humility, the non-consistency (that) is our holiness to us, devoid of religious significance, holiness proper to the Stranger[8]" (Laruelle 2007, 83). Lastly, freeing man from his consistency ensures his ultimate freedom from the pretentions of the philosophical decision. It is the freedom of the determination in-last-humanity, the autonomy of the axiomatic decision exercised in the field of historical Christianity, its dogmas and concepts that are now liberated, if not from their content at least from their onto-theological essence. In this, non-philosophical mystique fulfills the aims of the ancient mystics.

Humans as Futures

The "old" mystics have always employed the imperfect tense in their descriptions of the One-God. Nevertheless, the immanence of Man-in-Man cannot be spoken of neither in the present of actuality nor in the memory of the past- the subject has to be a messianic *Came-without-coming (Venu-sans-Venir) a Came (Venu) that is not the object/result* of an operation of coming. This means that the Man-in-Person is never a thing accomplished or already given but a being-performed, living and acting *in-real-Time.* Down to its pragmatic

---

[8] Finally found in the Stranger its strategically most adequate concept of man, more exactly of the subject as existing beyond the real immanence that it nevertheless is in its ultimate cause. Determined-in-the-last-instance by the real or radically immanent Ego, the subject exists in certain transcendental and aprioristic functions produced by the real Ego cloning them on the basis of the occasion that is the World. (Laruelle 1998,71)

action, "the Vision-in-One is in fact called in the radical future, it is the "in-Real-Time" since,"the way of the future is to be an effectuation of the universal past under the conditions of the time-world" (Laruelle, 1998, 81). This signifies that the future exists not in the sense of a time to come but in that of a transcendental identity turned towards the present. This ultimatum of time affects the mystic subject and "prevents it from coinciding unitarily with itself" (Laruelle 2007, 139). If eternity is a co-presence that traverses the temporal dimensions, the Man-in-person is an "eternal" future, meant to be determined-in-the-last-days or by the Last Days, not in the end of time but *in-real-Time*. It is by a heretical thought that time is dismantled and its three orders liberated to their manifested being.

Christ subject: the clone

Given the transfiguration of the ideas of God, Man and the World, how are we to perceive the historical figure of "Christ"? According to the non-philosophical reading of Christianity, it appears as a restricted interpretation of the Son (*le Fils*) not of God, since the One is liberated from its theistic content, but of the universal man. Non-mystique allows another use of Christ firstly as a simple symptom and secondly as a particular interpretation of the mystical subject. In this new context, He is no more a sacrificed Son of God but a Son cloned by Man and thus a messiah *for* the World who will "expose the a priori component of a philosophical dyad as a fantasy of transcendence precipitated by the indifference of the One toward philosophical thought" (Reszitnyk, 2014, 49).

The cloning of Son of Man has symptoms in the old mystique in the forms of *henosis* or deification, incarnation of *logos*, union of God and man. What all these notions have in common is, however, a synthesizing principle that relies on the convertibility of God and man. The problem that Laruelle sees here is that the confusion that affects the relations of filiation forbids thinking the science of men according to them. This results in alienating the life and threatening it by God while God lacks the human identity and is lost in a "super essentiality", in a "super consistence" (Laruelle 2007, 177). For all intents and purposes, "mysticism can no longer accept living the life of another, of God, instead of living its own life" (ibid.) From this springs the need to humanize the subject rather than deify it, since the determination in-the last-instance liberates God Himself and makes this divine aterial a variable of the Son of Man. If *theosis* is a transcendent donation, cloning[9] is other than

---

[9] The transcendental clone is the true minimal phenomenal essence or *identity of the double*, its identity without synthesis or its being-in-One-in-the-last-instance. (Laruelle 1998, 32)

becoming-man of God, more of becoming-God of man where God is seen emerging *as* Son. In its heretical radicality, the mystic subject does not seek God. Neither does he desire Him *as* God but as transcendental identity of the subject-God. He invents the divine more than he desires it, by deducing it from the Vision-in One as "this originary cloning of the One is the surest destruction of metaphysical doubling or philosophical doublets, it is even, if we can say this, *double('s)-identity as such [l'identité telle quelle (du) double]*"(Laruelle 1998, 138). The surest destruction of the metaphysical double, God-man as well its radical identity is to ensure that "philosophical material is identical-in-the-last-instance with a real that is radically autonomous with respect to it, and that this identity does not constitute sameness" (Reszitnyk, 2014, 48). If the Christ subject is born from this simple articulation that is the clone, the cloned being is no really an image of God, it is the possibility for radical immanence to transmit itself without losing the nature of its non-essence. The transcendental identity of the Christ subject in not a double of the One nor in the image *of* the One but a unilateral image of the World, a wave to one side, not to two sides as the entity reflection-thing in mirror" (Laruelle 2007,180).

To break immediately with the circle God-Man means to refuse to distinguish Man from the World. Cloning is not an accompaniment of transcendence by immanence but the unilateral extension of the in-One towards the World, the diffusion of its identity to the world without an act of diffusion. There is no divine revelation but the Vision-in-One, no Son-mediator, either. The Vision-in-Man is the reveal-without-revelation involving an experimentation of the World, a revelation in the form of cloning, a birth without process, a being-born-itself. In this non-procedural process, Man-in-person seizes the world in which he exists as Son.

The heretical fight for the World

Cloning is the transcendental operation of the Real through which the transcendent World is seen in every way as given immanently but only in-last-Identity. Because the One is foreclose to "its" knowledge and even "its" thought, it is able to determine them in-last-identity as knowledge of the World and no longer of the One. Hence, the world is given "in-One" but not in the sense of a divine creation. "Being-seen-in-One" signifies being given rather than thought, or thought but insofar as thought must be also given in-the-last-instance-in-One.

Traditionally, religion despised the world and has sought, similarly to philosophy, to integrate a broader experience of the World that could be thought philosophically. Thus, expressions such as "World mysticism," "God-world," "Christ-world," all define historicosystematic entities in a self-encompassing style. The concept of the world is transformed in non-philosophy, by being determined by the Man-in-person in the form of a theorem. It is enlarged by the fusion of two opposites, one of which is always philosophy as form-world (fusion of philosophy and the world, philosophy and mysticism, etc.) and second the transcendental identity of this concept determined and cloned by human Vision-in-One. In future-mystique, the immediate object of philosophy, which is the world, has always the internal form of this latter. The philosophical apparatus enriched by the supplement of the Christ experience supposes to reinforce the dimension of reality. This mixture is the element that allows philosophy to surpass itself with its own means and to meet the challenge of the burden of the divine and mysticism to conceptualize its ends and the type of reality to which it aspires. This will be better understood through the idea of fight *for* the world (Lutte *pour* le Monde) for which the Son-in-Man and we all, as Futures come.

The introduction of mysticism to man means that he frees himself from the sufficiency of hell by being his own kingdom and his own heavens. This is not a simple deviation from dogma or a recapture of heretical identity. Fiction-mystique aims at appropriating these heavily loaded religious concepts and heretically transfiguring them for a worldly use by the Christ subject. In the philosophical fight against representation and the mystical fight against positivity, non-philosophical mystique substitutes the heretical struggle against the world. The world as well as time is given in order to be transformed, appropriated in the identity of a clone. When the Subject Christ "clones" the One on the basis of a particular instance of philosophico-mystical material, he shows as Andrew Reszitnyk explains, "the transcendental component of philosophical decision to be identical in-the-last-instance with the real, and causes the real to assume a transcendental function a propos philosophy." (Reszitnyk 2014, 48) He measures the World according to Man-in-Man. Measured thus, "World" is whatever falls in the "World," "Time," as what falls in "Time," and the same goes for evil and even man, "it is the fall in sufficiency" (*la chute dans la suffisance*). However, in relation to what has fallen, we call "World" the identity (of) the World that extracts the sufficiency out of what falls within its domain treating it as a symptom. If the philosopher is the man who escapes *from* the world, the Christ subject goes *to* the world. His immanent identity, far from enclosing him in himself, vows him to the world and to fighting against its sufficiency. More generally, Futures (*les Futurs*) being the transcendental organon *for* the World, they come not *in* the World but *for* the World and respond to its solicitation because "our aversion for the sufficiency of the World rather than for the World in itself does not keep us away in an eidetic flight but we turn "to" him" (Laruelle, 2007, 215). It is not thus a question of a war but of a fight with the matter of the world in order to appropriate its intelligence in a new, non-consistent form. It is not as if Man had to fight against the transcendental illusion of the World in the name of an ideal, or under a divine duty, "the practice determined by the Man-in-person is this struggle *for* the World" (Laruelle 2007, 216). In the context of this heretical fight, the world is called "Hell" (*enfer*) on the basis of an axiomatic decision; it is the *first name* of its sufficiency. This associates it less with the idea of sin than with that of *the hallucination of the Real*, understood as the faith in the sufficiency of religion and philosophical reason. Hence, "to go to the World" (*aller au Monde*) is not at all a religious withdrawal, an ascetic escapade towards God. Rather it is a reduction of faith to the world, a reduction that man offers to the world as a gift (without donation). Because, as Laruelle explains, "it suffices less of a god than of a Christ subject supporting his rigor of the human to save the world from the complacency in which it is lost" (2007, 218).

The *a priori* of erotic ecstasy

The onto-theology of union to and separation from the World and God finds a last usage, albeit a symptomatic one, in a practice of non-unitional-unison, cloning with only the world (thus with God too). It is a practice of erotic unison pertaining to the mystic affect but the future heretic no longer aspires to divinization and even less to deification. This not because he does not desire but because he exists as ultimately performed according to a *primacy-without-primacy*. Nevertheless, this does not mean that the desire for God is now turned to a desire for the world.

By its structure, the Fiction mystique is a unified theory not only as explanation and usage of Christian mysticism, a kind of experimental science but also as an erotic and amorous pragmatic as claimed by the Neo-Platonists. If these lovers of harmony, viewed philosophy as a *happy life* and mysticism as *beatitude of the wonderer*, "the theoretical beatitude acquired a priori by the intellect will take another meaning as beatitude of the amorous union, as an erotic a priori constitutive of the mystical subject" (Laruelle 2007, 276). The beatitude sought by all the mystics of the past has changed status and is now viewed as an "extatico-erotic structure in which the amorous unison of human subjects is consumed."(ibid.), because nothing is given with man if it is not (in) himself. It is not possible to apply to Man-in-Person the method of unison that guaranteed the traditional convertibility of man to God while the opposite would still be a part of the structure of philosophical decision. Neither is it a question of trusting the mystical adventure in the hands of man rather than in God's. Rather, it is "to transfigure our heretical experience, mystical as well as erotic of the human such as it becomes capable of a form of unison with itself as unique Other" (Laruelle 2007, 277). It is not an illusory transformation of Man or of his relation to

God or the World but a transfiguration in view of acquiring a knowledge that would be identical to the constitution of his own personal existence. Hence, non-philosophical knowledge is not opposed to amorous sensibility, it is a theory made sensible in an a priori erotic way. Between its heretic cause rooted in the separated-without-separation and its erotic destination, it is here seen as entirely transformed, "what was simple means or pathos of union with Christ becomes organon of the One-in-One and structure of the subject" (Laruelle 2007, 277).

Eleni Lorandou, PhD Candidate, Lancaster University,
e.lorandou@lancaster.ac.uk

References

Kearney, Richard. *Anatheism: Returning to God After God*. Columbia University Press: New York, 2011.
Laruelle, François. *Philosophie et non-philosophie*. Mardaga: Liège/Brussels, 1989.
Laruelle, François. *Mystique non-philosophique à l'usage des contemporains*. L'Harmattan: Paris 2007.
Laruelle, François. "The End Times of Philosophy." *Continent*. 2.3 (2012): 160-166.
Laruelle, François. "The Call and the Phenomenon." *Journal of French and Francophone Philosophy / Revue de la philosophie française et de langue française*, Vol. XXI, Nr. 2 (2013): 105-117.
Laruelle, François. *Principes de la non-philosophie*. PUF: Paris, 1996.
Laruelle, François et Collaborateurs. *Dictionnaire de la non-philosophie*. Kimé: Paris, 1998.
Laruelle, François. *Le Christ futur, une leçon d'hérésie*. Exils: Paris 2002.
Resnitnyk, Andrew. "Wonder without domination. An introduction to Laruelle and Non-Philosophy." *Chiasma: a site for thought*. 1 (2014): 24-53.

STANIMIR PANAYOTOV (Sofia)

Non-Theurgy: Iamblichus and Laruelle

Abstract

Mysticism, theurgy, non-philosophy: this text will experiment with the three in an attempt to perform a non-philosophical hijacking of so-called theurgy (theurgia). I will experiment with a comparison between Iamblichus' theurgy, Laruelle's non-philosophy, and the notion of the Vision-in-One. I claim their point of convergence is their allegiances to the theory of the One, derived from Plato's Unwritten Doctrines. The ancient notion of the One is subject to a similar procedural gesture in both Iamblichus and Laruelle, namely, the procession of the One from the noematic to the aesthetic realm. What connects them is their rejection of the theory that the soul's descension from the One to the visible realm represents a degeneration of the Nous. In a concept akin to the very idea of theurgy, Laruelle proposes his Vision-in-One, which is to think from the One rather than the One. The Vision-in-One is an attempt to materialize the disembodied fate of the noema against realistic skepticism.

Keywords: Iamblichus, Laruelle, non-philosophy, theurgy, the One

I. On Theurgy

Theurgy was a set of ritual practices among Neoplatonists and other late antique circles to invoke the gods and unite with the divine – it allegedly involved incantations/chants and sacrificial offerings, of which we know very little. The historical evidence for its existence is flimsy and esoteric. Indeed, it is this flimsiness that invites for imaginative re-performance based on quasi-religious speculation and esotericism, which I take up here and call it non-theurgy, in an attempt to synthesize Iamblichus and Laruelle.

Iamblichus' exposition of theurgy already offers a redemptive design of the divine which, as I suggest later, embodies some of Laruelle's ideas and his reception.[1] By way of speculative designing of a "non-philosophical theurgy", I call for embodied practices (sound/chants/prayers) to suggest the body of the theurgist – be it Iamblichus or Laruelle –

---

[1] There is a kind of enthusiastic ritualism and anything-goes Gnosticism attached to Laruelle's reception going on.

is the vehicular agency of embodying the One on this unilateral side of the Real/World. The body of the theurgist must become the receptacle of absolute non-thinking so that the Divine can arrive and descend into the embodied One of unilateral reality.[2]

I will experiment with a comparison between Iamblichus' theurgy and Laruelle's non-philosophy and the notion of the Vision-in-One. I claim their point of convergence is their allegiances to the theory of the One, derived from Plato's Unwritten Doctrines. However, I try to update the Laruellian engagement with the One by *gnosticizing* and de-philosophizing theurgy. The ancient notion of the One is subject to a similar, but not identical, procedural gesture in both Iamblichus and Laruelle, namely, the procession of the One from the noematic to the aesthetic realm. What connects them is their rejection of the theory that the soul's *descension* from the One to the visible realm represents a degeneration of the Nous. In a concept akin to the very idea of theurgy, Laruelle proposes his Vision-in-One, which is to think from the One rather than the One (Laruelle et al. 2013, 165-168). Iamblichus' exposition of theurgy already offers a similar redemptive design of the divine.

What we know for sure is that theurgy represented a set of practices for the invocation of the divine. It was a spiritual practice in the heights of what Hadot insistently terms "philosophy as a way of life" (Hadot 1995, 264-277). Theurgy was a radical way of bringing back the role of and exercising the divine in human life. In modern times, theurgy is associated with some strands of occidental magic(k), i.e., Hermeticism, white magic, and Ordo Templi Orientis (see Webster 2016, 149-153).

According to Proclus, theurgy is "more excellent than all human wisdom, and which comprehends prophetic good, the purifying powers of perfective good, and in short, all such things as are the effects of divine possession" (Proclus 1816, 81). It is a veritable zeal to outscore the centuries-long Platonic intellection syllogistically and to condense it into an "irrational" short-cut to becoming one with the One. This ambition to create a spiritual "shortcut" to the Divine often downgrades theurgy to an irrational aberration of late Neo-platonism, and deep into the early 20th century studies and interest in it were suppressed by sidelining it as a parascholarly infatuation. Dodds partially corrected this pattern, though famously calling Iamblichus' *On the Mysteries of Egypt* "a manifesto of irrationality" (Dodds 1959, 287), while some retribution has been done on the *Chaldean Oracles* by the

---

[2] As a first and experimental example of an already existing non-theurgical prayer I will suggest here the work of Hunter Hunt-Hendrix of Liturgy. Consider, in his own words: "What I am doing is trying to spin out a new kind of system of philosophy – just like, say, Hegel's system, but more mobile: an RSS feed, album, actions, diagrams – all gesturing at a logic of becoming and an ethics but never landing on one, because in any case this is not possible to do, as I think Laruelle's philosophy of immanence has shown." (Rothbarth 2016)

likes of Majercik (Majercik 1982); thus, theurgy entered the scholarly world of investigating late antique philosophies quite of late. Theurgy was as close as becoming an official Roman doctrine with the rule of Julian (332-363 CE) whose commitment to theurgy and influence of Iamblichus almost led him to an ecumenical version of theurgical paganism, with an emphasis on prayer. Julian, describing the celestial workings of a henadic cosmology, strikes a powerful balance between rational and irrational, which defies Dodds' insistence on irrationality and opposition to mysterial thought, by saying

> [...] confining the appellation of hypothesis to the doctrine of the sphere: for the truth of the former is testified by men who audibly received this information from gods, or mighty daemons; but the latter is founded on the probability arising from the agreement of the phaenomena. Hence, if any one should esteem it better both to praise and confide in the former, such a one, whether I am trifling or in earnest, will meet with my esteem and admiration. (Julian 1932, 73)

If Iamblichus and Julian sought more manifest forms of the One in/as ritual, this was because it was preceded by Plotinus' *henosis* (oneness, unity). The idea comes from his henology as developed in the *Enneads* (see Plotinus 1988, 327-331), where Plotinus advocates a meditative withdrawal of thought from the highest hypostasis of the One. In Plotinus, for the One to be identical with itself, it cannot be ever thought (see ibid., 319-323). This precept, of course, is an idea juxtaposed to his more elaborate teaching of emanationism – the processual emanation of the world of beings from the One in four stages. But Plotinus never went as far as to suggest that lack of thought of the One can be *performed* in an embodied way. Plotinus advocated contemplation, while Iamblichus sought the path of incantation. A similar enthusiasm in the reception of Laruelle's work is being manifested today, one ripe with voluntarist ritualism and mysticism.[3]

The major sources for theurgy we have are the anonymous *Chaldean Oracles* and Iamblichus' *Mysteries*. In the *Oracles*' famous fragment 153, we read: "The souls that are re-established in this (pentad) come under the sway of destiny, says the oracle: 'For the theurgists do not fall into the herd which is subject to Destiny'" (Majercik 1982, 181). In her commentary (ibid., 386-387), Majercik clarifies that the theurgist is not subject of passion (the herd) and is one of the "few" (*hoi oligoi*). Now, Iamblichus clearly singles out the

---

[3] It is thus not by chance that non-philosophy has entered the Anglophone academia with more success in arts programs rather than philosophy departments. See as examples the event "Dark Nights of the Universe" (2012) and the subsequent publication (Thacker et al., 2013), as well as the video based on the same work, directed by Aaron Metté (2012).

theurgists as the "few," and in this respect, he is a sound Platonist. What is odd is his theurgical insistence on incorporeality:

> A certain few individuals, on the other hand, employing an intellectual power which is beyond the natural, have disengaged themselves from nature, and turned towards the transcendent and pure intellect, at the same time rendering themselves superior to natural forces. ... Those, on the other hand, who conduct their lives in accordance with intellect alone and the life according to intellect, and who have been freed from the bonds of nature, practice an intellectual and incorporeal rule of sacred procedure in respect of all the departments of theurgy. (Iamblichus 2003, 258-259)

In the *Oracles*, the Supreme God is nothing less than the Nous/The Father. In Neoplatonism the highest hypostasis is not a God, but nonetheless its gender is quite ambivalent. This gendering, which we now see as a sign of embodiment, does not in the least bother late antique writers. But the insistence on incorporeality and disembodiment in Iamblichus' version of ascending to the One is odd for the simple reason that the theurgist's body does remain a material obstacle to henosis; and it is an obstacle because the One cannot be contaminated with division caused by thought. Iamblichus' theurgy was a way to overcome this problem: it is, however, and remains, a spiritual ordeal, not a materialistic quasi-Platonism. What matters here is that Iamblichus defends the descending of the soul from the One as *non-degenerative* of henosis. The text of *Oracles* does not espouse, however cryptic and enchanting its nature, reverence to de-conceptualized abstractions of divinations. "What can be affirmed of the Chaldean father is the fact of his transcendence" (Majercik 1992, 8-9). The Father is still second intellect, because it is divided in nature. Therefore, a way must be established for the theurgist to sideline transcendence, and that way clearly cannot account for *logoi*.

In Imablichus' *De Mysteriis* [*On the Egyptian Mysteries*], the emphasis put in his version of (bypassing) emanationism is that, in theurgical practice, nothing emanating from the One is lost to the lower spheres of beings and becomings. The practice certainly invites imitation of the gods, having in mind that no morsel of the desired henosis degrades the One to the realm of anthropic existence. In this regard, Iamblichus' supposed "irrationality" is indeed an even more radical form of Platonic monism. What bothers post-Iamblichean Platonism is the peculiar idea that a representative of the "few" can paradoxically utilize embodiment to achieve such a ritualistic shortcut to the One. Actually, the first recorded mention of "theurgia" in fragment 153 already affirms that those "few" are but a standard subset of the philosophers chosen to commune with the One. But why invent another name, the theurgists? There must be some sort of deficiency in "philosophy."

It is to this philosophical deficiency that I now turn to claim a proximity between theurgy and non-philosophy later. The theurgist compensates something for the philosopher: in divination and ritual *for* the One, s/he performs God-work, not God-talk (Clarke, Dillon, and Hershbell 2003, xxix). Iamblichus has been versed in the hermetic literature and aware of the *Oracles*, as well as Orphism, which he intimates. To understand this God-work and move on to the comparison with Laruelle, one should know that the *Mysteries* are an answer to a Christian Neoplatonist, Porphyry. The text is a reply that seeks to provide answers in three areas: philosophy, theology and theurgy. We should also remember that "Iamblichus felt that his task of producing a written defense of theurgy was inherently impossible" (ibid., xlix) and that, thus, "philosophical speculation is futile." But is/was performation/ritual the answer? Theurgy is certainly very akin to the contemporary theories and practices of performance, but it is devoid of performance's inherent noumenal skepticism. It is a passage from philosophy and logos to theosis, not from philosophy to theosophy. The skepticism for philosophy comes from a religious critique of Hellenism, which is not the same as anti-rationalist ritualism. In his own words, having lost the power of prayer,

> [the things] are endlessly altered according to the inventiveness and illegality of the Hellenes. For the Hellenes are experimental by nature, and eagerly propelled in all directions, having no proper ballast in them; and they preserve nothing which they have received from anyone else, but even this they promptly abandon and change it all according to their unreliable linguistic innovation. (Iamblichus 2003, 301)[4]

Iamblichus contends that the "Greeks" as philosophers are degenerating to the level of the herd, and the herd is fate-ridden. (This critique should not be conflated with Socrates' critique of speech.) His response to Porphyry aims to liberate the few from fate and bring them to revelation. The providential motif of liberation is laid out clearly at the very end of the *Mysteries*:

> But this part (sc. of philosophy) is not, as you suspect, "overlooked" by the Egyptians, but is handed down in an appropriately pious manner. Nor do the theurgists "pester the divine intellect about small matters," but about matters pertaining to the purification, liberation and salvation of the soul. (ibid., 353)

---

[4] Note the semblance carried by this passage from *Corpus Hermeticum*: "For the Greeks, O King, who make logical demonstrations, use words emptied of power, and this very activity is what constitutes their philosophy, a mere noise of words. But we [Egyptians] do not [so much] use words (*logoi*) but sounds (*phônai*) which are full of effects" (translation from *Corpus Hermeticum* adapted by and cited in Shaw 2016, 109 n.6). See further reflection, especially with regards to the use of words like barbarism, in Iamblichus 2003, 301-302.

In Book X, just before his final exhortation, we find the place where Iamblichus *claims* (again, this is not a "defense") that theurgy is the only salvific path to the good (ibid., 345-346) – or whatever good there is in "predicting the future" (Porphyry's concern):

> Does truth not co-exist in its essence with the gods, and not merely in harmony with them, based as it is in the intelligible realm? In vain, therefore, are such allegations bandied about by yourself and some others. And not even those gibes with which some ridicule those who worship the gods as "vagabonds" and "charlatans," the like of which you have put forward, apply at all to true theology or theurgy. (ibid., 345)

Iamblichus' projection of theurgy is not riddled with the consequences that Porphyry seeks in his "predicting the future." By insisting on moving on beyond philosophy (an interpretation I suggest but which clearly needs more detailed work) to theurgy, or the God-work, Iamblichus offers a pragmatic account of the original meaning of henosis. For what use is there in the pessimism that the One is unachievable if that will render the philosophical life not-Good? Therefore, there is something wrong with words and something good in sounds. However paradoxical it might seem, sound is closer to the imperative of *not changing the prayer*. The elaboration of theurgy is thus a pragmatic and instrumental update of the philosophical life. Iamblichus operates with the polarity utility vs futility:

> Only divine mantic prediction, therefore, conjoined with the gods, truly imparts to us a share in divine life, partaking as it does in the foreknowledge and the intellections of the gods, and renders us, in truth, divine. And this genuinely furnishes the good for us, because the most blessed intellection of the gods is filled with all goods. ... along with the foreknowledge, they [the theurgists] receive Beauty itself, and the order which is both true and appropriate – and also present with this its utility. [...] whenever this (uncertainty) does not matter for this purpose, and foreknowledge rather is advantageous to souls for saving and leading them upwards, then the gods implant in the midst of their essences the foreknowledge inherent in divination. (ibid., 347-349)

All of this is consistent with the definition of theurgy as ritualized cosmogony. Because nothing is lost to the lower spheres of being, intellection cannot achieve the One – and giving it up means resorting to Gnosticism. The noosphere is supra-rational and in a way supra-transcendental. Iamblichus does not (at least consciously) try to be a gnostic, but the theurgical few constitute an elite circle of divine correspondence with matter. There is an *unknown* in theurgy which is, in the Laruellian sense, philosophically sufficient. Iamblichus neither presents a defense of theurgy nor philosophizes the ritual. But this does not mean theurgy is not philosophically sufficient.

In such context, it is understandable why scholarship is divided on the question where to place theurgy in the dyad rationality-irrationality, as it seems to discursively destroy the very idea of henosis: whether it is a cult of the Sun or mysterious incantations, theurgy is largely grasped as a nuisance to Plotinian emanationism.[5] Given all the emphasis on ritual, one could infer that it is not irrationality that was jettisoned from the post-Neoplatonic Platonism and imperial Christian dogmas: it was the *ritualistic rationality* that was degraded. The Empire found *eucharistia* later, without, as usual, ever accounting for antecedent forms of condensed rational motifs. Yet both sides of the dyad rationality-irrationality are contemporary depletions of the ideal of anthropological self-perfection in late Hellenism and leading a philosophical life, which, as Hadot claims, was just the beginning of that life (1995, 82-83), and not its final destination.

II. On Non-Theurgy[6]

To offer a practice of theurgy today, to collaborate with non-philosophy and spirituality, to impoverish Iamblichus' theurgy: these are the aims in conceptualizing non-theurgy. It is in effect a *fuite-en-avance* before Neoplatonism. Therefore, let us first clarify the status of the One and the remainders of henosis in Laruelle juxtaposed to the Neoplatonic tradition.

The One is what is already-given prior to any thought of it (Srnicek 2010, 3). Srnicek calls the One "infinitely conceptualizable." Because the One has always already determined in-the-last-instance everything in the world (on determination, see below), every object pertaining to reality is already a perspective on/from the One. Within the confines of Laruelle's attack on philosophical sufficiency and decisionism, "[s]ince a decision is external, any particular philosophy is incapable of thinking its own decision; rather the decision is its blindspot" (ibid., 5). If philosophy remains blind to this decision in order to operate, non-philosophy is then defined as the science of philosophy. This science of non-

---

[5] The way we can approach this problem is through the work of Sara Ahbel-Rappe and her findings on the operations of "non-discursivity" in late Neoplatonism. For her, this is the blending of doctrinal and ritualistic thought (Ahbel-Rappe 2000, xiii).

[6] The only writer I have seen mentioning both theurgy (not Iamblichus) and Laruelle is Steven Craig Hickman in a blog post called "Laruelle: Prophet or Charlatan? - Or, Philosophy as Neo-Baroque" at his blog *Social Ecologies* (see Hickmann 2012). However, it is just that - a mention, claiming Laruelle is "a Mystagogue or Therapeutiae or Theurgic Mystic of a darker Neoplatonism, or of an inverted gospel and anti-philosophy." A more general and similar comment is made by Woodard (2009); whether Laruelle could be seen as a modern-day Neoplatonist is an ongoing debate.

philosophy is not productive of metaphilosophical positions, because it remains uninterpretable (Brassier 2003, 25) and is not part of philosophy itself.

The standard objection/question to Laruelle is: How does he escape the decisional character of philosophy? By going back to the ancient notion of the One and by maintaining a non-decisional relationship to it, where non-decisional means internal (in as much as "decision" is external to philosophy). The desired pragmatics of non-philosophy is to "suspend the decisional authority of philosophy" (Srnicek 2010, 5) and the blindspot of the One. In a concept akin to the very idea of theurgy, Laruelle proposes his Vision-in-One, which is to think from the One rather than the One. Smith explains that in proceeding from the Vision-in-One, thought is "according *to* the Real," and not *of* the Real. As well as the subject, all things become equal before the Real (Smith 2013, 55). It is this non-decisional relation to the One and the Real that carries the spirit of anti-correlationism. Laruelle states:

> In any case, vision-in-One "gives" the One and it alone; it is "the" given entirely, the given as the identity (of the) given, as given-without-givenness, outside-the-fold or the doublet of the given and givenness. It is thus radical phenomenon without the phenomenological hinter-world in its broadest sense: without Being behind the phenomenon or connected with it, without givenness behind the given or connected with it. (Laruelle et al. 2013, 167)

For Laruelle the One is "in effect indifferent to what it determines" (ibid., 44). This is so because whatever it determines, it does so a) in-the-last-instance and b) through its being-foreclosed. "In-the-last-instance" means that the One effectuates a refusal to split objects (in the way philosophy does that); that in trying to overcome philosophical dualisms (the result of its decisionism) it relates unilaterally to them; in this, it is not temporal but real (Smith 2013, 87-88, with the precise definition of in-the-last-instance found on p. 89). "Being-foreclosed" means that the One is foreclosed to thought and is thus relationally unilateral to thought. Laruelle also defines the One as: "[a]n ancient transcendental utilized as a first name under the forms One-in-One, One-in-person, vision-in-One" (Laruelle 2010, xxvii). For Smith, the One in Laruelle is "a kind of 'spiritual element,' which he calls relative transcendence […] in addition to something that outstrips philosophy, that is foreclosed to philosophy: this is what he calls the One" (Smith 2012, 23).

Non-philosophy as a science does not remain blind to its being reliant on the Real. In non-philosophy there is a Real which is not malleable to synthesis and is beyond its own description: a rupture "between the real and its intellection." (Plotinus' One is a good example of such an ineffable rupture.) The "thinking" of this rupture is exercised by the human-in-person through the practicing of the Vision-in-One: a subject that thinks from the Real.

The practice of non-philosophy distinguishes it from philosophy; it does so by non-philosophy practicing the One, which is best expressed in Laruelle's "Vision-in-One" (Brassier 2012, 117). The Vision-in-One is thinking from the One, not for the One (Smith 2013, 87), and therefore it is its practice, because in thinking from the One the collapse between thought and reality is superseded. To understand non-philosophy's One is to understand formally the practice of non-philosophy in its Vision-in-One. Under the rubric "Vision-in-One (One, One-in-One, Real)" we find the following definitions:

> Vision-in-One is radically immanent and uni-versal; this is why it gives-without-givenness the givenness of the world-thought-World. [...] Non-philosophy formulates an open series of axioms on the One understood as vision-in-One and no longer as desire One:
> 1) The One is radical immanence, identity-without-transcendence, not associated with a transcendence or a division.
> 2) The One is in-One or vision-in-One and not in-Being or in-Difference.
> 3) The One is the Real insofar as it is foreclosed to all symbolization (thought, knowledge, etc.).
> 4) The One is given-without-givenness and separated without-separation-of givenness.
> 5) The One is that which determines or gives in-the-last-instance world-thought as given (object of a givenness). (Laruelle et al., 2013, 165-156)

Now, to approach something like "non-theurgy," several issues should be addressed.

First, to account for the inherent reversing of Neoplatonism in Laruelle. It is this Neoplatonic reversal that could serve first and foremost for the *de-religionizing of the One* and philosophy, and consequently Christian gnosis.[7] The initial result is divination *from* the One. In Neoplatonism, the function of the One can be largely defined as serving to divide noesis from soma. This division depends on a spiritual and scholarly synthesis reliant on the quiddity of an ineffable real, and what sort of telos and question confront the theurgist. At any rate, in Neoplatonism and theurgy we can speak of divination *of* the One. Yet in Laruelle the question is: How to *see* the One? This is not the same as the Neoplatonic question: How to *know* the One?

A quick comparison with Plotinus' One will help to elucidate how Laruelle's hijacking of the term subverts this rather disembodying ideal. Srnicek says that, unlike philosophy, non-philosophy abandons the idea that it should aim at knowledge of the One. Since

---

[7] This is an important step in clarifying the matter, because Neoplatonism can very rarely be read as a gnostic body of literature (it could, for example, only with regard to the non-Christian Sethian treatises in *Nag Hammadi*).

"philosophy has always framed the Real in its own philosophically-saturated terms, rather than letting the Real itself act" (Srnicek 2010, 3), the Real is unshackled by the epistemological program of philosophy's and Neoplatonism's One. With the changed question, Neoplatonism (more precisely its doublet One-Being) is reversed by non-philosophy, since the idea of knowing the One is questioned by the idea that the Real gives us access to knowledge: in Laruelle, the Real-One is radically unilateral and alien to thought. Unilaterality breaks away with decisionism. But it does not undo the question of how to see the One. For the One is an instance of (non-theurgic) embodiment that is utterly blinding; so blinding that its might and radiation made the Neoplatonists see it as the evaporating figurality of disembodiment. Laruelle's One annunciates a primate of unilateral theory of the embodied One. He achieves this (treating the world/philosophy, and also the One, as materials) through the procedure of "unilateralization," which turns philosophy's dualisms into "materials" (Smith 2013, 88). Unilateralization manifests that philosophy is an object determined by the One, instead of the One not determining anything in the world. The practice of the Vision-in-One by the human-in-flesh is determined in the last instance by non-philosophy's unilateral relation to the Real and therefore its non-decisional character.

Second, to conceptualize something like "non-theurgy" is to pollute the philosophically sufficient practice (and theurgy is still such a practice, despite all the mysterial objections of Iamblichus favoring the phoneme) with the undetermined real of the non-philosophical thetic posture of thought. It is, in practice, not only to de-religionize the Neoplatonic One, but to also willfully *gnosticize* theurgy.[8] The result of gnosticizing theurgy is non-theurgy (and not all of Neoplatonism). But how to do this outside the boundaries of religion? Does not gnosticizing theurgy also imply that theurgy in particular should be de-religionized? Absolutely. Other than conceptualizing "non-discursivity" in late Neoplatonism, we need to address the problem of how do we actualize theurgy as a modern-day pluralistic concern of spirituality.

Haar Farris offers that we introduce interdisciplinarity as a form of theurgy beyond the framework of religious studies. In this way one is free of the shackles of both confessionalism and ecumenism. This would be an "*enactive* understanding of the sacred" (Ferrer and Sherman cited in Haar Farris 2016, 121). He suggests that interdisciplinarity, then, is a

---

[8] In a conversation with Laruelle in June 2015 in Ohrid, Macedonia, he told me that as a younger scholar he did read voraciously Iamblichus. When I asked him whether he sees a possible proximity between Iamblichus and his work he did respond that this is a very likely comparison to be done (although I have not found any mention whatsoever of Iamblichus in his oeuvre so far). I take the freedom to bring in Gnosticism to the comparison. Again, gnosticizing here does not mean that Neoplatonism is a gnostic corpus; the procedure only entails a non-philosophical subsumption of philosophically impoverished theurgy.

"form of scholarly theurgy" (ibid., 127). He too defines theurgy as practical collaboration (with the divine): "Interdisciplinary scholarship can be conceived as theurgic practice that aspires to work in the context of a sacred plurality" (idem). This is a model that indeed allows for the creative polluting of theurgy with non-philosophy and vice versa. Haar Farris' proposal, however, relegates theurgy to the realm of philosophia, while I contend that theurgy as interdisciplinarity and the desired result here – non-theurgy – is not only de-religionizing but further gnosticizing theurgy. If both of these premises are followed, then non-theurgy is a possibility. The problem with theurgy as philosophia within participatory interdisciplinary research is that it relies on the impossibility of monolingualism and universality (a Derridean reliance on God as n+1, *plus d'Un*).

Non-theurgy, as with the entire project of non-philosophy, would be first and foremost a ritualized impoverishment of theurgy and its corollary of the impossible and the ineffable, for the non-philosophical spiritual venture is to practice the One in this world in its infinite effability. When theurgy is impoverished of its non-alterability, non-philosophical speculation on non-theurgy is productive rather than futile. Offering non-theurgy implicates it bears a spiritual, and not only mantic, quality. But what is the spiritual element of non-theurgy? It is the impoverished Neoplatonic One as the Laruellian Vision-in-One without a hinter-world of Being and with a human-in-person. For the Vision-in-One is an attempt to materialize the disembodied fate of the noema against realistic skepticism. This Vision does not need to remix or be confined to a Gnostic/sectarian Christianity should we resort to interdisciplinarity modeled as theurgy.

Just as Iamblichus offers a ritualized and, per Haar Farris, a "participatory" shortcut to the divine, we can update Haar Farris' (Derridean) interdisciplinary theurgy by not allowing it to serve as a philosophical blindspot. It would mean to betray both Iamblichus and Laruelle, for both of them *have impoverished* philosophy's transcendental processualism: the first by opposing Porphyry, the second by opposing Derrida. Only that Iamblichus did not go far enough in impoverishing the Greeks' philosophia.

Third, we need to address the relation of non-theurgy to Christianity. Thus, a final determination of non-theurgy is that both theurgy and non-philosophy are of non-Christian character. "Unlike Porphyry, who was a formidable opponent of Christianity, Iamblichus seems to have taken little notice of the new religion, whose full domination of the empire he did not live to see. In no extant work does he specifically mention the Christians" (Clarke, Dillon, and Hershbell 2003, xxviii). In the concluding pages of *Future Christ*, Laruelle says:

> Having thus avoided a philosophical-idealist deviation and a scientistic deviation within the method, what material is utilized for this operation, what exactly models so that we do not fall into another deviation, this time "Christianist," that comes from an excess of Christianity's presence alone in the object? "The-gnosis" may be that way of universalizing "the-Christianity" from the point of view of the experience to model. ... Re-activate the heretical posture in its challenging of every worldly authority, revive its long and burning struggle with the Church and its hatred of heresy, combine them in a unified posture of faith and knowledge of salvation, this does more than intensify Christianity, it carries it to the *non*-Christian universality that applies to every man beyond his religion and confessional background. (Laruelle 2010, 127).

Strictly speaking, here Laruelle does not call for the de-religionizing of universality; the spasmodic syllogism of the "non" is not anti-spiritual, it is merely heretical. Thus, gnosticizing theurgy should build not on a programme to de-spiritualize religious affects and thought, but to reignite them through a generic hereticism, which "applies to every man." And to manifest the heretic in a generic modality would mean to destroy the last bits of philosophical sufficiency in Neoplatonism.

Because the One has always already determined the Real and because the latter is unilateral, non-theurgy proceeds with/as Vision-in-One and can thus be beneficial for spiritual circles and practitioners only by totally depleting the Iamblichean sufficiency of the prayer's non-alterability.[9] Envisioning non-theurgy implodes theurgy's core of henosis, without becoming a science. The very idea of a non-philosophical update of theurgy is political: if non-theurgy is not envisioned from the perspective of a generic humanity, then it does remain with the oligarchic critique of the herd.

Fourth, and final, even though Laruelle submits his reading of Christianity to the banner of "science," non-theurgy cannot be a science, a "scientific ritual," in the spirit of a Science-in-Christ (see Laruelle 2015, 31 ff.), for theurgy remains too philosophical in its doctrinal dissent to "the Greeks." Iamblichus is not an anti-philosopher – by being a theurgist, he tries to be a *better* philosopher. We can become (better) non-theurgists by being austere non-philosophers with theurgy. Non-theurgy should remain in the realm of spirituality, the sacred and the divine within the limits of (Valentinian and Carpocratian) gnosis, not of the (Hebraic) Good News. And it cannot be any more Iamblichean than in its insistence of prayer – and any non-philosophically envisioned prayer should be alterable. The faith of non-theurgic prayer is alterity under the banner of unilaterality.

---

[9] It is no wonder that chaos magick and its practitioners, as Webster shows, have so voluntaristically not followed Iamblichus' admonishment.

But how to achieve this prayer without the extortionism of the phenomenological ineffable? We cannot bring the blindspot back into theurgy as a *plus d'Un*. However, we can override the ineffable by employing Laruelle's notion of the Vision-in-One in our prayers. Non-theurgy is – and could be – a subset of philo-fiction. All non-theurgic prayers are fictions on the side of embodied unilaterality and spirituality. Non-theurgy amplifies the kernel of the Real, in the sense that the lived of the Real is of the human, and the human-in-person. Thus, the practice of non-theurgy is both not-philosophical and non-philosophical and does not devolve to metareligious concerns, since it is enactable participation *with* the divine. Both of these premises are already contained in the Vision-in-One. Non-theurgy is an under-scientific manifestation of the Vision-in-One; it is underdetermined by the unilateral One and remains under the scientific ritual of generic gnosis. We could say that in trying to define non-theurgy we see in Laruelle something like henosical ritual that is universal to man in the sense of generic humanity.

Stanimir Panayotov, PhD candidate, Central European University, Budapest/
Institute of Social Sciences and Humanities, Skopje, spanayotov@gmail.com

References

Ahbel-Rappe, Sara. *Reading Neoplatonism. Non-discursive Thinking in the Texts of Plotinus, Proclus, and Damascius*. Cambridge: Cambridge University Press, 2000.
Brassier, Ray. "Axiomatic Heresy. The Non-Philosophy of François Laruelle." *Radical Philosophy*, No. 121 (September/October 2003): 24-35.
Brassier, Ray. "Laruelle and the Reality of Abstraction." In John Mullarkey and Anthony Paul Smith (eds.). *Laruelle and Non-Philosophy*. Edinburgh: Edinburgh University Press, 2012. 100-122.
Clarke, Emma C., John M. Dillon, and Jackson P. Hershbell. 2003. "Introduction," in Iamblichus. *De Mysteriis*, trans. by Emma C. Clarke, John M. Dillon, and Jackson P. Hershbell. Atlanta: Society of Biblical Literature, 2003. xiii-xlviii.
"Dark Nights of the Universe." *Archive*, May 5, 2012. <http://www.archive.org/details/DarkNightsOfTheUniverseEtNoxSicutDiesIlluminabitur>.
Dodds, Eric Robertson. *The Greeks and the Irrational*. California: University of California Press, 1959.
Haar Farris, Matthew S. "Some Admittedly Bold Interdisciplinary 'Participatory Turn' Hypotheses for Scholarly Collaboration with the Divine." In Joshua Ramey and Matthew S. Haar Farris (eds.). *Speculation, Heresy, and Gnosis in Contemporary Philosophy of Religion. The Fragile Absolute*. Lanham, Maryland: Rowman and Littlefield, 2016. 117-133.
Hadot, Pierre. *Philosophy as a Way of Life*, trans. by Michael Chase. Oxford: Blackwell, 1995.

Hickman, Steven Craig. "Laruelle: Prophet or Charlatan? – Or, Philosophy as Neo-Baroque." *Social Ecologies*, December 11, 2012. <http://www.socialecologies.wordpress.com/2012/12/11/laruelle-fraud-or-prophet>.

Julian. *Two Orations of the Emperor Julian One to the Sovereign Sun and the Other to the Mother of the Gods*, trans. by Thomas Taylor. London: Hermetic Publishing Company, 1932.

Iamblichus. *De Mysteriis*, trans. by Emma C. Clarke, John M. Dillon, and Jackson P. Hershbell. Atlanta: Society of Biblical Literature, 2003.

Laruelle, François. *Future Christ: A Lesson in Heresy*, trans. by Anthony Paul Smith. London and New York: Continuum, 2010.

Laruelle, François et al. *Dictionary of Non-Philosophy*, trans. by Taylor Adkins et al. Minnesota, Minneapolis: Univocal, 2013.

Laruelle, François. *Christo-Fiction. The Ruins of Athens and Jerusalem*, trans. by Robin Mackay. New York: Columbia University Press, 2015.

Majercik, Ruth. *Chaldean Oracles: Text, Translation, Commentary*. Doctoral Dissertation, University of California, Santa Barbara, 1982.

Metté, Aaron. *On the Black Universe in the Human Foundations of Color*. Vimeo, April 24, 2012 <http://www.vimeo.com/40918311>.

Plotinus. *Enneads VI.6-9*, trans. by Arthur Hilary Armstrong. Cambridge, Massachusetts: Harvard University Press, 1988.

Proclus. *On the Theology of Plato*, Vol. 1, trans. by Thomas Taylor. London: A.J. Valpy et al., 1816.

Rothbarth, Adam. "Hunter Hunt-Hendrix (Liturgy, Kel Valhaal): 'I Like to Trigger Emotion and Undercut It at the Same Time.'" *Tiny Mix Tapes*, August 3, 2016. <https://www.tinymixtapes.com/features/hunter-hunt-hendrix-liturgy-kel-valhaal>.

Shaw, Gregory. "The Neoplatonic Transmission of Ancient Wisdom." In Nathaniel P. DesRosiers and Lily C. Vuong (eds.). *Religious Competition in the Greco-Roman World*. Atlanta: Society for Biblical Literature, 2016. 107-119.

Smith, Anthony Paul. "Thinking from the One: Science and the Ancient Philosophical Figure of the One," in Mullarkey, John and Anthony Paul Smith (eds.). *Laruelle and Non-Philosophy*. Edinburgh: Edinburgh University Press, 2012. 19-42.

Smith, Anthony Paul. *A Non-Philosophical Theory of Nature. Ecologies of Thought*. London: Palgrave, 2013.

Srnicek, Nick. "François Laruelle, the One and the Non-Philosophical Tradition." *Pli: The Warwick Journal of Philosophy*, No. 22 (2010): 1-9.

Thacker, Eugene et al. *Dark Nights of the Universe*. Hong Kong: NAME, 2013.

Webster, Sam. "'More than Human,'" in Ramey, Joshua and Matthew S. Haar Farris (eds.). *Speculation, Heresy, and Gnosis in Contemporary Philosophy of Religion. The Fragile Absolute*. Lanham, Maryland: Rowman and Littlefield, 2016. 147-157.

Woodard, Ben. "The One: Plotinus, Laruelle and Deleuze." *Naught Thought*, February 23, 2009 <http://www.naughtthought.wordpress.com/2009/02/23/the-one-plotinus-laruelle-and-deleuze>.

AMEEN METTAWA (Madrid)

Non-Philosophy and the uninterpretable axiom

Abstract

This article connects François Laruelle's non-philosophical experiments with the axiomatic method to non-philosophy's anti-hermeneutic stance. Focusing on two texts from 1987 composed using the axiomatic method, "The Truth According to Hermes" and "Theorems on the Good News," I demonstrate how non-philosophy utilizes structural mechanisms to both expand and contract the field of potential models allowed by non-philosophy. This demonstration involves developing a notion of interpretation, which synthesizes Rocco Gangle's work on model theory with respect to non-philosophy with Laruelle's critique of hermeneutics. I use Alexander Galloway's interpretation of "The Truth According to Hermes" as a case study of the limits non-philosophy sets upon its use as a basis for philosophical models, in contrast to arguments by Gangle regarding non-philosophy's greater genericity in comparison to philosophy.

Keywords: Model theory, hermeneutics, axiomatic method, the secret, generic

1. The "Meaning" of Non-Philosophy

In his review of François Laruelle's 1986 text *Philosophies of Difference*, Graham Harman criticizes what he perceives as Laruelle's obtuse style. In keeping with the tradition of such critiques, Harman offers a decontextualized quote from the book, followed by some commentary:

> The sentence is certainly not 'meaningless.' Taken in context, its meaning is clear enough - eventually, after some minutes of labor. But to compile the chapter summaries above was never a pleasurable experience for this reviewer, and was often a downright painful one. Laruelle will get away with it only if he can prove that the payoff is sufficient to warrant the effort. (Harman 2011)

Rather than diagnosing Harman's pain as rooted in his philosophical modeling of Laruelle (i.e. the chapter summaries), Anthony Paul Smith responded with a defense of Laruelle's "style" itself:

> [Laruelle's] style is actually quite playful in the French, not at all sober and academic as Harman suggests, and this playfulness comes through even as he lays a lot of stress on the importance of non-standard syntax for thinking non-philosophically. He also plays with and mimics the style of others […] I think Rocco [Gangle, translator of *Philosophies of Difference*] captured this excellently in his translation and so reading him is no more difficult than reading Derrida, Henry, or Deleuze (and they are all difficult to read)" (Smith 2011).

One year after the original publication of *Philosophies of Difference*, in the article "The Truth According to Hermes," Laruelle addressed the very issue this exchange centers around, namely the relationship between non-philosophy and hermeneutics. In that essay, Laruelle criticizes both the decipherment of meaning and the communication of truth. However, the statements of both Harman and Smith demonstrate their adherence to a standard hermeneutics, which takes exactly these practices as its own. Harman, in what he seems to believe amounts to paying the devil his due by acknowledging that Laruelle's writing "is certainly not 'meaningless'," effectively misrepresents non-philosophy as participating in "hermetology," which "postulates that truth needs meaning" (Laruelle 2010, 19). Smith, by suggesting the hermeneutic heuristic of deriving meaning from Laruelle's texts by triangulating them in conjunction with his interlocutors, relinquishes Laruelle's project to the philosophized mode of interpretation which characterizes Harman's reading, offering readers an interpretive lens which non-philosophy intends to shatter.

In a later text, Laruelle writes that "non-philosophy is rationally incomprehensible within its presupposed but can be rendered philosophically intelligible through its modeling" (Laruelle 2012, 168). The latter claim, regarding the possibility of creating philosophical models of non-philosophical thought, is demonstrated in this case by Harman's attempt at a philosophical summary of *Philosophies of Difference* (and we will discuss modeling more below). The task of this paper is to demonstrate the former claim, that "non-philosophy is rationally incomprehensible within its presupposed." I will demonstrate this within a limited scope through a structural analysis of "The Truth According to Hermes." This analysis will allow us to contrast "Hermes" itself with Alexander Galloway's attempt at a philosophical model of the content of "Hermes" in *Laruelle: Against the Digital*, and will illustrate the tension between non-philosophy's rational incomprehensibility and the possibility of constructing philosophical models of non-philosophy. Although I designate my approach as "structural," I hope to demonstrate the identity of structure and content in "Hermes." Although I will not argue that all non-philosophical texts are "rationally incomprehensible," at least not in the same manner as "Hermes," the argument I put forward does suggest generalization from "Hermes" on the basis of the centrality of the axiomatic method to non-philosophy.

2. The Axiomatic Method

In 1995's *Principles of Non-Philosophy*, Laruelle elaborated a description of non-philosophy, and specifically of its syntax (more on this below) through the axiomatic method. Prior to Philosophy III (the period of *Principles*), Laruelle had introduced non-philosophical axioms but had not yet formally used them in his major works as the basis for performing non-philosophy through the axiomatic method itself. However, two short texts from the Philosophy II period, "The Truth According to Hermes" and "Theorems on the Good News," make experimental use of the axiomatic method in a manner subtly, but illuminatingly, different from the relatively standard form in which the method appears in *Principles*.

Regarding the standard form, anyone familiar with Spinoza's *Ethics* will recognize philosophical appropriations of the axiomatic method, or what is sometimes called the "geometric" method (due to its use in Euclid's geometry). First principles are stated outright and are themselves categorized and differentiated. For instance, Euclid employs the categories "definitions," "postulates," and "common notions," with postulates and common notions both serving as what we would today call axioms. Spinoza's first principles are "definitions" and "axioms." Both Euclid and Spinoza make use of their demarcated first principles to derive "propositions" by way of proofs, which, when successful, rely entirely on the first principles, or on other propositions already proven on the basis of the first principles. Later implementations of the axiomatic method, including in Laruelle's work, name propositions as "theorems." An axiomatic system's method of proving theorems is structured according to inference rules:

> Such rules are supposed to be truth-preserving in the following sense: as far as the axioms are true the theorems derived from these axioms are also true. Further, these rules are supposed to be not specific for any given theory: one assumes that the same set of rules of inference applies in all axiomatic theories (logical monism) or at least that any complete set of such rules applies in some large class of theories (logical pluralism). (Rodin 2011, 1)

Inference rules function, like axioms, as fundamental features of the logical architecture through which theorems are proven. Like axioms, they are not themselves proven. Inference rules are often only implied, yet they are discernible in the truth-preserving transformations undergone by axiomatic elements over the course of a proof.

In the section of *Principles of Non-Philosophy* titled "Transcendental theorems on the idiom of the One," Laruelle explicitly lists his definitions, axioms, and rules of inference (or what he calls "operations"), and then the theorems derived from these first principles. Prior to this, Laruelle experimented with an axiomatic method which did not explicitly state any axioms. Take the following example, from "Theorems on the Good News," first published in 1987, the same year as "The Truth According to Hermes":

"Theorem 0 or the Transcendental Theorem,
On Nontransferable Identity,
Nothing can, except through illusion, substitute itself for man and for his identity. And man cannot, except through illusion, substitute himself for philosophy, for the Other, etc. Man is an inalienable reality. There is no reversibility between man and philosophy.

Theorem 00,
On the Proof, as Transcendental or By Way of 0
The previous theorem is demonstrated (for) itself, that is, non-thetically. The present theorem and those that follow derive from the previous" (Laruelle 2014, 41).

Theorem 0 is simply a specific case of the law of identity (A=A), which would conventionally be treated as an axiom. The law of identity, which here becomes man=man, is taken as given by almost all philosophers (this should be our first clue as to why Laruelle would not call Theorem 0 an axiom). Laruelle makes the absent-presence of axioms even more explicit by having Theorem 00 say that Theorem 0 "is demonstrated (for) itself." This phrase, "demonstrated (for) itself," indicates a certain kind of self-evidence. However, self-demonstration is not equivalent to the direct self-evidence, without need for demonstration, of axioms such as Descartes' "clear and distinct perceptions." Nevertheless, Theorem 0 functions "axiomatically," insofar as it is that from which all the other theorems are derived. Why call Theorem 0 a theorem then, since it functions like an axiom and does not rely on derivation from some other axiom? Even more strangely, Theorem 00, which attributes self-demonstrating power to Theorem 0, is itself said to derive from Theorem 0. Self-demonstration here, rather than being definitional of Theorem 0, which would bring Theorem 0 closer to a self-evident axiom, is instead derived from Theorem 0, *from* itself, and thus demonstrated according to a derivation (accomplished by Theorem 00), rather than in Theorem 0 *by* itself. Theorem 00 retroactively performs an axiomatization-effect upon Theorem 0, which floats without ground, following Theorem 00's derivation from Theorem 0.

3. The Non-Euclidean Analogy

The exercise in which Laruelle is engaged in "Theorems on the Good News" effectively constitutes an attempt at producing axiomatic thinking without deciding upon any axiom in particular as the ground for that thinking. Although, as we know from *Principles*, later iterations of the axiomatic method will be explicitly grounded in non-philosophical axioms, this earlier text suggests an experiment in genericity, which bears on the famous analogy between non-philosophy and non-Euclidean geometry. Non-philosophy is said to be like non-Euclidean geometry because non-philosophy suspends certain intransigent philosophical axioms in the same manner and to similar effect as non-Euclidean geometry's suspension of the parallel postulate. Gangle provides the following elaboration:

> The analogy translates to the case of non-philosophy and philosophy as follows: if philosophy is conceived as the analogue of Euclidean geometry, it is clear that an analogous 'subtraction' of one or more of philosophy's 'axioms' (roughly, its enabling presuppositions) will in no way negate or disqualify philosophy as such. Instead, it will open up a wider range of possible models for the 'reduced' or 'simplified' system. All the philosophical models will be included in this larger class, but so will additional models that the now subtracted axiom(s) would have excluded. In this sense, non-philosophy is understood to extend philosophy, that is, it opens a more general domain of which philosophy represents only one restricted subdomain. By calling the mode of thinking that proceeds in-One or according-to-One non-philosophy, Laruelle intends simply to designate that a less restricted form of thinking than that of philosophy (one involving fewer presuppositions) is thereby more general. In this way, non-philosophy engages a 'space' of thinking that includes (the models of) philosophy while also including other models that philosophy axiomatically excludes. (Gangle 2013, 53)

According to Gangle, non-philosophy is, in part, an attempt at thinking in a manner which is more generic than philosophy, insofar as it is more model-inclusive. Part of non-philosophy's effort at increasing philosophy's genericity is the suspension of philosophical axioms which are taken as constraints on thinking (or on what counts as thinking), so that more thought may be included within, or modeled on the basis of, a new and less limiting non-philosophy. Gangle's characterization of the non-Euclidean analogy lets us see the experiment of "Good News" as the construction of a radically generic axiomatic method which proceeds without the constraints of axioms at all, while simultaneously maintaining the axiomatic method's rigorous formal structure through the use of axiomatization-effects.

4. Models

Before proceeding to an account of how "The Truth According to Hermes" fits into (and contests) this characterization of the non-philosophical appropriation of the axiomatic method as a genercization of philosophy, I will first offer some comments on what Gangle means by "model." As Gangle explains with regard to the axiomatic method, "while perfectly rigorous theorems may be generated deductively from an axiomatic system, precisely *what* those theorems refer to remains underdetermined. Indeed the *what* to which the axioms apply is determined only up to and precisely no farther than the system of deductive consequences generated by the axioms themselves" (Gangle 2013, 51). A theorem formulated through the axiomatic method, as an abstract system for the production of such theorems given a set of grounding constraints, is not inherently indexed to a referent outside of the system within which the theorem is derived. In order to determine that to which axioms and theorems may coherently refer, one uses model theory, which Gangle describes as establishing "the conditions under which systems of objects and relations may be said to 'satisfy' a determined set of axioms" (Gangle 2013, 50). A formal definition of these conditions may go as follows (note that theorems are a subset of well-formed formulas):

> A well-formed formula **B** is said to be true for the interpretation **M** iff every sequence in Σ (the set of all denumerable sequences of elements of the domain of **M**), satisfies **B**. **B** is said to be false for **M** iff no sequence in Σ satisfies **B**. Then an interpretation **M** is said to be a model for a set Γ of well-formed formulas iff every well-formed formula in Γ is true for **M**

In other words, an interpretation of some axiomatic system is an attempt at mapping the "combinatorics" of that system onto things external to the system in such a way that the syntax of the system is preserved. Gangle defines "syntax" as "the purely formal operations that regulate and transform strings of symbols or formulas" (Gangle 2013, 44). When a mapping, or interpretation, of an axiomatic system onto something else is successful (i.e. when the mapping preserves the system's syntax), this constitutes a model.

Returning to Gangle's comments regarding the greater genericity of non-philosophy compared to philosophy, we can now understand this greater genericity as something, which would be demonstrated by the applicability of the non-philosophical axiomatic system to a larger set of thinking processes than those to which one may apply an axiomatically formulated version of conventional philosophy. Accordingly, non-philosophy would have the capacity to provide the syntactical coordinates upon which one could mount a coherent interpretation of thinking processes excluded by philosophy, in addition to philosophical thinking processes. If this proved true, we could then characterize non-philosophy as being more open to modeling than philosophy, and thus more generic.

5. The Truth According to Hermes

Laruelle's other 1987 experiment with the axiomatic method, "The Truth According to Hermes," is either an exception or a challenge to this characterization of non-philosophy, for reasons given in the argument below. These same reasons compel me not to offer my own interpretation of this text, but instead a summary of the interpretation Alexander Galloway makes in *Laruelle: Against the Digital.*

According to Galloway, Laruelle claims that the "media principle" is a governing structure of metaphysics, hermeneutics, and communication (Galloway 2014, xxi). It amounts to the assumption of a connection between truth and "a human agent" which communicates truth (Galloway 2014, xx). Laruelle dismisses the idea that truth can be communicated by a human agent as an idea based in an epistemologically limiting, "narcissistic" anthropocentrism (Galloway 2014, xxi). The secret, which Galloway takes as another name for Truth, the One, and the Real, is never revealed to anyone, but "the fact of it being communicated" is (Galloway 2014, xxii). Because Laruelle doesn't want knowledge of the secret to be tainted by human bias, he rejects hermeneutics and phenomenology as methods of accessing truth, since they function according to the media principle (Galloway 2014, xxii). Galloway then lists other philosophers and philosophical traditions Laruelle explicitly or implicitly rejects, but qualifies this as not exactly a rejection but more of a reduction to a state of materiality at which point non-philosophy engages them (Galloway 2014, xxiii). Galloway describes the practice of such an engagement precisely: "Non-philosophy means, essentially, to select an existing philosophical system, hermeneutics say, and to analyze it exclusively for the generic logics that exist within it. These logics are what remain once the human, the person who decides to do philosophy, is removed" (Galloway 2014, xxiii). Despite being unable to communicate truth, or the secret, all philosophies contain these "generic logics" which are conditioned by truth, and thus all philosophies have some connection to truth (Galloway 2014, xxiii). Non-philosophy would then be the practice of elucidating this connection through an analysis of generic logics.

Galloway's reading is marked by a systematic misidentification of Laruelle's theorems as "theses." Theorems imply derivation from axioms, while theses lack this implication. Furthermore, Laruelle will later distinguish between demonstration through the axiomatic method and argument through "philosophical theses" on the basis that the latter cannot provide acceptable accounts of "the real or phenomenal experience" (Laruelle 2013, 5). However, Galloway's reading is a philosophical interpretation of "Hermes," and should be judged according to the conditions for successful modeling, as discussed above. We will examine Galloway's interpretation to determine if it is a model, in which case it would interpret Laruelle's text in a manner, which preserves its syntax.

We encounter our first problem when we consider that "Hermes" rejects interpretation as such. As Galloway says himself, "Alienation, translation, interpretation, reflection—these many vectors of the human mind are all steadfastly resisted by Laruelle" (Galloway 2014, xxi). And yet Galloway is undoubtedly producing an interpretation of Laruelle's text and, moreover, he does so on the basis of introducing a grounding rejection of "correlationism" (Galloway 2014, xx). All of Galloway's remarks regarding the limits of human cognition have been inserted by him in his attempt to model "Hermes" as a philosophical attack on correlationism. Galloway is able to turn the text into a critique of the limits of human understanding because he has assumed the text's axiom to be something like: "there is no correlation between Truth and its communication." However, the closest we get to such a formulation is in Laruelle's first theorem, where he says "hermeto-logical Difference is the indissoluble correlation, the undecidable coupling of truth *and* its communication" (Laruelle 2010, 19). This theorem, however, must be understood as itself derived from an implicit axiom or axioms, and not considered the ground of the text itself. Although it is acceptable to axiomatize theorems which have been properly derived from a system's axioms according to the inference rules governing that system, it is at the very least careless to treat one theorem as that from which all other theorems are derived when one knows neither the system's axioms or inference rules, considering that any given theorem may be insufficient for the derivation of some other(s).

Galloway's erasure of the axiomatic structure of the text allows him to covertly axiomatize the rejection of correlation. Galloway effectively reads "The Truth According to Hermes" as though it was a non-hermeneutics in the following manner: a hermeneutics which suspends the axiom of correlation. This would allow for a comparison between

"Hermes" and the general non-philosophical project of doing philosophy without certain philosophical axioms, as discussed above through Gangle. The problem is that, elsewhere, when Laruelle is engaging in that general project, his axioms are clearly stated (such as in *Principles*). Laruelle does in fact suspend the hermeneutic axiom of correlation, but this is not what provides the systemic architecture for the derivation of his theorems. The suspension of this axiom is accomplished within the theorems, which have themselves been derived from another axiom.

Let us attempt to find another model for this text, to better understand its structure. Theorems 1 through 7 closely parallel parts of Heidegger's lecture "What Is Metaphysics?" wherein he substantializes Nothing as the origin of negation. In that lecture, Heidegger argues that (1) science rejects the Nothing as an object of thought, while (2) nevertheless employing negation. Through a phenomenological analysis of moods, however, we can discover that (3) negation comes from a more primordial experience of the Nothing. This appears to map the syntax of Laruelle's text when summarized as follows: (1) generalized hermeneutics rejects the possibility of an uninterpretable truth, while (2) nevertheless relying on concealment (secrets, understood as something occulted but theoretically knowable; and all things for generalized hermeneutics become secrets to be deciphered); (3) the process of decipherment of what is concealed is a process which "emerges" from the more primordial uninterpretable secret (Theorem 4: "[the secret] is itself the uninterpretable from which an interpretation emerges"). This Heideggerian interpretation takes Laruelle's disconnected theorems and hallucinates an argument through them on the basis of Heideggerian presuppositions. If we come to Laruelle's text with Heideggerian assumptions, or if we insert these assumptions as axioms and prove the theorems on that basis, Laruelle seems to provide a system which allows for a model in the form of the Nothing argument. We can thus map Laruelle's terms (generalized hermeneutics, the Uninterpretable, interpretation) onto Heideggerian terms (science, the Nothing, negation). Further, given that Laruelle provides no proofs for his theorems, we would import Heidegger's own rules of inference.

However, to get this far would be to ignore every broad antagonism toward Heidggerian philosophy found in the text: "[the secret] is an immediate transcendental given, an immediate that is absolutely pre-dialectical and pre-differential, pre-Hegelian or pre-Heideggerian" (Theorem 6); "[the secret] is the One, understood in an absolutely immanent and finite way; it excludes the play of Being" (Theorem 9); "The unitary philosopher (the philosopher of Being, then of difference) was always a representative, emissary, and civil servant of the Postal and Telecommunication Ministry" (Theorem 16). If Heidegger's argument on the Nothing is conditioned by an investigation of Being (which, of course, it is), then the content of Laruelle's theorems has sufficiently ruled out the possibility of a Heideggerian model of the text.

This exercise can be repeated for each of the philosophers and philosophical presuppositions Laruelle explicitly or implicitly rejects throughout the text. Galloway is correct in stating that, with "Hermes," "Laruelle has essentially barred himself from entry into the intellectual currents of the twentieth century" (Galloway 2014, xxiii) by way of its resolutely negative theorems. In addition to Heidegger and all of hermeneutics, Laruelle explicitly rejects Hegel, Nietzsche, "conflict of interpretations" theory (Ricoeur), philosophies of "the structure of Difference in general" (Deleuze), and "play in general" (Derrida). Laruelle has constricted, in the broadest possible strokes with regard to the philosophies of his predecessors and contemporaries, the possibility of modeling the text philosophically.

A major difference between "The Truth According to Hermes" and "Theorems on the Good News," with regard to their implementations of the axiomatic method, is that while "Good News" experiments with thinking axiomatically without axioms toward radical genericity, "Hermes" structurally operates against genericity by occluding the possibility of philosophical models. Although, like "Good News," "Hermes" lacks an explicitly stated axiomatic ground (remembering that axiom-suspension, for Gangle, corresponds to greater genericity), two factors collude against interpretations which aspire to model the text: (1) the broad rejection of the nearest philosophical ideas, and (2) the incommunicability of the secret. By "concealing" the axiomatic basis of the text, Laruelle has effectively positioned this basis *as* the secret. The secret, as a concealment without content which interpretations lack access to but nevertheless continuously posit in corrupted form, is immanently axiomatized within the text. We cannot attribute meaning (understood as an interpretation, which qualifies as a model) to the text given that the theorems of the text are derived from an uninterpretable truth, and thus can only exist within their own inapplicable axiomatic system.

Ameen Mettawa, La Escuelita, Centro de Arte 2 de Mayo,
ameen.mettawa[at]gmail.com

References

Galloway, Alexander. *Laruelle: Against the Digital.* Minnesota: University of Minnesota Press, 2014.

Gangle, Rocco. *François Laruelle's Philosophies of Difference: A Critical Introduction and Guide.* Edinburgh: Edinburgh University Press, 2013.

Harman, Graham. "Review: Philosophies of Difference: A Critical Introduction to Non-Philosophy." *Notre Dame Philosophical Reviews.* University of Notre Dame, 2011. Web. 11 August 2011 <ndpr.nd.edu/news/philosophies-of-difference-a-critical-introduction-to-non-philosophy/>

Laruelle, François. *Principles of Non-Philosophy.* London: Bloomsbury, 2013.

Laruelle, François. *Struggle and Utopia at the End Times of Philosophy.* Minnesota: University of Minnesota Press, 2012.

Laruelle, François. "Theorems on the Good News." *Angelaki* Vol. 19, Nr. 2 (2014): 41-43.

Laruelle, François. "The Truth According to Hermes: Theorems on the Secret and Communication." *Parrhesia* Nr. 9 (2010): 18-22.

Rodin, Andrei. "Doing and Showing." *ARXIV.* Web. 31 August 2011. <arxiv.org/pdf/1109.4298.pdf>

Smith, Anthony Paul. "So What?: On Graham Harman's Abominable Review of Laruelle's Philosophies of Difference." *An Und Für Sich.* Web. 15 August 2011. <itself.blog/2011/08/15/so-what-on-graham-harmans-abominable-review-of-laruelle/>

DAVID BREMNER (Paris)

Non-Standard Stainless: Laruelle, Inconsistency and Sense-impressions

Abstract

"Stains" can serve as a metaphor for the role allotted to meaninglessness not only by partisans of the deterritorializing force of "brute matter", but also by diagnosers of symbolic incompleteness. For both, the blindspot that will lead to the disturbance of a given regime of meaning must be determined through a smear or glitch which that regime cannot sublate: the mark of a Real stripped of systematising mediation. However, we argue that it is all too easy to allow the stringency of this Real to be undermined by the inflation in its name of merely contingent empirical instances. Such blockages to theoretical and artistic practice can be removed with the aid of the articulation of incompleteness and inconsistency implied by François Laruelle's conception of the Real as non-consistent but hyper*complete "radical immanence". À* rebours *of Laruelle himself, different types of meaninglessness can then be distinguished, de-metaphorized, and conceptualized as "noise".*

Keywords: Laruelle, incompleteness, identity, sense-impressions, substance, incommensurability

Introduction

The awkward teetering of the "stain" between metaphor and concept provides us with a means of isolating philosophical problems relating to the role of meaninglessness.

Three types of meaninglessness loom large since the break with classical metaphysical rationalism: meaninglessness as genetically primitive ground of meanings; meaninglessness as excessive overspilling of the sterility of meanings; and meaninglessness as the empty gap of the incompleteness of meanings. Gains won in the drawing of these distinctions have led to losses elsewhere. Namely, on the one hand, in the stifling of the question of the role of spatio-temporal and qualitative-intensive stain-forms – such as in Stockhausen's music or in the bristles of Philip Guston's paintbrush, or Goya's – and of our desire for them. And, on the other hand, in the stifling of the question of what specific relations may obtain between *different types* of meaninglessness or purported "formlessness" and *different types* of meaning and form – within any one of, or cutting across, the three categories.

We will argue that, by upping the ante of the competition to strip away conditionality from the Real, François Laruelle's "non-standard philosophy" helps us to better reformulate these non-trivial open questions, which are hardly even askable from the dead-ends into which it is all too easy to be forced. Laruelle's theory has been elaborated in a – still expanding – series of works over the past four decades, and we hope to give a glimpse of the conceptual innovations putting it shoulder to shoulder with his as yet more famous peers.

Introducing Laruelle's formidably abstract – but, we suggest, practically urgent – intervention will require a relatively lengthy prefatory historical survey, in our first section, of two problems and a crux. Firstly, we will review a problem regarding David Hume's sense-impressions and the classical metaphysical conception of "substance"; secondly, a full-bloodedly speculative problem emerging between Bergson and Deleuze regarding the link, or lack thereof, between the infinitesimal vibrations of sensation and the dividing line between the possible and the impossible; and, finally, a crux reached at the point where meaninglessness is purified by Žižek so as to become a kind of "void".

By fleshing out these three moments it is hoped that the best possible springboard will be provided for a relatively snappy exposition, in the second section of the article, of Laruelle's highly original reworking of Kant's thing-in-itself. This will lead, in the third section, to our "pay-off" argument that non-standard philosophy allows us – somewhat against the grain of Laruelle's own commitments – to shake off the shackles of our crux, such as to prize open and multiply our questions in a way that is newly fruitful, albeit ragged. The issue of meaninglessness in art will be foregrounded, and we will briefly discuss two video works by Amanda Beech, and will suggest that if something like a desire-for-the-stain constitutes a pertinent artistic drive, this drive should be untethered from an exclusive marriage to "sheer sensation", in order to avoid suppressing art's capacity for conceptual discovery.

The methodology of non-standard philosophy is, for reasons to be sketched, radically non-linear, and so our exposition will be obliged to proceed through a lurching series of broken loops. The article will close with a coda in which we will glancingly crystallise a query we may want to pose to Laruelle himself.

A hint of what non-standard philosophy will do with the stain may be given before we launch into our historical survey by citing – for now cryptically – his use of the geometrical figure of the fractal, a pattern (scribble or regular polygon) reiterated self-similarly so as to take on unexpected complex properties as it scales up. Leaving hanging a quotation or two may give a sense of Laruelle's scrambling of the philosophical registers of "concrete" and "abstract", a crucial de-reification which we will salute and try to unpack starting from our second section. "[F]ractality is not only in the World, it is just as much in your head and your eye" (Laruelle 2011, 131), which makes possible "a fractal practice of philosophy at the same time as a 'de-intuitivation' of the fractal itself; and an ontological or real use of the fractal extended beyond physical or geometrical intuitivity at the same time as a refusal of the metaphorical use to which a 'fractal vision of the world' inevitably leads." (Laruelle 2011, 140).

I. The stain between impression and substance: a motley history in two problems and a crux

1. The problem of sense-impressions and auto-intelligible substance

1.1. *Hume's "impressions" and the triangle-in-general*

Hume's empiricism makes sense-impressions – the raw data impinging upon sight, hearing, touch, taste, and smell – the primitive building-blocks of the theory dealing with the possibility and acquisition of knowledge. We will sketch first of all a certain reading of Hume's argument associated with the Kantian "critical" current – for this is the tradition which Laruelle will seek to push to its n-th degree.

This critical reading is sympathetic to Hume's goal of striking a blow against idle metaphysical speculation by refuting its question-begging positing of a purely spiritual faculty of mind capable of acceding to "refined perceptions" (Hume 1956, 183) from some ethereal realm. It is seen as entirely fair and just that Hume should take umbrage with Descartes' claim that our capacity to form an idea, for example, of the abstract essence of the triangular-shape-in-general, detached from any particular triangles we have in fact seen drawn in chalk on blackboards, is accounted for *simply* by the fact that upon introspection it appears to us "clearly and distinctly" that contained in the idea of a triangle are the properties of having three sides and angles adding up to 180°. These are purely formal, non-sensible determinations, such that this triangular-shape-in-general is "neither isosceles nor scalenum, nor [...] confined to any particular length and proportion of sides" (Hume 1956, 183), and yet for the classical rationalist these constraints are *objective*. For Hume this recourse to apparent logical-geometrical clarity and distinctness is nothing other than woeful obscurity, because the genesis of the knowledge in question remains obfuscated.

However, on the critical reading the worry regarding Hume's attack is that, in order to "destroy this artifice" by means of which philosophers are wont to "cover many of their absurdities" (Hume 1956, 183), he may have been obliged to presuppose that the sense-impressions in question – those accounting for the genesis of ideas – are able to reveal and transmit *their own* content, directly and – as it were – of their own accord, without the aid of any mediating structures, *to* the mind's system of ideas. If "*all our ideas are copied from our impressions*" (Hume 1956, 183) – "impressions" presumably being a certain species of spatio-temporal and qualitatively intensive forms – and if impressions and ideas are distinguished only in "the degrees of force and liveliness with which they strike upon the mind" (Hume 1956, 167), then the question of how exactly "force and liveliness" allows the impression to cross the threshold from meaningless physicality to cognitive intelligibility is now puzzling. It may be that Hume here requires – against his own explicit commitments – the assumption of certain aspects of the classical metaphysical characterization of *substance*. A historical detour regarding substance will here be worth the trouble.

1.2. "Substance" from Aristotle to Spinoza

In his *Categories*, Aristotle defines substances as individual bodies, these individual bodies being the ultimate bearers of linguistic predication, such as themselves to not be sayable of anything else (Aristotle, *Categories* 2a11). He gives the examples of "man" and "horse". Let us consider the horse Red Rum, who is fast and reddish-brown. Neither "fast" nor "reddish-brown" are substances, for they require attribution to something else, namely the particular horse Red Rum. Not even "horse", it turns out, meets the stringent criteria of "that which is called a substance most strictly, primarily, and most of all" (Aristotle, *Categories* 2a11), because "horse" is a *species* and so requires individual instances of horses of which it can be predicated. According to this key strut of the classical definition, Red Rum is a *primary substance* only as a strictly individual body in the very coincidence of his flesh and blood with itself. Substance is therefore that which is *identical to itself*. In Aristotle's *Metaphysics* a certain nuance is added: the *matter* of living tissue (or stone for a house, or fire for a flame) is distinguished from the essential *form* of the being, and it is this latter which takes the role of substance qua subject of predication and change (another property given in the *Categories*), without which it would be impossible for any of the being's attributes to exist. This remains a guiding thread throughout the scholastic Medieval period: substance is able to furnish the explanation of why a horse runs, neighs, and seeks nourishment insofar as the identity-to-self of the animal's substantial form causally guarantees that these goals have been added to the otherwise mechanically law-bound material stuff from which the horse is constituted.

In the seventeenth-century Spinoza breaks with the scholastic tradition, but does so precisely by rendering explicit and elucidating a tacit presupposition which had, arguably, been present since Aristotle. It transpires that substance is that which contains within itself both its own cause and, by the same token, the capacity to intelligibly auto-unveil its own form and properties to the philosopher. Rejecting the unexplained teleological explainer of a substantial form-essence for every organic species and empirical thing, Spinoza assimilates their goals and functions seamlessly into the causal order of matter. A "substance" is now that and only that "which is in itself and is conceived through itself, that is, that whose concept does not require the concept of another thing, from which it must be formed." (Spinoza, *Ethics* ID3[1]). The consequence is that there is *only one* substance, because there can be only one self-caused cause of the totality of all those non-substantial things (phones; ink blots; sodium chloride; the concept of finitude) which need to be conceived through something other than themselves (a compuction to communication; a leaky pen; electrostatic attraction; distinguishment from the concept of infinity).

As we hope will become clear, Laruelle can be viewed as pressing this collapse of substance to its extreme terminus, but only if we note that he will seek to rend asunder the short-circuit of transparent reciprocity between ideal thought (justified understanding) and real thing (material causality) upon which we clearly see that Spinoza relies. Spinoza's substance – taking on the name of God – is able to directly ensure the intelligibility of *everything*, in the guise of *anything's* ultimate cause *and* sufficient explanation. And this is why he views all logical possibilities as actual in real terms – including Descartes' purely geometrical-ideal triangle-in-general. This latter is not internally contradictory, as would be a square circle, and so for Spinoza it is real, because the intimacy with thought of his unified-and-unitary substance qua both *causa sui* and universal *explanans* fuses the conceivable – i.e., the non-contradictory – with the real (… at the price of robbing contradictions of reality, and hence of philosophical interest; a loose thread for our open questions later).

1.3. *A hidden presupposition in the impression's eclipse of the abstract?*

The problem with Humean impressions, alotted the role of most basic source of the content of thoughts – "basic" as in, not analytically decomposable, and supposedly explanatorily sufficient – is that they seem to need the very auto-bestowing intelligibility of classical metaphysical substance in order to transmute the acephalic, uniform meaninglessness, excessive ubiquity, and overwhelming density of spatio-temporal and qualitatively intensive stains into organized and potentially classifiable *ideas* (Humean or otherwise). This threatens to undermine Hume's distaste for abstract objects, such as the generalized, formal-

---
[1] Definition 3 of the first Part of the *Ethics* (Spinoza 1996, 1).

ly construed triangle, but also his aim – which we strongly reaffirm – of having done with the foggy presupposition of an unconditioned faculty of transparent and reciprocal intellectual intuition between thought and real. Notwithstanding Spinoza's welcome collapse of metaphysically teleological substances, and as philosophically earth-shattering as it undoubtedly was, his elision of cause and reason can only count as an instance of such a question-begging pre-established harmony.

The progressive, naturalizing thrust of Hume's assault upon unscrupulous presumption risks ending up mired in a self-imposed – and equally complacent – stubbornness vis-a-vis his requirement of a moment of intuitive verification before any postulate can be declared to count as true knowledge. The theory of the lively and forceful impression would appear to not be coherent in the places where it would need to be coherent in order to disqualify the reality of the abstract triangle. Genesis is, in the first instance, irrelevant to intelligibility, whether operational or deductive, and its prioritization entails a vicious circularity. To reject intellectual intuition *à la* Descartes and Spinoza is not to refute their attribution of an autonomy, of a certain kind, to formal determinations defined through axiomatic stipulation or construction – the bare bones of which relative autonomy we will attempt, through Laruelle, *also* to strongly reaffirm. Without a very good reason, allowing the stain to solidify into a halting-point blocking practices involving abstraction can only be abhorrent to the very spirit of Hume's own project of emancipation from – in Kantian language – dogmatic slumber.

2. The problem of the continuity of sensation and infinite incompossibility

A second possible stance which affirms that it is the sensorial stain, which occupies the position of "brute" underivable reference-point aims to entirely upset the stability of the system of ideas. Henri Bergson, in seeking an answer to the venerable question "What is time?", separates out two types of "multiplicity": discrete and continuous. Discrete, discontinuous multiplicities tend to be those which are implicated in analytic thought and mathematico-scientific calculation – for example: mutually exclusive categories; numerical degree; and extended space qua metrically measurable, simultaneously in any direction. In contrast, examples of continuous, "smooth" multiplicities would include intermingling feelings, or the gapless succession of graded shades in the colour-spectrum, or a climbing sonorous pitch graphically figureable as a sound wave of which the contiguous peaks and troughs grow ever closer as its frequency increases. Time itself – which, for Bergson, is, qua pure "duration", a continuous multiplicity – will only be reached by purifying sensuous intuition of the clutter of discrete multiplicities.

The waxing of memory through lived experience – always singular and, at each new moment, holistically recalibrated – on this account puts us in touch with the Absolute insofar as, on the level of sensuous intuition, prior to any skewed analysis proceeding along the lines of biased criteria, the vibration of *our own* duration can be integrated with the vibrations immediately surrounding it, both faster and slower in frequency (cf., for example, Bergson 1992, 149-152). Deleuze, at least in *Difference and Repetition*, appears to retain from Bergson this privileging of the a-semantic *sentiendum*, which, at least in the central chapter of the book, remains purportedly untouched by the slightest mediation (Deleuze 2004, 176-178). This radically meaningless stain is alloted the crucial role of instigator of the cascade of shocks which disturbs the habitual, banal accord of the faculties of mind, forcing them to snap out of the representational mode, wherein anything exterior is commensurated with pre-established frames of scale and categorization, and into a direct coitus with their own ontological substrates.

One must of course grant that space and (not just) time, as the dimensions of sensuous intuition are – as Kant specifies – infinitely divisible continua, registering degrees of strength and weakness in matter's affection of intuition so unbroken as to become, at their most fine-grained, infinitesimal: infinitely and unmeasurably small. But why should the ribbons of phenomenal smoothness – by all accounts themselves synthetically derivative, and *ideal* qua phenomenal and apparent as opposed to (meta-)physical – be unified and allowed to swell up, bloating once again on the model of substance, so as to erect yet another barrier and halting point to our investigation into the relations between meaningless stains and meaningful non-stains?

The vibration or sine-wave is but one possible model of the behaviour of raw matter, or of metaphysical temporality. And Deleuze's declared intention is, after all, to scatter Spinoza's uber-substance onto its non-substantial modes, fulfilling its collapse by deriving it from them in order to attain an immanent and non-closed dispersal of sufficient explanations, thereby warding off the risk that Spinozist univocity be ideologically operationalized as a totalized, domineering unexplained explainer (Deleuze 2004, 50). Possibility – construed as ontological-real, rather than epistemic – is to be unboundedly infinitized such as not to be allowed to exclude incompossibilty and incommensurability from within itself. As this is attempted in *Difference and Repetition* via the altogether *conceptual* thought-experiment of a dice-throw reiterated to infinity, permitting the affirmation of the necessity of chance as a whole (Deleuze 2004, 248-249), the question is all the more urgently begged as to why it should be a *sentiendum,* rather than something thoroughly abstract and cognitive – such a square circle, or an even less banal contradiction than this – that is permitted alone to provide the friction of discovery.

3. The crux of non-trivial meaninglessness suppressed by empty indeterminacy

A final preparatory loop will bring us to our crux. A third strategy for undermining the auto-sufficiency of meaningfulness, elaborated in Lacanianism, involves focusing on the meaningless structure underpinning semantics. We may be obliged pragmatically to treat the world as a coherent totality, but the non-existence of any neutral meta-language, and the discovery that a set containing all sets is a logico-mathematical paradox, undermine the stability of the boundaries of the symbolic order upon which we rely and reveal that it functions only thanks to its disavowed structuration around the "void" constituted by its fractured openness to its own exterior.

Thus for Žižek the "stain" of meaninglessness is at one and the same time the disturbing eruption of the inconsistency of the real and the manifestation of the dislocated gap of the subject's unconscious desire. He cites the tramp in Chaplin's *City Lights*, who in the film's first scene is found when a newly minted statue is uncovered by the mayor, asleep in its lap, only to be awoken by the noise of the surprised audience, who are provoked to laughter by his embarrassed scrabbling attempts to get out of the way. Žižek notes that the tramp "is always interposed between a gaze and its 'proper' object, fixating upon himself a gaze destined for another, ideal point or object – a stain which disturbs 'direct' communication (…) leading the straight gaze astray, changing it into a kind of squint" (Žižek 1992, 5). Mistaken again and again for someone else – a rich benefactor – by a flower-seller girl who is blind and in need of funds for an operation, the tramp finally presents himself to her without hiding behind this confusion. "This is the moment of death and sublimation: (…) his being is no longer determined by a place in the symbolic network, it materializes the pure Nothingness of the hole, the void in the Other (the symbolic order)" (Žižek 1992, 8).

Identifying the stain-disturbance with *meaningless per se and as a whole* allows Žižek to de-metaphorize it by cauterizing it sharply in the sequestration of a (purportedly) non-relational, purely empty void. However, there is cause for hesitation here. The unsublatable "void" is no doubt central in the psychoanalytic register of unconscious desire, but as we understand him Žižek's philosophical commitment is that such a void (to which we will return via Laruelle) is the precondition *of any and all intelligibility whatsoever*. If that which throws a spanner in the works of meaning is construed as *always* being the twin void of desire and symbolic incompleteness, we may be left wondering why the possibility of a nuanced discernment of *different types of meaninglessness* should have thus been excluded. This is the nub of our crux: is there not more to be said about what separates an a-signifying musical riff or ritornello, or an unrecognizable smear of paint, from an a-semantic anomaly in scientific observation, and these from an incompossibly over-semantic superimposition of clashing beliefs?

II. Laruelle's "non-standard philosophy":
the indifferentiation-of-the-last-instance of concrete and abstract

1. Hyper-Kantianism

Laruelle intervenes here first of all by encouraging us to concede the Kantian point that *any* perception or experience or thinking is *conditioned* by operations of shaping or enabling determination which are transcendental with respect to it. "Transcendental" in this broadly Kantian sense is to be understood in the skeletal, metaphysically threadbare sense of "minimally necessary condition of possibility, without which the very intelligibility of the thing in question is lost".

Kant insists that to have an experience you need to have had a synthesis of *both* a sensible stuff *and* a form-giving function or "concept". Moreover, the matter of sensation is itself no longer all that "brute" by the time it arrives at the faculty of understanding to be stitched in to classificatory-categorial concepts selected via logical-propositional judgments, for it has already been – as it were – industrially squeezed through the spatio-temporal filters constituting the pure a priori dimensions of sensible intuition. "Matter" is faceless, whereas sensuous perception is *per se* formed. Knowledge of the operativity of classificatory categories and rules for their connection is not derived from metaphysical principles but transcendentally deduced from what knowledge inescapably knows about its own structure. A Laruellean question mark already pops up regarding how one might hope to empirically distinguish a privileged instance of *matter* from amongst transcendentally shaped *forms*.

Euclidean three-dimensional simultaneous metrical extension *partes extra partes*, for space, and linear succession, for time, are for Kant not to be mistaken for properties of the bare things-in-themselves, even though we rely on these forms to attain knowledge of any things at all. The nineteenth-century neo-Kantians, among them Hermann Cohen, take the further step of de-reifying these specific forms, which were in fact peremptorily nailed down and frozen by Kant in an ahistorical snapshot as unsurpassably necessary "forms of intuition" – in spite of his unlatching of them from metaphysical constraint. On the neo-Kantian account, there is no in-principle barrier to our coming in the future to conceive of – if not intuitively experience – as-yet-unconceptualized spatio-temporal modalities, as had in fact happened with the eighteenth-century discovery of non-Euclidean geometries – which follow from the cancellation of Euclid's "fifth postulate" proscribing the touching of parallel straight lines, a cancellation achieved through the plotting of the parallels on the surface of a sphere – or with Einstein's elaboration of general relativity.

Aiming to radicalize this transcendentalist stance, non-standard philosophy will, among other things, seek to definitively unstick the unsatisfactory category of "the matter of intuition" – with its shifting models: sine wave, particulate atoms, unbalanced clashing forces, and so on – from what it will view as its arbitrary, methodologically incoherent nomination as metaphysical primitive. We will now adumbrate a few of Laruelle's central ideas, which we will argue are indispensable for escaping the clasp of our crux.

2. Radical immanence

Laruelle's innovation hereupon lies in his contestation that to think in a thoroughly immanent, non-representational manner involves accepting the "Identity-of-the-last-instance" of thought itself with the Real, the *indifferent* unseparation of the two, in such a way as to acknowledge – in a seeming paradox – the sheerness of the *scission* between transcendentally conditioned and determined forms, of any kind, and that which is entirely undivided and identical to itself, and hence no longer the slightest bit ideal, but real and only real. Laruelle's Real is given the name of "radical immanence" or "the One", and is apodictically deduced and axiomatically defined as precisely that which is not muddied by even the slightest hint of transcendence, or of any *relativity to* anything – other than itself.

The merest scrap of empirical data will always imply a split or division between its conditional occasionment and that unconditioned Real which is immanent only to itself, rather than to anything else, and which "gives nothing of itself and receives nothing of itself except the modality in which it is given. This is only possible if it is the one or the indivision, the Without-division, which is given to itself in its specific (that is, indivisible) modality" (Laruelle 2010, 22). Thus, the One is in-principle separated from and *foreclosed to* any type of thought: not only to sensuous phenomenal palpation, but also to the operations of representation, as well as to any philosophical manoeuvre relying upon the glue of substance to hold it together: it is "*index sui* prior to any indication" (Laruelle 2010, 22).

According to Laruelle, thought must therefore distinguish itself from the One, while the One does not distinguish itself from thought in return. Its foreclosure is tied up with this irreversible, untransparent asymmetry. Empirically given data – be they numbers or smudges – are, as per Kant, determinate (exhibiting certain specific characteristics rather than others), as well as synthetically unified (not to mistake them for thing-in-themselves). But the fact that determinacy must *per se* be distinguished from indeterminacy, does not warrant any hypostatization of the gap between the two, for how could one flesh-out a narrative describing the emergence of the condition of possibility of narrativization? Such an attempt would reify what is a skeletal, merely intelligible transcendental necessity into a story held hostage by the very contingent empirical experiences it is supposed to account for.

We are thus forced to confront the undeniable split between conditioned and unconditioned as an epistemic lacuna which pulverizes any pretension we may have had to diaphanously discern, in a representational mode of truth-as-correspondence, the relations of causality and conditioning which are in fact in play. A blindspot which, further, undermines the sufficiency of the very notions of "causality" and "conditioning" to the task of binding the phenomenal appearances together at a safely regulated distance from the unbound indeterminacy of the Kantian negative noumenon, that cut of withdrawal cauterizing our finite cognition from its own outside. Thus, in the theoretical practice Laruelle is recommending, the non-standard theoretician does not contemplate or represent anything, but rather *does* something, slicing into overinflated co-optations of the Real illegitimately construed, on the model of substance, as a totality of relations which the philosopher might exhaustively survey. This action requires the *axiomatic* affirmation of the "determination-in-the-last-instance" of the determined *per se* – whether it ends up being occasionally determined, via whatever transcendental operations of objectivation, as this or as that, as a headache or Fermat's last theorem – by the purely immanent Identity-of-the-last-instance of everything with the Real. The mainstay of non-standard philosophical practice – the word *practice* being heavily emphasized – is the carrying out of this act, which "unilateralizes" philosophical decisions.

3. Determination in the last instance and Unilateralization

Who is really acting though? Laruelle often nominates the subject of non-standard philosophy as none other than the "human" or "Man-in-person", whose immediate "Lived Experience" is, in-itself, said to be perfectly irreflexive – i.e., subsisting prior to the closing of the loop of linguistic self-reference through which philosophy, according to Laruelle, tries to plaster over its own dislocation from the Real. However, on this point we will prefer to look at an instance of a conflicting tendency in his work, whereby the ultimate irreflexive instance of Identity in itself – strictly in-itself, rather than through any of its mediations; that which applies the negative "pressure-from-below" which dislodges the attempt to substantialize conceptual synthesis – is construed as being simply the One itself. If we are to carry out a thorough criticism of the auto-sufficiency of conceptual synthesis, why would the "human" and "lived experience" be let off the hook? (For two powerful variants of this quibble, see Fox 2017 and Brassier 2012.)

"Determination in the last instance" means then,

> among other things, that the One does not act by itself and through a part of itself which it would alienate into the World and which it would identify with this latter; and also that the finite act upon the World is identically, immediately, its distanciation from the One, the affirmation of its non-unitary non-confusion with the One. The One acts *in the last instance only*, and it acts on the World by determining it to not be the One. (Laruelle 1985, 140; my translation, D. B.)

> 'Last instance' does not indicate a first or final cause in a causal continuum (the famous indefinite progressions or regressions in the conditions of a conditioned), nor does it respond to the complementary qualm regarding stopping the causal chain [...] *It is not in the slightest to these problems that the theory of determination in the last instance responds but rather to their 'exclusion', more exactly to their unilateralization.* (Laruelle 1985, 141; my translation, D. B.)

So, as hinted at above, the Real is *not a condition* but is rather the determinant of any determinacy whatsoever, insofar as the latter is *per se* separated from the undetermined. The determined thing ends up being shaped thus and so, rather than otherwise, by *contingent* occasional instances of conditioning, but this only makes sense if the determined thing is distinguished in its general sharp (or hazy) *ipseity* from the blankness of Identity qua Identity, i.e., from the facelessness from which *ipseity* is distinguished insofar as it is identical to itself rather than to "nothing", this latter being the form that pure Identity qua Identity in isolation must take. However, every phenomenon is in fact itself identical-in-the-last-instance with the Real qua the One, because anything and everything can and must, in – and only in – the last instance, be seen to fall under the mode of indivision. Indivision ultimately gains the upper hand in the parallax between, on the one hand, the perspective upon things viewed in so far as they are Identical and undivided, stripped of mediation (Laruelle's "Vision-in-One"), and, on the other, the perspective upon things viewed within the synthetic discourse-Worlds in which philosophical decisions envelop them. The latter needs the former, but not *vice versa*.

As we will see, the undivided has Identity but no unity, such that the "splintering off" from the One of the particular, specific transcendental operations by which thinking objectivates and organises things cannot be philosophically hardened into a *metaphysical* transcendence, because the ontological status of the processes leading to the separation of object from subject and subject from object, as well as the criteria for their successful mapping, have been epistemically scrambled ("fractalized"). That is, no recourse to substance can be made in trying to put one's finger on how precisely they might work. It is not only that it is structurally impossible for a conditioned experience to glance airily back over its own shoulder in order to glimpse the mechanisms of its own conditioning – of which it is, therefore, in the first instance oblivious – but also that any fleck of experience must be exposed in its non-reciprocal dependency upon – its irreversible distinguishment from – the One, by the operation of unilateralization.

This uni-directional severment, applying indifferently across the schematic stratifications of thought to fragments and atoms just as much as to the relations between these terms, is also the annulment of any hope for the auto-intelligible or self-unveiling automatic mapping and connection of these determinations. Thus the very distinction between thinking and non-thinking itself will take the form of a *unilateral* duality or "Identity-without-unity": a duality with only one side, here that of thinking, which distinguishes itself from non-thinking without non-thinking distinguishing itself from it in return. More precisely, *both* terms, thinking (ideality), and non-thinking stuff ("materiality-without-matter", let's say), are unilateralized through the revelation of their equal relativity to the blindspot of real negativity. Thought needs the Real, but the Real does not need thought.

4. Inconsistency, incompleteness, and the de-substantialization of the void

For Kant, the appearances are of course endowed with self-Identity, having certain specific empirical properties rather than others, but so too is the noumenon, with the difference that its Identity-to-itself is non-empirical and unknowable, beyond being limited by Kant to the principle of non-contradiction. But what if the – so to speak – acidic (or oxygenating) underdetermination and non-relationality of the noumenon cannot be held back from seeping into the appearances and untethering the stifling extra layer of relational mediation with which unearned metaphysical presumption decides to arbitrarily unify and organize the otherwise splendidly immediate and unrelated singularities occurring in the realm of the determined? And what if the non-relation which asymmetrically determines relational determination entails that even by speaking of the thing-in-itself as "non-contradictory" one was illegitimately reifying it as a bound relational determination, serenely set over in front of the mind's contemplating eye, in a manner redolent of Aristotelian substance? These are the questions Laruelle asks, and his non-standard philosophical reply is that, when it comes to philosophy, this is indeed what has always already happened.

It transpires that "unity" (in contradistinction to Identity) is always synthetically constructed, because unification requires totality and totalization is always a synthetic operation. Thus the manner in which one totalizes a field of objects always follows off the back of a supplementary decision of thought, tying together groupings of things into extraneously marshalled assemblages by catching them in a spider's web centred upon a selected principle. In the case of Bergson and certain moments in Deleuze, the Laruellean reading has it that, far from unmediated escape, we have the selection of an operational principle, which takes stochastic seriality as a necessary and reversible *name* for the very bridge supposed to let the Real flow into thought and thought flow back into the Real. This is a name for *scission itself* allowing its modelling as a smooth, continuous variation and auto-distantiantion, folded back into its determinant and said to be a necessary property of it, i.e., of that unscissioned without which scission doesn't make sense. Identity (in contradistinction to unity) is for Laruelle not synthetic or transcendental but simply immanent – that is, irreflexive, and precisely *lacking* any unified horizon, limiting bound or halting point which could provide the basis for the recuperation of self-identical forms into a closed set such that a scale and a principle for the commensuration of them which each other could be found.

The uncorking of totality, however, is a familiar idea, and we seem here to be not a million miles away from being back at the Lacano-Hegelian position which we earlier claimed sacrificed the ability to distinguish between different types of meaninglessness to the void of symbolic incompleteness, thereby getting stuck in a crux with which we were not content to rest satisfied. At this stage there indeed springs up the danger of falling into the assumption that the Real's "rupturing" of the order of the conditioned World implies a *substantial crack* between the two. This may perhaps be the risk run by Žižek, and one which Laruelle might be able to dodge.

From Laruelle's perspective, the gap at stake here cannot be substantialized, because this would require that it be totalized, and, as per the above, *unity* can only be the product of a synthetic operation. Division too requires the unification of terms into a grouping separated from the undivided. This is not the case for our conceptualization of Identity or indivision itself, which can and must be defined negatively (or rather, positively, insofar as we are dealing with the cancellation of a constraint not unlike the removal of a speed-limit (cf. Brassier 2007, 146)) through the procedure of the lifting or crossing-out of division. Epistemic formlessness qua the Real qua Identity qua the One has been rendered so thoroughly vacuous by Laruelle as to "constitute *a hole in nothingness itself*" (Laruelle 2003, 175). In Brassier's words, it lacks "even the minimal consistency of the void" (Brassier 2007, 137). What does this mean? The precise sense we give to "consistency" here is important. The Real is *in*consistent because it does not "hang together", surpassing any synthetic unification. However, it is crucial to note that, for this very reason, it is *not* "incomplete", to use this term in an extended Gödelian-logical sense as meaning, roughly, "lacking something it should incorporate".

The question of logical completeness can only arise with respect to a system of stipulated rules and statements which is *consistent*, i.e., not allowing any contradictions to be derived from the propositions which constitute it, since (in classical logic at least) from a contradiction anything follows (the "principle of explosion"). If we're dealing with a set of properties of a thing or a model of a thing's functioning, logical consistency can only be determined through a contradiction-free propositional characterization of the object. Positive consistency, to be logically coherent, has to be *systematic*, even if only in the exiguous sense of the disjunctively juxtapositional negation or exclusion from the object of what is opposed to it. Overspilling even opposition, and a stranger to the possibility of contradiction, Laruelle's Real is *hyper*complete, at the same time as being absolutely non-consistent. This *negation of* consistency is, we recall, itself not question-begging, because non-consistency is indexed by *indifference* to the distinction between contradictory and non-contradictory – that is, by the operation of lifting or crossing-out consistency, the suspension of the pretention to substantial sufficiency of the synthetic operation upon which consistency relied in the first place. Non-consistency is therefore not the mere product of another supercilious decision, and this Real non-object – even though it cannot be propositionally encapsulated; or rather, precisely because of this, but *only* under these stringent procedural conditions – is not just one more dogmatic and queasy philosophical confection-fantasy.

We thus arrive at an injunction to remain vigilant against any facile or simplistically intuitive conception of *inconsistency*. As Žižek and Deleuze insist, the Real is not a closed totality, and so is as indifferent to the category of essence as it is to the distinction between autonomous self-causedness and heteronomous causation. But the default of totalization *for this very reason* does *not* at all mean that particular objects, whether concrete *or abstract*, lose their own reality, integrity, or relative autonomy. Slime and other types of oozing gunge may topple from a state of hanging together towards one of falling apart, but only in a register already presupposing the tacit consistency of a system of quasi-logical relations to associate them with, and distinguish them from, more stolid objects. And the void, once desubstantialized, is shown to remain relative to non-voids, the opposition between void and non-void plenum or atom having been, as a whole – both of its poles – unilateralized or pushed over onto the separatedly relational side of the scission between what is relational and the absolutely non-relational and unseparated One. The non-consistent One is always glued to the heel of any minimally thinkable determination, as its determinant-of-the-last-instance. Neither slime nor holes are therefore any more straightforwardly emblematic of the Real than chess-pieces, Pythagoras's theorem, or partial-differential equations, which they cannot, in the first instance, be taken to swallow up, corrode, crush, or reduce.

III. Art & noise

Laruelle may attain the *nec plus ultra* of French anti-dialectical suspicion, but doesn't the above point in the direction of reopening, or keeping open, the unreified dialectical placement of sensation in art? In this section we will allow ourselves to briefly stray from the letter of non-standard philosophy, in order to deploy it in a manner at odds with Laruelle's own stated goals, such as to formulate some important open questions which risked being suffocated by our crux.

We thus note, with respect to sensorial stains, that if they suspend their own classification in order to do things with spatio-temporal materials, then, for a start, this suspension depends on classifications being in play, rather than not. Obscurity is grasped as such in distinction from clarity, however provisional or fake. Are there particular types of clarity or pseudo-clarity in relation to which specific types of innovation in the shaping of sensorial form become especially pertinent? And what are the reasons why we might have come to desire to separate out sensorial smearing as worth pursuing in isolation from other kinds of cognitive disturbance?

Art does not just confront us with sensorial blurring, undermining our workaday representational complacency (which is not to deny that since at least Cézanne it does do this). It also (*cognitively*) confronts us with the *cognitive* breakdown entrained by our necessary lack of a full synoptic grasp or schematic overview of our own intrication within ideological machines and global systems, presenting systemic complexity *qua* systemic complexity. Is not another goal the production of new incommensurabilities through the deployment of the various rule-bound games which constitute art's own clichéd lines of least resistance, as well as its opportunities for breaking with these? A desideratum on both counts being to help stave off false substantial-Aristotelian totality. And shouldn't art bring to light something specific we didn't know about our desires now?

It might therefore be useful to supplement a desubstantialized conception of the stain with the quasi-information-theoretic function of "noise", glossed as interference in the communication of a message – not an in-principle occluded non-informational substrate of information, but rather the presence of too much information. If the sensorial stain no longer enjoys a special privilege, it makes sense to blur and efface the lines demarcating it from the array of other types of meaninglessness, as a first step precisely towards a more nuanced taxonomy of these. Our hunch is that the blindspot which harbours the most truth in any given situation may turn out to be locatable thanks only to its mediation with the determinate meaningfulness at play in the situation. The absolute meaninglessness of the One would then be the spur to accepting that the most fecund contradictions are only discoverable through a laborious, slow and gropingly proceeding investigation of the entailments and incompatibilities implicated in the occasional resources which happen to be lying around in our current situation. This is of course not a suggestion likely to enthuse Laruelle, whose ultimate *bête-noir* is the Master-dialectician Hegel.

By way of examples, chosen with the intention of maximally prizing open the reach of our open questions, two video works by Amanda Beech contain plenty of the multifaceted type of noise we have in mind. Firstly, in "Gz and Hustlas" (2003)[2], a mash up of Apocalypse Now and Snoop Dogg, scenes from the film have been chopped up and edited together against the eponymous rap track, as if to construct a slick promotional clip. Instead of Snoop, we admire preening helicopters, puffed-up soldier-laden boats, and bridges being dynamited in synch with the snare. The artist has filmed the movie playing on her own TV, so the quality of the image is degraded by the electronic smudge of fuzzy pixels. But there is also an enormous amount of systemic and narrative noise. The globe-trotting machinery of military power is shoved in our face, and one is revolted, and at the same time, *thrilled* by the ludicrous, but somehow apt, surfeit of machismo, Realpolitik, and sheer blockbuster entertainment. A repellently *jouissif* contradictory entanglement in capital-power, made a bit more explicit.

Secondly, "Sanity Assassin" (Beech 2010). Creeping zooms upon an opulent but stark Californian interior, with grand piano and floral arrangements, but also on clandestine masonic paneled ceilings; rough side-of-the-freeway landscape glimpses; the inky infinity of interstellar space, with some kind of chemical snow falling, or architectural models gliding with utilitarian efficiency in and out of shot, in sharp relief in the foreground; floating: what appear to be spaceships, made of curious oblong surfaces plastered with homey wallpaper, and rendered in low- to mid- fidelity CGI.

Gain corporate enfranchisement, ushered into mahogany chambers behind closed doors? Or pursue public transparency in circulating through municipal precincts? Which is better? Upon what can I fall back to help me decide? The work enacts the deprivation of any would-be metaphysically-given pointers by juxtaposing and superimposing uncanny cosmic intimations of the acephalic modality of indivision with normatively grasped, desire-baiting social conundrums. However, as the sci-fi-utopian charge of interstellar space grabs us propositionally-conceptually – as does the very notion that (the notion of) modal indivision is in play –, we are dealing here with the *concept of* outer space and its attendant culturally sedimented baggage. The unease felt in face of the work's contradictions is cognitive and social at the same time as pulsional.

---

[2] This video is not available online, but others are, at: http://www.amandabeech.com.

Coda: Incommensurability

We contest that unilateralization unblocks an obstruction to philosophical and artistic activity by showing that *nothing* in radical immanence qua radical immanence can furnish any criterion for success. The deprivation of any short-circuit between the Real and the conditioned for Laruelle liberates determinate singularities from smothering envelopment by what is for him that otiose extra layer of philosophical mediation forcibly commensurating them – be they "concrete" forms *or* "abstract" ones – with arbitrarily decided-upon metaphysical yardsticks. The slick but vicious circularity of philosophical auto-sufficiency is thereby broken and dislocated.

We would like to suggest that two conclusions should be drawn from this. Firstly, that philosophy, science, and art must be seen to be labouring under the necessarily unmitigated charge of an effortful experimentation, investigating their determinate situations through hypothesis-testing and the setting and resetting of fungible axioms. This is our attempted dialectical twist on non-standard philosophy's anti-dialectical dismemberment of terms from relations. And secondly – a slightly more Laruellean claim, though not straightforwardly so – that philosophy's insufficiency to definitively patch up its own blindspots entails that incommensurabilities, which are necessary in order to kick against false engluements of totality, have to be *constructed*, for, against what we have interpreted as Deleuze's modal realism, no reservoir of *prêt à porter* infinite incompossibilty will be found lying around ready to be leveraged in the Real.

The *fractal*, then, can be read as a figure of that specific indifferentiation resulting from the default of substance: identical to itself and modally undivided across its phenomenally broken scales and stratifications, but no longer offering any simply given yardstick-criterion from which to infer the principles governing its (in effect) absolutely chaotic internal mappings. The query to be addressed to non-standard philosophy, then, concerns the worry that this under-determined, blankly infinite complexity may after all harden into yet another precipitate halting point. To fractalize substance may be to get close to its definitive collapse. But must the Real as inconsistent zero-degree rule out the very possibility of non-substantial criteria for determinate truth?

David Bremner, PhD Candidate, University of Kent /
Université Paris 8, db404@kent.ac.uk

References

Aristotle. *Categories and De Interpretatione*. Trans. J. L. Ackrill. Oxford: Clarendon Press, 1963.

Beech, Amanda. "Sanity Assain," Web. 2 November 2017. <http://amandabeech.com/works/sanity-assassin/>.

Bergson, Henri. *The Creative Mind: An Introduction to Metaphysics*. Trans. Mabelle L. Andison. NY: Citadel, 1992.

Brassier, Ray. *Nihil Unbound*. Basingstoke/NY: Palgrave Macmillan, 2007.

Brassier, Ray. "Laruelle and the Reality of Abstraction," in Mullarkey, John and Anthony Paul Smith (eds.). *Laruelle and Non-Philosophy*. Edinburgh: EUP, 2012. 100-121.

Fox, Dominic. "Under Pressure: Marx, Metaphysics and the Cunning of Abstraction. (Response to Katerina Kolozova)." Symposium contribution, 2017. Web. 2 November 2017. <https://syndicate.network/symposia/philosophy/toward-a-radical-metaphysics-of-socialism/>.

Deleuze, Gilles. *Difference and Repetition*. Trans. Paul Patton. London/NY: Continuum, 2004.

Hume, David. *A Treatise of Human Nature*. Excerpted in Isaiah Berlin (ed.). *The Age of Enlightenment*. NY: Mentor, 1956.

Laruelle, François. *Une biographie de l'homme ordinaire: des Autorités et des Minorités*. Paris: Aubier, 1985.

Laruelle, François. "What can non-philosophy do?" Trans. Ray Brassier. *Angelaki* 8:2 (August 2003): 169-189.

Laruelle, François. "The Truth According to Hermes: Theorems on the Secret and Communication." Trans. Alexander R. Galloway. *Parrhesia* 9 (2010): 18-22.

Laruelle, François. *The Concept of Non-Photography*. Trans. Robin Mackay. Falmouth/NY: Urbanomic/Sequence, 2011.

Spinoza, Baruch. *Ethics*. Trans. Edwin Curley. London: Penguin, 1996.

Žižek, Slavoj. *Enjoy Your Symptom! Jacques Lacan in Hollywood and out*. New York: Routledge, 1992.

YVANKA B. RAYNOVA (Sofia/Vienne)

"L'âge de la non-philosophie":
Martin Heidegger et François Laruelle

Abstract

"The Age of Non-Philosophy": Martin Heidegger and François Laruelle

In his lessons at the College of France, Merleau-Ponty noticed that something ended with Hegel and that we perhaps entered in an age of non-philosophy. This poses the question if philosophy is coming to an end or if it can be rebuild from within by retaining its essence. While Merleau-Ponty is trying to restore philosophy from the inside, Heidegger and Laruelle open two different paths of a non-philosophical thinking from the outside. The purpose of the article is to compare these two paths more in detail in order to articulate their differences as to the problems of identity, of the "thing of thought" (Sache des Denkens), of the role of science etc., and to show the radicality of Laruelle's undertaking, which aims not a Verwindung *(recollection), nor an* Überwindung *(overcoming) of philosophy but its appropriation in a new unified theory of thought. One of the main thesis of the author is that Heidegger should not be considered only as a "philosopher of difference" (Laruelle) but also as a thinker of identity as he has expounded four different identity concepts. Hence, it is argued that if Laruelle's critique of the convertibility of Erignis' identity is legitimate, his critique of Heidegger's amphibology of the One is questionable.*

Keywords: Marin Heidegger, François Laruelle, metaphysics, difference, identity, non-philosphy

Introduction

Quelque chose a fini avec Hegel. Il y a, après Hegel, un vide philosophique, ce qui ne veut pas dire que les penseurs que les génies aient manqué, mais que Marx, Kierkegaard, Nietzsche commencent par une dénégation de la philosophie. Faut-il dire qu'avec eux on entre dans un âge de non-philosophie? Ou bien cette destruction de la philosophie en est-elle la réalisation? Ou bien en conserve-t-elle l'essentiel, et la philosophie, comme l'écrit Husserl, renaît-elle de ses cendres? (Merleau-Ponty 1968, 141-142)

La constatation de Merleau-Ponty que "quelque chose a fini avec Hegel" n'est pas nouvelle. On se rappelle que Marx et Engels avaient qualifié le processus de décomposition de l'esprit absolu du système hégélien de "caput mortuum" (Marx/Engels 1968, 42). Pour eux ce qui avait fini avec Hegel, c'était la philosophie comme idéologie, c'est-à-dire la foi superstitieuse que le monde est dominé par des idées qui constituent les principes déterminants de la réalité (ibid., 40). Ce qui est plutôt original, c'est l'idée de Merleau-Ponty que la philosophie a abouti à une sorte de non-philosophie, qui selon lui commence avec la dénégation de la philosophie et aboutit à sa destruction – on pense ici à la destruction de la métaphysique de Heidegger. D'où la question, s'il la philosophie est arrivée définitivement à sa fin ou si elle peut renaitre à nouveau à partir de ce qui constitue son essence, c'est-à-dire être transformée par l'intérieur. Alors que Merleau-Ponty va prendre plutôt ce dernier chemin (cf. Raynova 2010, 78-98), des philosophes comme Heidegger et Laruelle suggèrent que pour dépasser les limites de la philosophie il faut sortir "hors" d'elle. Ainsi, selon le jeune Heidegger, la philosophie de Hegel a abouti à sa fin puisque le penseur allemand tournait en rond autour des problèmes sans pouvoir s'en sortir. Il aurait fallu, au contraire, recommencer la philosophie à partir du centre de ce cercle problématique (GA 24, 400). Plus tard, après le tournant, la question de "la fin de la philosophie" est posée par Heidegger dans un contexte plus large identifiant la philosophie avec la métaphysique et son histoire. En montrant les impasses de la philosophie/métaphysique, Heidegger propose alors une autre voie, qui sera d'importance cruciale non seulement pour les "philosophies de la différence" et les projets de déconstruction, mais aussi quant à l'articulation la plus radicale de la non-philosophie de la part de François Laruelle.

L'objectif de la présente étude est par conséquent d'analyser et de comparer les deux alternatives d'approche non-philosophique que nous offrent Heidegger et Laruelle, afin d'articuler leurs différences essentielles quant aux problèmes de l'identité, de la "chose la pensée" (*Sache des Denkens*), du rôle de la science etc. et de montrer en quel sens la conception laruellienne est plus radicale. Une des thèses principales, que j'essayerai de démonter, est que Heidegger n'est pas seulement un "philosophe de la différence", comme le suggèrent certains de ses interprétateurs y compris Laruelle, mais qu'il est de même un penseur de l'identité qui en a esquissé plusieurs concepts.

Je dois dire en avance que je ne suis ni heideggérienne, ni laruellienne mais que j'utilise ici, comme ailleurs, la méthode d'une herméneutique comparée inspirée par l'approche de Paul Ricœur (cf. Raynova 2010, 16; idem. 2017, 12). Je suis bien consciente que par-là je serais prise entre deux fronts, d'autant plus que je n'essayerais pas à faire comme Ricœur des efforts de médiation entre les positions contraires[1], mais de montrer leur incompatibilité. Néanmoins, je prends volontairement le risque d'être accusée par les uns d'avoir de la sympathie pour Laruelle, qui aurait défiguré la pensée de Heidegger, et par les autres pour utiliser les vieilles méthodes de l'histoire traditionnelle de la philosophie (Laruelle 2015, 7), voire même de "l'hermétologie" unitaire et autoritaire (Laruelle 1987, 398).

1. Le pas en arrière et le saut "hors de la philosophie"

> *Den Schritt zurück aus der Philosophie in das Denken des Seyns dürfen wir wagen, sobald wir in der Herkunft des Denkens heimisch geworden sind.*
> (GA 13, 82)[2]

On a abondamment commenté la conception heideggérienne de la fin de la philosophie. Or, ce qui frappe dans ces commentaires, c'est que beaucoup d'auteurs analysent la conférence "La Fin de la philosophie et la tâche de la pensée" (1964) sans même mentionner des textes antérieurs comme "Qu'est-ce que la philosophie" (1955), "Identité et différence" (1957) ou "Le tournant" (1949)[3]. Lire le texte pour lui-même et par lui-même, comme le fait p.ex. Jean-Luc Marion (cf. Marion 1986), est une approche intéressante quant à certains détails, mais à mon avis l'importance de ce texte ne peut être saisie que si l'on essaye de capturer sa place dans l'évolution de la conception heideggérienne de la philosophie qui a beaucoup changé depuis le cours de 1919/1920 *Grundprobleme der Phänomenologie* (GA 58) à la conférence de 1964. Donc ce que je voudrais montrer ici, par une esquisse à grands traits, c'est qu'on ne peut pas vraiment comprendre "La Fin de la philoso-

---

[1] Faire la médiation ou essayer de mettre Heidegger et Laruelle en dialogue ne fera pas de sens, car comme le dit Laruelle lui-même "il n'y a pas de conflit ou de guerre des deux Hermès [celui de la phénoménologie ou l'herméneutique et celui de la non-philosophie], et peut-être même pas de 'dialogue' entre eux" (Laruelle 1987, 400).

[2] Je propose la traduction suivante: "Le pas en arrière nous pouvons oser de sortir hors de la philosophie pour entrer dans la pensée de l'Estre (Seyn), du moment où nous sommes autochtones dans l'origine de la pensée". Il s'agit donc pour Heidegger de sortir *hors de la philosophie* (*aus der Philosophie*) afin de remonter à l'Estre (*Seyn*) ce qui ne devient pas clair de la traduction d'André Préau: "Nous pouvons risquer le pas qui ramène de la philosophie à la pensée de l'Etre, dès lors qu'à l'origine de la pensée nous respirons un air natal". (Heidegger 1990, 33).

[3] Ces textes font partie du tome 11 de la *Gesamtausgabe*. Certains furent publié en français dans *Questions I et II*, tandis que "La fin de la philosophie et la tâche de la pensée" ainsi que "Le tournant" furent publié dans *Questions IV*. J'utilise ici *nolens volens* les éditions françaises, mais étant donné que les traductions de Heidegger doivent toujours être employé avec précaution, je me permettrai de proposer là où il me semble nécessaire des traductions alternatives en suivant les textes de la *Gesamtausgabe*.

phie et la tâche de la pensée" sans les textes précédents et, par conséquent, l'alternative de non-philosophie, proposée par Heidegger comme le pendant de la métaphysique.

Quand Heidegger déclare dans "La Fin de la philosophie et la tâche de la pensée" que "philosophie, cela veut dire métaphysique" (Heidegger 1990a, 282), ceci parait à première vue un postulat qui nécessite des explications. Il est vrai qu'il ajoute: "La métaphysique pense l'étant dans son tout – le monde, l'homme, Dieu – en regardant vers l'être, c'est-à-dire en tenant le regard fixé sur l'articulation de l'étant dans l'être" (ibid.). Mais cela explique peu et la nécessite de justifier la thèse de l'équivalence "philosophie = métaphysique" devient d'autant plus urgente quand on prend en considération qu'ailleurs, dans "Qu'est-ce que la métaphysique?" (1937), Heidegger présente une vue différente de la métaphysique en utilisant la métaphore de Descartes qui décrit la philosophie comme un arbre, dont les racines sont la Métaphysique, le tronc la Physique, et les branches qui sortent de ce tronc les autres sciences (Heidegger 1968, 23). En remontant au fondement ou l'essence de la métaphysique, Heidegger aboutit à l'équivalence " métaphysique = Dasein":

> Die Metaphysik gehört zur 'Natur des Menschen'. Sie ist weder ein Fach der Schulphilosophie noch ein Feld willkürlicher Einfälle. Die Metaphysik ist das Grundgeschehen im Dasein. Sie ist das Dasein selbst.[4] (GA 9, 121-122)

Donc, si l'on prend Heidegger au mot, il s'ensuit que la métaphysique appartient de telle façon à l'être du Dasein qu'il soit impossible d'envisager sa fin sans envisager la fin du Dasein même. Or, si la philosophie est métaphysique, est-ce que la fin de la philosophie sera-t-elle la fin du Dasein? Il semble que personne ne s'est posé cette question, y compris Marion. Pourtant ce n'est pas un hasard qu'il indique que l'identité étroite entre philosophie et métaphysique pose de problèmes:

> ... il [Heidegger] précise que 'Philosophie est métaphysique', en stricte équivalence; il traite donc bien de la fin de la métaphysique. Il se peut, pourtant, que l'on doive discuter cette équivalence; car si Heidegger s'offre en guide incomparable pour entrer dans la question de la fin de la métaphysique, il se pourrait aussi qu'il ne nous conduise plus aussi fermement en l'entreprise d'en finir avec cette fin même. Quel but donne une fin à la fin de la métaphysique? S'il ouvre cette question, Heidegger la laisse libre. (Marion 1986, 23)

---

[4] Je traduirais ce passage de la façon suivante: "La métaphysique appartient à la 'nature de l'homme'. Elle n'est ni une discipline de *Schulphilosophie* (philosophie de l'école), ni un champ d'improvisation avec d'idées arbitraires. La métaphysique est l'évènement fondamental (*Grundgeschehen*) à l'intérieur du Dasein. Elle est le Dasein même." L'équitation "métaphysique = Dasein" fait défaut dans la traduction de Corbin: "… la Métaphysique com-pose la 'nature de l'homme'. Elle n'est ni la spécialité d'une philosophie d'école, ni un champ clos pour extravagances fantaisistes – elle est l'historial qui, fondement de la réalité humaine, s'historialise comme réalité-humaine" (Heidegger 1968, 71).

Effectivement, si l'on demeure dans le cadre de la conférence "La fin de la philosophie et la tâche de la pensée", cette question restera ouverte. Etait-ce peut être l'intention de Heidegger?

Notons d'abord que cette conférence a été préparée à l'occasion d'un évènement particulier: le colloque "Kierkegaard vivant", organisé par l'UNESCO à Paris du 21 au 23 avril 1964, auquel ont participé un grand nombre de philosophes célèbres, notamment Gabriel Marcel, Karl Jaspers, Jean-Paul Sartre, Jean Wahl, Lucien Goldmann et Jacques Derrida. Le texte de Heidegger fut traduit et présenté par Jean Beaufret. Il est évident que dans le cadre limité de son propos Heidegger ne pouvait expliciter toutes ses idées sur la philosophie et la métaphysique. De ce fait pour les auditeurs sans connaissance plus avancée de ses écrits cet exposé pourrait avoir l'air d'une provocation. Et en effet, Heidegger a su provoquer l'intérêt, car on pouvait bien se demander après la conférence qu'est-ce qu'elle avait à faire avec Kierkegaard, qui ne fut même pas mentionné? Jean Beaufret, qui essayé de donner une réponse à cette question, souligne:

> Il n'est pas, dans ce texte, question de Kierkegaard qui, dans Sein und Zeit, est pourtant si présent. Kierkegaard est en effet, aux yeux de Heidegger, sinon un philosophe, du moins un maître de la littérature existentielle dont l'apparition, à la fin de la philosophie, est parfois d'autant plus concordante avec la tâche de la pensée. (Beaufret 1990, 279)

Mais il est douteux que l'approche existentiel de Kierkegaard était en accord quelconque avec "la tâche de la pensée" telle qu'elle fut envisagée par Heidegger, comme nous le verrons tout à l'heure. Si je tiens à articuler ce doute, c'est qu'il est important de mettre au clair que selon Heidegger personne – sauf lui-même – n'avait compris la véritable tâche de la philosophie, que celle-ci est demeurée dans toute l'histoire de la philosophie *l'impensé*, même pour des rebelles comme Nietzsche et Kierkegaard. Il a articulé cela assez clairement dans un passage de *Qu'appelle-t-on penser?* que je voudrais rappeler ici:

> Concept et système sont au même titre inconnus à la pensée grecque. C'est pourquoi aussi elle demeure fondamentalement d'une autre nature que le nouveau style de pensée de Kierkegaard et de Nietzsche, qui certes pensent expressément contre le système, mais qui par là même restent prisonniers de la tyrannie du système. Kierkegaard, par l'intermédiaire de la Métaphysique de Hegel, reste du point de vue philosophique enlisé d'un côté dans un Aristotélisme dogmatique qui ne le cède en rien à celui de la Scholastique médiévale, et d'un autre côté dans la subjectivité de l'Idéalisme allemand. Aucun esprit sensé ne voudra nier l'impulsion donnée par Kierkegaard en ce qui concerne l'attention renouvelée que l'on porte à 'l'existentiel'. En revanche,

Kierkegaard n'a pas le moindre rapport à la question décisive qui porte sur l'être de l'Être. (Heidegger 1973, 197).

La question décisive pour Heidegger, qui est donc celle de *l'être de l'Être*, constitue ce qu'il appelle *die Sache des Denkens*, c'est-à-dire la chose qui préoccupe la pensée ou qui constitue l'affaire de la pensée[5]. "La fin de la philosophie et la tâche de la pensée" est consacrée justement à ce thème. Heidegger reprend là une tentative qui n'a jamais cessé de le préoccuper depuis *Être et Temps*, à savoir la critique immanente de la *Sache des Denkens*, en posant deux questions:

1) En quoi la philosophie, à l'époque présente, est-elle entrée dans son stade terminal?
2) Quelle tâche, à la fin de la philosophie, demeure réservée à la pensée?

Il déploie la réponse à la première question par la thèse déjà mentionnée que "philosophie, cela veut dire métaphysique" et que la métaphysique est arrivée à son achèvement. Toutefois, précise-t-il, achèvement ne veut pas dire parachèvement au sens de perfection. Si l'on considère l'allemand *Ende*, qui veut dire aussi lieu, le mot pourrait être interprété comme rassemblement à un lieu. La fin de la philosophie désigne en ce sens un lieu, "celui auquel le tout de son histoire se rassemble dans sa possibilité la plus extrême" (Heidegger 1990a, 283). Un trait essentiel de cette "fin", c'est la ramification de la philosophie en sciences et leur émancipation de la philosophie, leur autosuffisance et, surtout, leur prise en charge des ontologies des diverses régions de l'étant – ce qui constituait naguère la tâche de la philosophie. La conclusion qui s'ensuit pour Heidegger, c'est que la pensée de l'Occident européen, née jadidans la Grèce antique, a abouti à une civilisation mondiale gouvernée par les sciences technisées (ibid., 286). Dans ce contexte il pose la seconde question, à savoir s'il y a une tâche de la pensée, issue comme "possibilité première" de la philosophie sans que celle-ci se n'en ai jamais rendu compte.

Heidegger approche cette seconde question au moyen d'une réflexion sur la *Sache des Denkens* en faisant résonner le *Gedanke* de Hegel. Rappelons que dans la troisième

---

[5] Beaufret traduit "*Sache des Denkens*" par "affaire de la pensée" ce qui rend seulement un aspect du sens et de l'usage du mot, p.ex. quand on dit "*der Sache nach*" (quant à l'affaire) ou "*das ist nicht meine Sache*" (cela n'est pas mon affaire). Or ce terme est utilisé par Heidegger dans sa polyvalence pour évoquer autant *die Sache* thématisée par Hegel que l'impératif husserlien "*zu den Sachen selbst*" (aller aux choses elles-mêmes). Dans le dernier cas Beaufret le laisse en allemand (cf. Beaufret 1990, 289) sans fournir aucune explication. André Préau, pour sa part, explique qu'il traduit *Sache* selon le contexte par "cause", "affaire", "cas", "propos", "chose" (cf. Heidegger 1968a, 276) ce qui fait. Or cette approche rend peut-être bien le contexte mais le mot *Sache* se perd de vue d'autant plus qu'il n'est pas mis en parenthèses.

partie de l'*Encyclopédie* Hegel thématise explicitement le penser (*das Denken*), la pensée (*der Gedanke*) et la chose de la pensée (*Sache des Denkens*):

> So ist die Intelligenz für sich an ihr selbst erkennend; – an ihr selbst das Allgemeine; ihr Produkt, der Gedanke ist die Sache; einfache Identität des Subjektiven und Objektiven. Sie weiß, daß, was gedacht ist, ist; und daß, was ist, nur ist, insofern es Gedanke ist; – für sich; das Denken der Intelligenz ist *Gedanken haben*; sie sind als ihr Inhalt und Gegenstand. (Hegel 1986, 283)[6]

Hegel présente donc la chose de la pensée comme *identité* du sujet et de l'objet ce qui amène Heidegger à la conclusion qu'en fait il ne s'agit que de la subjectivité thématisée d'abord par Descartes et ensuite par Hegel et Husserl: "Elle [la chose de la pensée] est pour Husserl comme pour Hegel et conformément à la même tradition, la subjectivité de la conscience" (Heidegger 1990a, 291). Or, dans l'appel *zur Sache selbst* chez Hegel et Husserl il reste, selon Heidegger, un impensé: c'est le fait que la chose entre dans la dimension du paraître et advient dans une certaine clarté qui se joue dans l'ouvert. Cet état d'ouverture, qui seul rend possible le "il y a" (*es gibt*) ainsi que la possibilité de monstration, est ce que Heidegger appelle *Lichtung*, clairière, et qu'il explique de la façon suivante.

> Le substantif *Lichtung* renvoie au verbe *lichten*. L'adjectif *licht* est le même mot que *leicht* (léger). *Etwas lichten* signifie: rendre quelque chose plus léger, le rendre ouvert et libre (...) Ce qui est *licht* au sens de libre et d'ouvert n'a rien de commun ni linguistiquement ni quant à la chose qui est ici en question, avec l'adjectif *licht* qui signifie clair ou lumineux. (ibid., 295)

Heidegger évoque par-là l'ambiguïté de la clairière comme un lieu ouvert autant pour la lumière et la présence que pour l'obscurité et l'absence et conclue qu'il serait faux de nommer "vérité" l'Ἀλήθεια au sens de *Lichtung*. Ce que Hegel nomme vérité, explique-t-il, c'est la certitude du savoir absolu et son adéquation comme accord de la représentation et de ce qui lui est présent. Mais ni Hegel, ni Husserl, ni d'ailleurs toute la métaphysique ne se sont jamais occupé de *l'être en tant qu'être*, c'est-à-dire de la présence qui en tant que telle ne peut être donnée que dans la clairière de l'Ouvert (ibid., 301-302). Ce qui reste aussi impensé, c'est que la clairière est autant ouverte pour la présence de l'être que pour son retrait, la Λήθη. D'où émerge la question si ce retrait, cette Λήθη, "appartient à l'Ἀλήθεια, non

---

[6] "L'intelligence connait ainsi en elle-même pour elle-même. *En elle-même* elle connait l'universel. Son produit, la pensée, est la chose même; c'est l'identité simple du sujet et de l'objet. Elle connait *pour soi*; car elle sait que ce qui est pensé est, et que ce qui est n'est qu'autant qu'il est pensé. La pensée de l'intelligence consiste à avoir des pensées. Ce sont les pensées qui font son contenu et son objet" (Hegel 1869, 205). On voit dans ce passage qu'Auguste Véra, excellent connaisseur de Hegel, traduit "die Sache" par "la chose même".

comme simple adjonction, pas non plus comme l'ombre appartient à la lumière, mais comme le cœur même de l'Ἀλήθεια ?" (ibid., 303). Dans ce cas, la chose même de la pensée ne devrait plus, selon Heidegger, porter le nom *Sein und Zeit* (être et temps), mais *Lichtung und Anwesenheit* (clairière et présence) et la tâche serait de savoir comment se fait-il qu'il y a (*es gibt*) la clairière.

Comme déjà indiqué, dans cette conférence Heidegger laisse cette question ouverte et c'est pourquoi il nous faut consulter d'autres textes pour voir où mène cette voie.

D'abord, pour aller au-delà de la philosophie, comme suggère le titre "La Fin de la philosophie et la tâche de la pensée", il faut savoir qu'est-ce que c'est la philosophie. Je laisserai de côté les premiers écrits de Heidegger, notamment la conférence *Grundprobleme der Phänomenologie* (GA 58), pour passer directement à la conférence "Was ist das – die Philosophie?" au colloque "Qu'est-ce que la philosophie? Autour de Martin Heidegger", qui a eu lieu du 27 août au 4 septembre 1955 à Cerisy-la-Salle sous la direction Jean Beaufret.

Heidegger commence son exposé avec la constatation que la question est trop vaste et indéfinie et qu'il faut donc l'aborder par un chemin. Celui-ci se trouve au fait "immédiatement devant nous", si l'on se tourne vers le mot même de philosophie. Provenant du grec φιλοσοφία, la philosophie "parle grec", souligne-t-il, ce qui veut dire qu'elle est "dans son être originel, de telle nature que c'est d'abord le monde grec et seulement lui qu'elle a saisi en le réclamant pour se déployer" (Heidegger 1968b, 15). Le mot φιλοσοφία nous dit en plus que la philosophie détermine non seulement le monde grec, mais aussi le cours intérieur de l'histoire occidentale-européenne (ibid.) Malgré que Heidegger s'oppose à maintes reprises à la position de thèses (Sätze), l'équivalence "philosophie = φιλοσοφία = philosophie occidentale-européenne d'origine grecque" est un postulat qui sert de base à l'assertion, assez proche à ce que soutient Husserl dans la *Krisis*, à savoir que la philosophie est le produit exclusif de l'Europe et des européens :

> L'affirmation: la philosophie est grecque dans son être propre ne dit rien d'autre que: l'Occident et l'Europe sont, et eux seuls sont, dans ce qu'a de plus intérieur leur marche historique, originellement "philosophiques". C'est ce qu'attestent la naissance et la domination des sciences. C'est parce qu'elles prennent source dans ce qu'a de plus intérieur la marche historique de l'Occident européen, entendons le cheminement philosophique, c'est pour cela qu'elles sont aujourd'hui en état de donner à l'histoire de l'homme sur toute la terre l'empreinte spécifique. (ibid., 16)

Du mot φιλοσοφία Heidegger passe sur l'autre partie du questionnement en expliquant que quand nous posons la question "qu'est-ce que...?" cela sonne en grec : τί ἐστιν.

> C'est cette manière de questionner que Socrate, Platon et Aristote ont déployée. Ils demandent par exemple: qu'est-ce que cela — le beau? Qu'est-ce que cela — la con-

naissance? Qu'est-ce que cela — la nature? Qu'est-ce que cela — le mouvement? (ibid., 16-17)

Ce τί, qui a été traduit en latin par *quid est*, renvoie à la *quidditas,* désignée en allemand par *die Washeit.* Cette quiddité fut déterminée de manière différente par les philosophes, p.ex. comme idée ou essence. Heidegger suggère par-là que ce qu'on cherche en posant la question: "Qu'est-ce que la philosophie?", c'est l'essence de la philosophie. On est donc renvoyé encore une fois au mot φιλοσοφία sans pouvoir s'en sortir de ce cercle qu'en le considérant de plus près. Ce n'est pas un hasard, dit Heidegger, que la langue de la philosophie est le grec, car "la langue grecque, et elle seule, est λόγος" (ibid., 20). Comme λέγειν, (ex)position, le Logos est une mise en présence sans intermédiaire de la chose même. Le mot philosophe, qui est composé par φιλεῖν et σοφόν, désigne au sens de Héraclite celui qui parle comme le Logos et correspond ainsi au σοφόν. Heidegger explique cette correspondance par une interprétation de Héraclite, que je vais reproduire ici entièrement, du fait qu'elle me semble d'importance majeure pour comprendre pourquoi Laruelle a résolument distingué son principe d'identité et d'immanence des notions telles que le Tout et l'Un.

> L'ἀνήρ φιλόσοφος aime le σοφόν. Ce que ce mot dit selon Héraclite est difficile à traduire. Mais nous pouvons l'élucider en suivant l'interprétation propre d'Héraclite lui-même. Conformément à quoi τό σοφόν dit ceci : Ἑν Πάντα, 'Un (est) Tout'. 'Tout' veut dire ici : Πάντα τά ὄντα, l'ensemble, la totalité de l'étant. Ἑν, l'Un, veut dire: ce qui est un, l'unique, ce qui unit tout. Mais, uni, est tout l'étant en l'être. Le σοφόν dit : tout l'étant est en l'être. Dit avec plus d'acuité : l'être est l'étant. Ici 'est' parle au sens transitif et ne veut pas moins dire que 'recueille'. L'être recueille l'étant en cela qu'il est l'étant. L'être est le recueil – Λόγος. (ibid., 21)

Or, selon Heidegger Héraclite et Parménide n'étaient pas encore des philosophes, ils étaient "*größere Denker*" (plus grands penseurs), car ils voyaient le Tout, c'est-à-dire ils étaient à l'unisson du Logos comme un Tout recueillant. La philosophie commence – il nous faut retenir en mémoire ceci, car c'est une importante spécificité de l'approche heideggérien – seulement quand on pose la question: qu'est-ce que l'étant en tant qu'il est? Cette question est le produit de l'étonnement qui est à l'origine de la philosophie: "L'étonnement est la disposition à l'intérieur de laquelle, pour les philosophes grecques, la correspondance à l'être de l'étant se trouvait accordée" (ibid., 35). Heidegger conçoit cette disposition (*Stimmung*) ou tonalité (*Grundstimmung*) comme *pathos*, non au sens de passion, mais au sens de "se laisser porter par" ou "céder" à l'appel de l'Etre. En même temps, on pourrait dire, en utilisant le vocabulaire de Laruelle, que par cette question la philosophie devient décision et opère une différence, une scission, qui va dominer toute la métaphysique depuis Platon. Heidegger qui voit dans la pensée d'Aristote l'apogée antique de la métaphysique rappelle sa définition selon laquelle la philosophie est la mise en marche vers la question: qu'est-ce que l'étant? Et, plus précisément: qu'est-ce que l'étantité de l'étant? (ibid., 23) Cette définition révèle d'une part que la philosophie est dans la modalité du correspondre qui s'accorde à la voix de l'Etre de l'étant et d'autre part que correspondre est un parler, un logos (ibid., 36-37). Elle mène aussi à la conclusion de Heidegger que sans une méditation sur le langage nous ne saurions vraiment ce que c'est la philosophie et qu'il faudrait donc thématiser le rapport ambigu entre Pensée et Poésie:

> Entre elles deux, pensée et poésie, règne une parenté profondément retirée, parce que toutes deux s'adonnent au service du langage et se prodiguent pour lui. Entre elles deux pourtant persiste en même temps un abîme profond, car elles "demeurent sur les monts les plus séparés" (ibid., 37).

Ainsi l'entretien "Qu'est-ce que la philosophie?" finit par ouvrir un autre grand thème, celui du rapport entre Pensée et Poésie, en le laissant bien ouvert, c'est-à-dire sans mettre au clair en quoi consiste l'abime entre les deux. Tout l'exposé de Heidegger semble se résumer dans l'idée que la philosophie est "une correspondance qui porte au langage l'appel de l'être de l'étant" (ibid., 37-38). Or, que veut dire cette correspondance? Il est bien évident que pour qu'il y ait une correspondance il faut deux choses et donc qu'il s'agit d'une différence, celle de l'Etre *et* de l'étant. Mais il s'agit d'une différence très particulière du fait qu'elle est en même temps une identité qui se rapporte à l'Etre *de* l'étant. Pour avancer sur cette question, qui occupera toute la philosophie contemporaine après Heidegger et surtout Laruelle, il faut se référer aux travaux ultérieurs de Heidegger autour du thème de l'identité et de la différence, réalisés entre 1956 et 1957.

Dans sa contribution sur "La constitution onto-théo-logique de la métaphysique" (1957) Heidegger souligne que "nous ne pensons l'être tel qu'il est que si nous le pensons dans la différence qui le distingue de l'étant et si nous pensons l'étant dans la différence qui le distingue de l'être. C'est ainsi que la différence nous devient proprement visible" (Heidegger 1968a, 296). Or, si nous essayons de nous représenter cette différence nous sommes aussitôt tentés de la concevoir comme une relation ajoutée par la pensée à l'être et à l'étant d'où la différence est rabaissée à n'être qu'une distinction de notre entendement. Pourtant si l'étant est ce qui *est* et l'Etre, ce que l'*étant* est, nous rencontrons l'étant et l'Etre déjà dans leur différence avant toute distinction ou adjonction de notre entendement. Pour concevoir la différence comme telle et l'Etre comme différence, souligne Heidegger, il nous faut reculer, faire un pas en arrière. Cela nous permettra de concevoir *le sens transitif* du mot "est" de "l'être *est*", c'est-à-dire l'être comme un passage vers l'étant. Or cette transition vers l'étant se passe sans que l'être quitte sa place, puisque l'étant n'existe pas auparavant pour recevoir l'être après et c'est pourquoi Heidegger parle de Survenue (*Überkommnis*):

> L'être passe sur et survient (de) ce que par cette Survenue arrive par soi en tant que non-voilé. Arrivée veut dire: s'abriter dans le non-voilement, durer dans l'abri, être étant. L'être se montre comme Survenue qui dévoile. L'étant comme tel apparaît dans le mode de l'Arrivée qui s'abrite dans le non-voilement. L'être, au sens de la Survenue qui dévoile, et l'étant comme tel, au sens de l'Arrivée qui s'abrite, se présentent ainsi différenciés du Même, résultant de la diá-krisis (Unter-schied). (ibid., 298-299)[7]

Cela mène Heidegger à décrire l'entre-deux (*das Zwischen*) comme un rapport, où la Survenue et l'Arrivée sont maintenues en rapport de réciprocité et d'écart. La différence de l'être et de l'étant, comprise comme diá-krisis (*Unter-schied*) de la Survenue et de l'Arrivée, est l'Accord (*Austrag*) dé-couvrant et abritant ou l'éclairement de ce qui se ferme et se voile. Plus encore, l'Accord révèle l'être comme un fond (λόγος, *Grund*) qui a lui-même besoin d'une fondation-en-raison appropriée, à partir de ce qu'il fonde lui-même en raison: c'est-à-dire qu'il a besoin d'une causation par la Chose la plus originelle et primordiale (*Ursache*) entendue comme *Causa sui*. C'est ainsi, souligne Heidegger, que Dieu comme *Causa sui* entre dans la philosophie et que la métaphysique, en vertu de l'unité unissante de l'Accord, devient à la fois ontologie et théologie. La constitution onto-théologique de la métaphysique procède de la puissance supérieure de la Différence, qui tient écartés et rapportés l'un à l'autre l'être comme fond et l'étant comme fondé et fondant-en-raison (ibid., 305). Bref, la Différence constitue le plan général (*Grundriß*) suivant lequel l'essence de la métaphysique s'est édifiée comme onto-théo-logie toutefois sans penser la Différence comme telle:

> Dans la mesure où la métaphysique pense l'étant comme tel dans sa Totalité, elle se représente l'étant dans la perspective de ce qu'il y a de différent dans la Différence, sans avoir égard à la Différence comme telle. (ibid., 305)

Il s'ensuit par-là que si l'on veut dépasser la métaphysique il faut aller au-delà de ce "plan général". Mais comment? Peut-être, comme le suggère Peter Trawny (Trawny 2003, 86), l'indice de ce dépassement est livré par le mot *Grundriß* qui signifie déchirure (*Riß*) du fond (*Grund*). Autrement dit, toute la philosophie comme métaphysique est une pensée de la différence qui représente une déchirure insurmontable dans le fond de l'être. Trawny a rai-

---

[7] Je propose ici une traduction plus différente de celle d'André Préau qui traduit p.ex. "Sein geht über (das) hin" avec "L'être passe au-delà et au-dessus". Mais Heidegger dit "geht über" et non pas "geht darüber hinaus". Ensuite Préau traduit "wesen als die so Unterschiedenen aus dem Selben, dem Unter-Schied" par "…s'accomplissent comme étant ainsi différents, ils le font par la vertu du Même, de la Dimension" (Heidegger 1968a, 299). Or, Heidegger emploie "wesen" dans le sens d'"être présent" et non comme "accomplissement". Ensuite il ne dit pas que l'être et l'étant soient "ainsi différents" mais qu'ils se présentent ainsi différenciés comme provenant du Même. Enfin, je me permets de traduire Unter-Schied par le grec diá-krisis (cf. Lindell, Scott, 1987, 847) pour souligner la distinction comme séparation (*Scheidung*) et en même temps pour indiquer la décision comme scission.

son quand il note que si l'on voudrait abolir cette déchirure du fond, il faudra abolir toute l'histoire de la philosophie (ibid.), mais il ne faut pas oublier que par la destruction de la métaphysique Heidegger ne vise pas à détruire la métaphysique ou la philosophie en tant que telle, mais d'éliminer les couches qui dissimulent le sens originaire (de la langue) de l'être. Rappelons dans ce contexte le mot de Heidegger au début d'*Identité et Différence* disant qu'il laisse au lecteur de trouver seul la réponse à la question "Comment la Différence procède-t-elle de l'essence de l'Identité?" (Heidegger 1968a, 256). Cette question inclue déjà une allégation fort importante, à savoir que la Différence ne peut pas être pensée *sans l'Identité de laquelle elle procède*. Et ce n'est pas un hasard que la *diá-krisis* comme acte de différenciation renvoie au Même en indiquant une Identité primaire. Cette question est discutée dans la première partie d'*Identité et différence* (cf. Heidegger 1968a, 257-276), où Heidegger montre que le principe d'identité, présenté souvent par la formule "A est A", révèle l'identité de l'être de l'étant comme "lui-même le même avec le même" (ibid., 260). Le point le plus important dans ce texte, sur lequel je voudrais spécialement attirer l'attention, consiste dans l'interprétation heideggérienne de Parménide. Heidegger s'adresse à Parménide parce que c'est chez lui que l'être de l'étant a trouvé le plus tôt un langage propre et ensuite parce que chez lui l'identique parle dans un sens qui presque extrême dans la sentence: "Le même, en effet, est percevoir (penser) aussi bien qu'être." Selon Heidegger cet énoncé veut dire que deux choses différentes, la pensée et l'être, sont appréhendées comme étant "le même", comme ayant place dans le même et se tiennent l'une l'autre *à partir de ce même*. Donc, à la différence de la métaphysique, pour laquelle l'identité fait partie de l'être, pour Parménide *l'être a sa place dans une identité*:

> L'être est défini [par Parménide] à partir d'une identité et comme un trait de cette identité – souligne Heidegger. – Plus tard, au contraire, la métaphysique a représenté l'identité comme un trait de l'être (...) L'identité de la pensée et de l'être, qui parle dans la sentence de Parménide, nous arrive de plus loin que l'identité définie par la métaphysique à partir de l'être et comme un trait de l'être. (ibid., 262)

Chez Parménide il ne s'agit donc pas d'une coappartenance comme identité (métaphysique), mais d'une identité qui vient "de plus loin" comme ce "à partir de quoi", comme l'*An-fang* (début capturant) de l'être et de la pensée. Or le terme directeur de la sentence de Parménide, τό αυτό, le même, demeure une énigme obscure, puisque Parménide ne le définit pas. Si Heidegger laisse cette énigme sans essayer à lever son voile, Laruelle ira bien plus loin, comme nous verrons.

Dans ce texte Heidegger présente donc deux conceptions très différentes de l'Identité. Avant de continuer, je voudrais signaler, qu'il y a une troisième conception, assez proche de celle de Parménide, que Heidegger découvre chez Schelling. Dans son cours sur Schelling (1936), Heidegger note:

> Dieu est toujours (...) avant tout fond et avant tout existant, et donc avant toute dualité (...) Schelling l'appelle 'fond primordial (*Urgrund*), ou plutôt sans-fond (*Ungrund*)' - "l'indifférence absolue", dont aucune différence, pas même l'ajoitement de l'Estre (*Seynsfuge*), ne peut être dit en prédicat. Le seul predicat de l'Absolu, c'est son 'sans-predicat', sans que par cela l'Absolu devient du neant. (GA 42, 213; trad. YR)[8]

Ces différents concepts d'identité, thématisés par Heidegger, montrent qu'il n'est pas simplement le penseur de la "différence comme différence", par opposition à Hegel, le penseur de l'identité, comme on a trop souvent affirmé (cf. Janicaud 1988, 150, 161; Gasché 1994, 75; Trawny 2003, 86ff), et encore moins celui qui a brouillé l'identité et la différence, comme prétendent certains critiques (cf. Ledic 2009, 526), mais aussi et surtout celui qui a ouvert une nouvelle perspective sur la question de l'identité et son rapport à la différence.

Si dans "Identité et différence" Heidegger conclue qu'il faut laisser à Parménide son obscurité en ce qui concerne le Même, c'est pour avancer en proposant sa propre interprétation de l'identité. Cette nouvelle interprétation est conçue comme contrepartie de l'accomplissement de la philosophie chez Hegel, qui identifie la chose de la philosophie avec l'être en tant que pensée, ce qui témoigne selon Heidegger de la *Seinsvergessenheit* (oubli de l'être)[9]. Par conséquent, Heidegger replace l'identification hégélienne de l'être et de la pensée par l'identité conçue comme co-appartenance de l'être et de l'homme. Dans l'époque du monde technique cette coappartenance apparait sous la forme de *Ge-stell*, d'Arraisonnement, qui est la mise en demeure qui place l'homme et l'être de façon qu'ils s'interpellent (Heidegger 1968a, 269).

> Dans l'Arraisonnement règne une étrange rencontre de dépendance, d'un côté, d'attention, de l'autre. Il s'agit pour nous de percevoir dans sa simplicité cette "propriation" (Eignen), par laquelle l'homme et l'être sont 'propriés' l'un à l'autre; c'est-à-dire qu'il s'agit d'accéder à ce que nous nommons das Ereignis, la Copropriation. (ibid., 270)

Pourquoi l'Arraisonnement (*Gestell*) n'est qu'un prélude à la Co-propriation (*Er-eignis*) est expliqué dans la conférence *Le tournant* (*Die Kehre*, 1949), où Heidegger déploie l'idée que

---

[8] "Gott ist immer ... vor allem Grund und vor allem Existierenden, also überhaupt vor aller Dualität ... Schelling nennt es den 'Urgrund oder vielmehr Ungrund' - die 'absolute Indifferenz', von dem keine Differenz, auch nicht die Seynsfuge eigentlich als treffendes Prädikat gesagt werden kann. Das einzige Prädikat des Absoluten ist die 'Prädikatlosigkeit', ohne daß damit das Absolute zum Nichts wird."

[9] Ceci est clairement énoncé dans les annexes "Beilagen zu: Die onto-theo-logische Verfassung der Metaphysik" (cf. GA 11, 107).

le *Gestell* se pose devant la chose et dissimule ainsi la proximité du monde. Pourtant même dans cette dissimulation, il y a un petit éclair, puisque le *Gestell* nous signale le péril de l'oubli de l'être et ne se donne pas comme un "destin aveugle", mais "comme ce qui sauve" (Heidegger 1990b, 318). Par cette mise en garde contre le péril, le *Gestell* nous renvoie à l'*Ereignis* comme un évènement plus initial et une relation plus authentique entre l'être et l'homme, une relation dans laquelle "le monde technique serait ramené de la condition de maître à celle de serviteur" (Heidegger 1968a, 271). Cette conception de l'*Ereignis* ouvre une nouvelle perspective sur l'identité: à la différence de la métaphysique où l'identité constitue un trait fondamental de l'être, Heidegger soutient que l'être autant que la pensée a sa place dans une identité dont l'essence procède de l'*Ereignis* comme 'laisser-coappartenir'. En ce sens, dit-il, "l'essence de l'identité appartient en propre à la Co-propriation" (ibid., 273), "Das Wesen der Identität ist ein Eigentum des Er-eignisses" (GA 11, 48). L'essence (*Wesen*) est ici entendue dans le sens de *Eigentümlichkeit*, de trait essentiellement propre à l'être qui renvoie à *Eigentum* (la propriété), non au sens de quelque chose qu'on possède, mais au sens de ce qui est *eigen* (propre) et par-là – à l'*Er-eignen* ou l'*Er-eignis* comme approprier (*eräugnen*, approprier par le regard) et Co-propriation.

Or, la question est: comment arriver à cette identité de coappartenance dans l'*Ereignis*? Heidegger utilise ici l'image d'un saut, qu'exige l'essence de l'identité même:

> [Il s'agit] d'un saut qui part de l'être comme fond (Grund) de l'étant pour sauter dans l'abîme, dans le sans-fond (Abgrund). Cet abîme, toutefois, n'est pas un néant vide et pas davantage une obscure confusion, mais bien la Co-propriation elle-même. En elle se fait sentir, dans sa pulsation, la propriété (Wesen)[10] de ce qui nous parle comme langage, comme ce langage que nous avons appelé un jour 'la demeure de l'être'. Les mots 'principe d'identité' désignent maintenant un saut qui est exigé l'essence de l'identité, parce qu'il lui est nécessaire, si la coappartenance de l'homme et de l'être doit parvenir jusqu'à la lumière essentielle de la Copropriation. (Heidegger 1968a, 273-274)

Penser l'*Ereignis* comme *Er-eignis* ou Co-propriation, c'est travailler, œuvrer à construire ce domaine pulsant et résonnant en soi. Ce travail se fait, selon Heidegger, au moyen du langage duquel la pensée reçoit les matériaux nécessaires, car le langage est la pulsation la plus sensible dans cette construction flottante et tout-comportante de l'*Ereignis*. Ou, autrement dit, c'est par le fait que notre propre être (*Wesen*) est approprié (*vereignet*) dans le langage, que nous habitons dans la Copropriation (GA 11, 46-47).

On voit donc que c'est par l'identité conçue comme *Er-eignis* que Heidegger boucle la boucle non seulement quant à la question de l'identité et de la différence, mais aussi

---

[10] J'ai changé ici la traduction "essence" par "propriété".

quant au sujet de la fin de la philosophie et la tâche de la pensée. Pour sortir hors de la philosophie comme métaphysique, il faut faire un pas en arrière afin de concevoir la différence comme différence, c'est-à-dire la décision métaphysique comme scission, et ensuite faire un saut dans *l'Ab-grund* de l'*Er-eignis*. C'est en cela que consiste la vraie tâche de la pensée. Or, ce saut n'est possible que si l'on renonce à chercher un fond/fondement (*Grund*) et une fondation (*Be-gründung*) de l'Etre. En ce sens on pourrait dire avec Gianni Vattimo que cet "affaiblissement" de l'être chez Heidegger ouvre le chemin vers la pensée faible (cf. Vattimo 1985; idem 1987, 125). Mais c'est plus que cela, car c'est aussi une rupture définitive avec l'onto-théologie comme un commencement par un fond suprême de l'Etre qui serait Dieu. Dieu, comme il montre dans son cours sur Schelling, ne pourrait pas être un fond (*Grund*). Le saut dans l'*Ab-grund*, c'est "la pensée sans-Dieu", la pensée qui abandonne le Dieu des philosophes, le *Causa sui*. Cette pensée plus ouverte et plus libre (*freier*) est, selon Heidegger "peut-être plus près du Dieu divin" (ibid., 306). Pourquoi? D'abord, parce qu'elle essaye de faire place à la *Lichtung*, c'est-à-dire au *lichten* qui – comme nous l'avons vu – rend ouvert et libre. Ensuite, parce qu'elle renonce à toutes prétentions d'un savoir sur Dieu. Notons ici, que déjà Kant avait démontré qu'il est impossible de donner de preuves ontologiques de Dieu (Kant 1905, 490ff) et par-là que Dieu constitue "le véritable abime de la raison humaine" (ibid., 503). Le "dernier Dieu", *der letzte Gott,* dont parle Heidegger dans les *Beiträge zur Philosophie: Vom Ereignis (1936-1938)* [GA 65, 403ff] ne doit pas être compris comme un être existant, car alors il serait objectivé en étant, ni comme l'Etre (GA 65, 437-439), mais conçu dans un sens négatif comme l'échec de la raison de penser un fond ultime, comme l'abime du sans-fond de l'Etre, du Tout, des Dieux (ibid., 472)[11]. Cette impossibilité réfère à l'attitude de silence de la *Sigetik* (ibid., 78-79), ainsi qu'à la retenue (*Verhaltenheit*) comme une tenue ou tonalité (*Grundstimmung*) qui seule peut nous situer "à proximité du dernier Dieu" et nous préparer à son passage silencieux:

> La retenue, le milieu concordant de l'effroi et de la crainte, le trait propre *traversant* la tonalité, c'est ce en quoi le Da-*sein* s'accorde sur le *silence* du passage du dernier Dieu. C'est en œuvrant à cette tonalité du Dasein que l'homme devient le gardien de ce silence. (ibid. 17; trad. YR)[12]

---

[11] Heidegger explique l'*Ereignis* comme l'aptitude du *Da-sein* de concevoir "le fond abyssal du sans-fondement des Dieux" (der abgründige Grund der Grund-losigkeit der Götter). Sur la question que veut dire le "dernier Dieu" chez Heidegger il n'y a pas un accord parmi les chercheurs mais plutôt un discours animé (cf. GA 65, 472).

[12] "Die Verhaltenheit, die stimmende Mitte des Erschreckens und der Scheu, der Grundzug der Grundstimmung, in ihr stimmt sich das Da-sein auf die Stille des Vorbeiganges des letzten Gottes. Schaffend in dieser Grundstimmung des Daseins wird der Mensch zum Wächter für diese Stille".

Ainsi, à l'obscurité de la pensée du Même chez Parménide et de l'identité entre Pensée et Etre chez Hegel, Heidegger propose l'alternative de l'abime de l'*Ereignis* et du dernier Dieu comme "l'autre commencement de la pensée" (*der andere Anfang des Denkens*). C'est cette pensée de l'être et de l'évènement comme "re-commencement" qui sera, en particulier, mise en question dans le "nouvel ordre démocratique de la pensée" de François Laruelle (cf. Laruelle 1996, 15).

2. La radicalité de la non-philosophie

Nous avons vu que selon Heidegger la philosophie est entrée dans son stade terminal et que par conséquent la question est de savoir quelle tâche est réservée à la pensée. Heidegger explique dans ce contexte qu'il ne s'agit pas d'une *Überwindung* (dépassement) de la métaphysique, puisque ce serait d'y tenir compte, mais de la "laisser à elle-même" et de s'impliquer dans l'*Ereignis* (GA 14, 29-30). C'est pourquoi il préfère de parler de *Verwindung* (cf. GA 9, 416), qui veut dire assomption ou recollection[13], pour souligner la nécessite d'une re-collection (*An-dacht*) de l'histoire de l'être (*Seinsgeschichte*) à travers la pensée gréco-occidentale et d'articuler l'essence de la métaphysique avec son oubli et son impensé. Cette démarche seule permettra, selon lui, un nouveau départ, non-philosophique puisque non-métaphysique.

Le projet de François Laruelle peut paraitre à première vue semblable du fait que lui aussi cherche à surmonter les défauts de la philosophie et de se placer hors d'elle. Mais son approche diffère radicalement de celle de Heidegger ainsi que de tous les autres philosophes qui ont tenté à élaborer une sorte de non-philosophie. Il souligne que la notion de non-philosophie n'est pas nouvelle, qu'elle émerge dans la philosophie allemande du 18ème siècle pour designer "l'état pré-spéculatif ou l'absence de philosophie, l'ignorance où se tient la conscience naturelle et populaire", qui est momentanée et destinée à être relevée ou relayée dans la philosophie (Laruelle 1996, 2). Chez Kant, Fichte, Hegel et Feuerbach elle émerge de la réflexion systématique sur la philosophie elle-même, sur ses limites et sa puissance. "Non- philosophie" désigne alors l'état pré-spéculatif ou l'absence de philosophie, l'ignorance où se tient la conscience naturelle et populaire, destinée à être dépassée dans la philosophie. Sous "non-philosophie" on désignera par conséquent une altérité, un résidu périphérique ou une condition externe-interne de l'activité philosophique.

---

[13] Françoise Dastur traduit *Verwindung* par "assomption" (Dastur 2006, 19-20), tandis que Gianni Vattimo interprète *Verwindung* comme recollection et distorsion (Vattimo, 1987, 13, 16).

> Chaque philosophie définit ainsi une marge de non-philosophique qu'elle tolère, circonscrit, se réapproprie, ou dont elle use pour s'ex-proprier: comme au-delà ou altérité à la maîtrise philosophique. Il s'agit alors d'un 'non-' dont le contenu et l'agent sont ontiques ou empiriques, ontologiques dans le meilleur des cas, mais dont la portée est limitée par cette maîtrise. (ibid.).

Selon Laruelle, Heidegger pousse cette autoréflexion de la philosophie sur elle-même plus loin jusqu'à l'idée de "la fin de la philosophie". Et c'est exactement en ce point que se dessine une des différences essentielles entre la critique heideggérienne et celle de Laruelle, qui rejette cette notion. Pour Laruelle "la fin de philosophie" est une expression philosophique non seulement en vertu de sa formulation mais aussi par sa signification et comme principe. Elle articule la philosophie dans son possibilité extrême, c'est-à-dire comme une rotation autour d'elle-même, comme un renfermement en soi et une technique qui se consomme en se retirant de la pensée laissant un espace vide. Heidegger et Derrida auraient ajouté certaines nuances importantes à ce schéma de l'essence de la philosophie comme autoposition et fermeture indéfinie, mais ils ne l'auraient pas dépassé. Or, ce schéma est voué à l'échec du fait qu'il est divisé par une différence ou une altérité qui reste subordonnée à son identité, l'ensemble formant une structure dyadique/triadique qui est simultanément ouverte et fermée (Laruelle 2013, 173). Selon Laruelle cette structure constitue l'invariable de la philosophie ou *la matrice de la décision philosophique* qui se traduit par une dyade, qui inclue et exclue simultanément son identité comme un troisième terme:

> Le trait invariant le plus universel de la philosophie est une matrice fractionnaire à 2/3 termes: elle se donne une intériorité et une extériorité, une immanence et une transcendance simultanément, dans une structure à synthèse ou hiérarchie, l'une l'emportant sur l'autre alternativement. Cette matrice dite de la 'Décision philosophique' peut se lire comme l'identité d'un double rapport de la philosophie à elle-même: identité du 2/3 (dans la mesure où le troisième terme, terme de synthèse, est immanent à la dyade, la philosophie étant en manque d'elle-même) et du 3/2 (dans la mesure où le terme de synthèse est transcendant à la dyade, la philosophie étant en excès d'elle-même). Par cette structure elle prétend se déterminer elle-même par-delà toutes ses déterminations empiriques dont elle ne fait le calcul que pour l'ordonner à une *autoposition* dont elle est titulaire, auto-compréhension ou auto-législation, auto-nomination, etc. Dans ce trait formel s'enracine la circularité de l'argumentation philosophique et de ses procédures d'auto-validation. (Laruelle 1996, 5)

On voit donc que si pour Heidegger la philosophie est métaphysique, pour Laruelle la philosophie est décision. Mais il faut souligner que la façon dont Laruelle conçoit la décision est tout à fait différente de la conception heideggérienne. Heidegger utilise le mot décision (*Entscheidung*) dans un double sens: dans le sens commun d'un acte humain libre et volontaire de choisir, de préférer une chose à une autre (Heidegger, GA 65, 87) et dans un sens spécifique de dé-cision, *Ent-scheidung,* désignant l'essence de l'Estre (*Seyn*) (ibid., 92). Dans ce dernier sens la dé-cision renvoie à l'Estre comme l'origine de toute scission, de toute séparation ou différence et de tout *Er-eignis*. C'est à partir de cette origine qu'il faut comprendre les décisions ultérieures des hommes comme "nécessités historiques" (*geschichtliche Notwendigkeiten*) qui appartiennent au devenir de l'Estre à travers l'histoire en décidant de son avenir. Ce qui se décide en fait à travers les différentes décisions humaines, tel que p.ex. si l'homme veut rester sujet ou établir le Da-sein, revient en fin de compte au même, à savoir si l'Estre se retirera définitivement ou si son retrait deviendra "le début autre de l'histoire" et de la pensée (ibid., 91; cf. 46). La décision résulte en ce sens de l'expérience de la détresse du délaissement de l'Estre avec une mission particulière qui est "l'abritement de la vérité de l'*Ereignis* de la retenue du *Dasein* dans le grand silence de l'Estre" (*die Bergung der Wahrheit des Ereignisses aus der Verhaltenheit des Daseins in die große Stille des Seyns*; ibid., 96) Il s'agit donc d'une décision fatale et c'est pourquoi Heidegger souligne que l'essence de la décision, c'est être ou non-être (ibid. 101).

Or, si pour Heidegger la décision est liée à la mission de l'abritement de la vérité et par-là à un "début autre" de l'histoire et de la philosophie (ibid., 173) qui sera à effectuer par le moyen de la non-philosophie au sens de non-métaphysique, pour Laruelle, au contraire, la décision est oubli et/ou occultation du Réel en tant qu'Un. Avant de poursuivre sa critique, il faut rappeler que Laruelle n'était pas le seul qui s'est aperçu de ce défaut, caractéristique autant pour l'herméneutique heideggérienne que pour toute la philosophie occidentale. Dans *L'écriture et la différence* (1967) Jacques Derrida avait déjà signalé ce problème en disant que la décision de la philosophie occidentale consiste, depuis Platon, dans son choix comme science, comme théorie (Derrida 1967, 65). Plus tard, dans *La Dissémination*, il poursuit:

> Or que décide et que maintient le 'platonisme', c'est-à-dire plus ou moins immédiatement, toute l'histoire de la philosophie occidentale, y compris les anti-platonismes qui s'y sont régulièrement enchaînés? Qu'est-ce qui se décide et se maintient dans l'ontologie ou dans la dialectique à travers toutes les mutations ou révolutions qui s'y sont entraînées? C'est justement l'ontologique: la possibilité présumée d'un discours sur ce qui est, d'un logos décidant et décidable de ou sur l'on (étant-présent). Ce qui est, l'étant-présent (forme matricielle de la substance, de la réalité, des oppositions de la forme et de la matière, de l'essence et de l'existence, de l'objectivité et de la subjectivité, etc.) se distingue de l'apparence, de l'image, du phénomène, etc., c'est-à-dire de ce qui, le présentant comme étant-présent, le redouble, le représente et dès lors le remplace et le dé-présente. (Derrida 1972, 220)

Cependant, même si Derrida se distancie de la décision 'platonicienne' ou métaphysique en suggérant la primauté de l'indécidabilité en tant que condition de possibilité de la décision (Derrida 1994, 94), ainsi que de la Différance comme ce qui précède toute différence (Derrida 1967a, 95; 1967b, 38), il ne quitte pas – selon Laruelle - le champ de la décision philosophique. Laruelle note que Derrida va plus loin que Heidegger en lui montrant ces propres omissions et inconséquences, mais il n'arrive pas à dépasser cette même manière de penser qui dénie l'Un (ibid. 24). Lui aussi, il reste dans la matrice philosophique: d'abord parce qu'il construit la Différance sur le modèle syntaxique général de la Différence, c'est-à-dire comme un "sous-système de la Différence" (Laruelle 2015, 12, 98), et ensuite parce qu'il refuse de dénouer la décision et la conserve comme aporie:

> Derrida est le penseur qui porte la décision philosophique au bord de la dislocation aporétique pure et simple mais qui, par une virtuosité d'équilibriste menacé, entend la ressaisir une dernière fois et maintenir la possibilité et la vérité d'une telle décision et se refuse à franchir le pas ultime. La décision philosophique non seulement s'accommode de ce risque et de ce côtoiement d'abîme, où elle oublie de plus en plus le problème de l'essence de son unité interne, mais elle confirme son essence unitaire, elle trouve de nouvelles forces dans cette épreuve (...) La déconstruction de la métaphysique est la 'vérité' de celle-ci, le grossissement et la radicalisation de ce qu'il y a de définitivement inconsistant, d'unité non-réelle, purement fictionnelle voire hallucinatoire, dans la philosophie en général. (Laruelle 2015, 98)

Si j'ai fait ici un détour en passant par Derrida, c'est pour pointer la prétention de radicalité de la non-philosophie laruellienne mû par l'ambition de dépasser autant la radicalité de la destruction heideggérienne que celle de la déconstruction derridienne. Dans une interview récente Laruelle explique qu'il avait dressé sa théorie de l'Un contre les philosophies de la différence, en particulier ceux de Deleuze et Derrida, puisque la différence allait devenir un nouvel absolu philosophique se substituant à l'Être. Il se rappelle: "Comme j'avais cherché à montrer ce qu'il restait à mon goût de trop philosophique dans la déconstruction, Derrida m'a dit: 'on se croirait à Chicago, vous vous emparez de mon arme et vous la retournez contre moi'" (Laruelle/Forestier 2015). Et en effet, Laruelle a tourné toute la critique de la décision gréco-occidentale de Derrida contre lui, en avançant que la philosophie en tant que telle repose sur cette matrice décisionnelle par laquelle elle prétend se déterminer elle-même pour l'ordonner à une auto-position dont elle est titulaire et de devenir ainsi même législatrice par rapport au Réel (Laruelle 1996, 5). Or, "l'arme" que Laruelle tourne contre Derrida et contre tous les philosophes, c'est le Réel lui-même en tant qu'indifférent à la différence et à la décision.

> Critique radicale: on entend ainsi la recherche d'une instance à la fois plus réelle et plus immanente que la Différence ou que l'Autre, et que nous avons trouvée dans l''Un' ou la 'vision-en-Un' entendus en un sens et avec des moyens précisément 'non philosophiques'. C'est à un changement global de terrain que nous avons dû procéder, abandonnant celui de l'Être puis celui de l'Autre pour celui de l'Un ou de l'immanence radicale qui nous a paru le Réel même. (Laruelle 1996, 4)

Comme je l'ai souligné ailleurs (Raynova 2017a, 7), le principe clé de la non-philosophie, c'est l'impératif de l'immanence radicale de l'Un par lequel Laruelle a suspendu et remplacé *la* question fondamentale (*die* Fundamentalfrage) de la philosophie (cf. Heidegger GA2, 6). Alors que les philosophies de l'immanence (Spinoza, Deleuze) ont posé l'immanence de façon transcendante, c'est-à-dire comme pensée *de* l'immanence qui pose celle-ci thétiquement, la radicalité de la non-philosophie exige de "traiter l'immanence de manière immanente" sans en faire un objet. Cette immanence (à) soi, c'est ce que Laruelle appelle "l'Un-en-Un" (Laruelle 1996, 169), à savoir ce qui n'est trouvable précisément que dans l'Un et non à partir de l'Etre ou de l'Autre, et qui possède une *autonomie radicale* par rapport à toute transcendance. Ce concept se dirige contre celui de la Différence qui, selon Laruelle, est l'essence ou le moteur de la philosophie alors que l'l'identité est son apparence objective. Si la philosophie réunit, c'est-à-dire si elle réunification, c'est parce qu'elle est et reste un partage transcendantal: "elle est de manière dominante une activité de décision et de division déterminante dont la pensée ne sort jamais" (Laruelle 1992, 19). Laruelle souligne, que même lorsque la philosophie vise l'identité, c'est sur le mode de sa division qu'elle la pense et quand elle pose le principe d'identité, ce n'est jamais A, mais A = A (ibid.). Cette critique de Laruelle est très importante, puisqu'elle nous renvoie à l'approche heideggérien. Comme nous l'avons vu, dans *Identité et différence* Heidegger part de ce principe d'identité, présenté par la formule "A = A" et qu'il traduit par l'identité de l'être de l'étant comme étant "lui-même le même avec le même" (Heidegger 1968a, 260)[14]. Contre cette approche – et plus en général contre la philosophie qui tient sur l'identité un discours double ou même multiple, celui d'une unité numérique ou celui de l'Unité transcendantale comme ingrédient de l'Etre et convertible avec lui ou avec l'Autre – Laruelle pose l'axiome fondateur de la non-philosophie selon lequel "l'Un ou le Réel est forclos à la pensée" (Laruelle 1996, VI). Il explique:

> C'est renoncer enfin au dernier mirage métaphysique, celui d'une 'science de l'Un' opposée à la métaphysique comme 'science de l'Etre'. La non-philosophie est bien une 'science première', mais parce qu'elle est selon-l'Un plutôt que de-l'Un. Une 'science de l'Un', comme celle de l'Etre, quoique plus subtilement qu'elle, reste prise dans l'ap-

---

[14] N'oublions pas que Heidegger réfute ce concept d'identité A=A en tant que métaphysique.

parence transcendantale qui nourrit la suffisance philosophique et n'est qu'une abstraction du complexe qu'elle forme naturellement avec celle de l'Etre. Y renoncer et surmonter cette frustration, c'est la condition pour instaurer une véritable pensée selon-l'Un qui puisse se rapporter, comme à son objet, à la philosophie qui est pensée selon l'Etre, c'est-à-dire par et pour lui. (ibid.)

Cette suspension de la *Fundamentalfrage* par la pensée selon-l'Un, compris comme Un-en-Un, entraine plusieurs conséquences qui nous permettent d'articuler les différences essentielles entre la pensée de Heidegger et la non-philosophie de Laruelle. Tout d'abord, le Un-en-Un est donné radicalement étant ainsi radicalement distinct du "es gibt" heideggérien et post-heideggérien:

> Phénoménalement, c'est un 'Donné-sans-donation' et de ce point de vue la non-philosophie formule les axiomes suivants, plutôt que les principes: a) Il y a du donné radical, il exclut de son essence la donation elle-même, c'est-à-dire le pli du donné et de la donation; b) Parce qu'il est en-Un, l'Un n'unifie pas, en lui ou hors de lui. (1996, 20)

C'est cette l'autonomie radicale de l'Un, son indifférence réelle à l'égard de l'Être et de la pensée, ainsi que de leur mélange, à savoir le "Même" comme objet ultime de la philosophie, qui "invalide une thèse ontologique majeure, celle de sa convertibilité avec l'Être, convertibilité à leur logos près; et limite la pertinence supposée première de la thèse de cette autre convertibilité, la Différence ontologique de l'Être et de l'étant" (ibid., 24). La non-philosophie effectue par-là une réorganisation de l'économie des grandes instances – Un, Être, Autre, Étant – à partir de la découverte première de la non-convertibilité de l'Un avec l'Être (l'ontologie des Anciens), ou avec l'Autre (les déconstructions contemporaines de l'ontologie) ou encore de son incommensurabilité avec l'Être-sans-Un (ontologie de l'Être-comme-Multiple). "Toutes ces formes positives ou négatives de convertibilité" – souligne Laruelle – "sont désormais éliminées par l'Un qui implique sinon la dissolution pure et simple de ces amphibologies (Un-Étant, Un-Être, Un-Autre) du moins leur non-pertinence quant au Réel" (ibid.). Dans ce contexte, ce qu'il reproche à Heidegger, qui attribuait à la métaphysique la confusion de l'Être-présence et de l'étant, c'est de confondre lui-même l'Un avec l'Être. Si l'Un est absolument indifférent à l'Être, c'est qu'il est non seulement d'essence absolument distincte (l'immanence radicale, le donné-sans-donation), mais de causalité originale précisément sur l'Être, c'est-à-dire Un-en-dernière-instance (ibid., 25).

De ce fait-là, l'identité n'est plus événementielle au sens de l'*Ereignis*, elle ne procède pas de lui. L'identité de l'Un-en-Un ne renferme plus aucune dualité ou différence comme celle de la différence ontico-ontologique ou celle de la Co-propriation. Dans une conférence intitulée "Identity and event" (1999), Laruelle note qu'il semble à premier abord que l'identité et l'évènement ne représentent que deux entités métaphysiques. Pourtant, dit-il, l'identité est impliquée dans l'évènement de façons hétérogènes (Laruelle 2000, 179)[15]. La grande différence entre philosophie et non-philosophie est que pour la première l'identité et l'évènement sont convertibles tandis que pour la seconde elles sont inconvertibles et forment une dualité unilatérale:

> If philosophy, regardless of its stance, defines the event in terms of identity plus a few other determinations, then it reciprocally makes of identity, as such, an event, albeit one that is doubtlessly special or extreme. Non-philosophy, on the other hand, refuses this convertibility, it does not turn identity into an event but determines the event unilaterally through identity as real presupposition of thought (...) as a Real that we shall characterize as being without essence, without donation, without consistency or form – for Identity 'in the flesh' [*l'Identité en chair et en os*] is in fact none of these things (Laruelle 2000, 179-180)

> The Real is initially in itself a condition sine qua non, one which is negative and necessary but not sufficient. But when the variable, as we shall say, 'effectuates' the Real or One, then the latter enters, without alienating itself, without losing its character as Real, into a transcendental function through which it relates to philosophy, or, more precisely, through which it brings forth philosophy as given-in-One. (ibid., 186)

Dans les écrits de l'époque du tournant de Heidegger, que nous avons examiné plus haut, cette convertibilité est présente de manière exemplaire dans les concepts de l'entre-deux (*das Zwischen*), de la Survenue de l'Etre, au sens de passage vers l'étant qui le dévoile, et de l'étant comme l'Arrivée qui s'abrite par ce dévoilement dans l'Etre d'où la diá-krisis (*Unter-schied*), ainsi que dans le caractère événementiel de l'*Ereignis*. Répétons qu'à la différence de la métaphysique, où l'identité constitue un trait fondamental de l'être, Heidegger soutient que l'être autant que la pensée a sa place dans une identité dont l'essence procède de l'*Ereignis* comme 'laisser-coappartenir' – "l'essence de l'identité appartient en propre à la Co-propriation" (ibid., 273), "Das Wesen der Identität ist ein Eigentum des Ereignisses" (GA 11, 48) Or, pour Laruelle le vice de la convertibilité réside dans le fait qu'elle implique une co-relation ou une corrélation qui suppose le Réel connaissable ou pensable. Par contre, la non-philosophie conçoit le Réel comme déterminant sans réciprocité la connaissance en articulant la véritable asymétrie destructrice de la corrélation, à savoir l'unilatéralisation la plus radicale de l'identité de l'Un-en-Un. Laruelle souligne dans ce contexte:

> Sur ce point le conflit gréco-moderne par exemple entre Aristote et Descartes, et que Heidegger a cru pouvoir relancer par l'accentuation de l'asymétrie de l'être et de la

---

[15] Etant donné que je n'ai pas trouvée la version française – je ne sais même pas si la conférence a été publiée en français – j'utilise ici la publication en langue anglaise.

pensée, par la (co)respondance de celle-ci à celui-là, puis la Déconstruction par l'asymétrie radicalisée de l'Autre au Logos, est sans pertinence et laisse à la position philosophique du problème son autorité. Le problème est plutôt de soustraire la relation... à la corrélation, à la relation d'inclusion disjonctive de réciprocité, de "communauté" ou de "système" qui est son élément nourricier et son essence, et de déterminer celle-ci par l'Ego dans la dépendance duquel elle se tient désormais. (Laruelle 1996, 130)

La question comment penser le Donné-sans-donation en tant que forclos à la pensée mène Laruelle à la question plus fondamentale: existe-t-il un Ego purement immanent? Il reprend ici les différentes critiques de l'Ego cartésien, notamment celle de Heidegger, afin de présenter une nouvelle théorie unifiée (non-cartésienne) de l'Ego. Heidegger – dit-il – a interrogé la réalité de l'Ego à partir du *sum* et non plus de la *cogitatio* en fonction du sens d'être de l'Etre et non plus de la pensée. Ce type de "déconstruction" porte certes la métaphysique à sa limite, mais il achève d'occulter la possibilité d'une autre "essence de la manifestation", plus immanente qu'est le Réel lui-même qui ne peut pas être objet d'une question et d'une déconstruction (ibid., 111). C'est pourquoi la question de type heideggérien: d'où tenons-nous le *sum*, quel est son sens d'être? devrait être remplacée par une question plus précise: d'où tenons-nous l'Ego?

> La philosophie – souligne Laruelle – ne se donne l'Ego qu'à travers un filtre qui, dès Descartes, annule la radicalité de son être donné, le diffère, le déplace, le soumet à une donation et en général à une opération extérieure (…) Chez Descartes lui-même et pas seulement chez Nietzsche, Heidegger, Lacan ou Derrida, l'Ego est d'emblée divisé, différé de lui-même et, c'est la même chose, son être-donné (l'Ego-en-Ego) est confondu avec celui d'un étant ou avec l'être en général (…) La non-philosophie postule au contraire que l'Ego est déjà manifesté avant la manifestation de l'être et de la pensée, et ceci sur son mode propre. Quant à l'identité de l'être et de la pensée (identité réelle-en-dernière-instance ou transcendantale en tant qu'elle se dit de l'être et de la pensée), elle formera un ordre premier mais dérivé de l'Ego – celui du sujet. Elle aura bien lieu par l'Ego, mais hors de l'Ego. (...) La non-philosophie, se donnant l'Ego comme déjà manifesté ou comme le Réel, ne le cherche pas, ne cherche pas une synthèse du sujet/objet comme sujet; elle procède en clonant l'identité transcendantale qu'est le sujet de l'identité réelle de l'Ego d'une part et d'autre part du matériau philosophique. (ibid., 115-116)

Afin de dissoudre l'amphibologie de l'Ego et de la philosophie et de produire une théorie non-cartésienne de l'Ego puis du sujet, Laruelle propose d'abandonner le concept philosophique de l'Ego et l'usage philosophique de la pensée, et de traiter l'"Ego" comme un nom premier dans une axiomatique transcendantale déterminée par lui en-dernière-instance. Si dans la philosophie les deux usages de l'Un comme être et comme pensée (Ego) relevaient du même Un, dans la non-philosophie les deux états de l'Un ne sont plus "le même" et ne sont identiques que par ce que Laruelle appelle le "clonage" transcendantal. Ce clonage ou fonction transcendantale ne modifie pas l'Un/le Réel tout en étant inconcevable sans lui: le Un transcendantal ou clone et le réel Un sont identiques en vision-en-Un ou, autrement dit, le clone transcendantal de l'Ego est identité en-Ego. "L'Un transcendantal est donc situé 'entre' le Réel même et un donné 'empirique', ici la différence abstraite et simple de la pensée et de l'être, la Distance non-phénoménologique" (ibid., 127).

De cette façon Laruelle élimine le sujet de la philosophie, ou le *Da-sein*, en le remplaçant par la force (de) pensée conçue comme la structure constituée de cette identité transcendantale, et propose le théorème suivant: "*l'Ego détermine-en-dernière-instance, c'est-à-dire par clonage transcendantal, le sujet comme force (de) pensée*" (ibid., 128). Or que veut dire ce théorème? Il dit d'abord que l'Ego comme immanence absolue ne pense pas et n'est pas une substance. Il est la "cause" non pas de la pensée et de l'être mais de l'essence de leur différence, c'est-à-dire cause "en-dernière-instance". Ensuite, la pensée n'est plus une substance et encore moins un objet, une essence, un but que l'Ego s'efforcerait d'atteindre, mais une "force" ou dualité unilatérale qui effectue pour la première fois la détermination en-dernière-instance et le clonage transcendantal. Enfin, "la force (de) pensée est le contenu phénoménal du 'sujet'. Si bien que l'Ego, purement immanent, ni objectif ni subjectif, peut être accompagné mais non nécessairement du sujet ou de la force (de) pensée. *L'Ego et le sujet cessent d'être confondus et distincts au sein de leur 'mêmeté': l'Ego jouit d'une autonomie radicale, le sujet d'une autonomie relative*" (ibid., 129). Du fait que l'Un/le Réel est radicalement autonome, il ne s'aliène pas dans son effet ou dans son objet qui ne possède qu'une autonomie relative. L'Un n'agit pas par lui-même sur cet objet qui lui est absolument indifférent mais c'est encore lui "en-dernière-instance" qui agit dans la "force (de) pensée", titulaire concrète de cette causalité. "Détermination-en-dernière-instance et force (de) pensée apparaissent à la suite de l'Un mais celle-là est l'essence transcendantale de celle-ci" (ibid., 146).

La science de l'Un réel comme radicalement autonome, non-convertible, indifférent et identique, comme un Donné-sans-donation qui ne diffère et qui n'agit pas, permet l'élaboration d'une conception tout à fait nouvelle, non-herméneutique de la vérité et qui s'oppose directement à celle de Heidegger. "Le conflit de l'Etre et du Dasein, de la vérité et du sens de l'Etre" – souligne Laruelle dans son article paradigmatique "La vérité selon Hermès" (1987) – "est lui aussi l'un des modes de ce conflit plus général, celui du secret – du supposé-secret – et du logos" (1987, 397). Alors que chez Heidegger la vérité est conçue come A-λήθεια, comme le non-voilé ou le non-caché (*Unverborgenheit*), qui inclue aussi bien la monstration que le retrait de l'Etre en renvoyant à l'ouverture de la clairière, pour Laruelle l'essence de la vérité reste un secret non-connaissable et non-interprétable.

> Il y a un autre Hermès à côté de l'Hermès unitaire ou autoritaire. Il détermine l'essence de la vérité comme secret, mais comme secret qui n'a pas besoin, pour exister et se faire connaître, de la lumière du logos, des ruses du sens, des stratégies de l'interprétation, des horizons du Monde, des formes transcendantes de la manifestation. La vérité comme secret existe de manière autonome *avant* l'horizontalité de la manifestation. Le secret jouit d'une précession absolue sur l'interprétation, il est lui-même l'Ininterprétable à partir duquel s'annonce une interprétation. (ibid., 398)
>
> Rien ne sert de remonter de l'herméneutique ou de la phénoménologie à leur condition possibilisante, dans *aletheia* par exemple. Ce sont là des effets à la surface du système de la Différence herméto-logique. L'essence du secret ne connaît pas les jeux du voilement et du dévoilement, la structure de la différence en général. C'est l'Un compris de manière absolument immanente et finie; il exclut le jeu de l'Etre et le jeu en général. (ibid., 399)

Le secret est en ce sens inaliénable dans une présence ou une transcendance. Pourtant, s'il faut lui donner une définition transcendantale, on pourrait dire que le secret est la forme strictement irréfléchie de la vérité qui se donne à elle-même sur le mode indivisible. Il est curieux que Laruelle semble à un certain moment rejoindre Heidegger quand il note que le secret "est plutôt ce silence ou cette ténèbre lorsqu'ils sont absolument dépourvus de transcendance, mais non de positivité" (ibid., 398). Or, ce n'est qu'une ressemblance apparente, car le silence du secret laruellien n'est pas une attitude – l'attitude de silence de la *Sigetik* provenant de l'échec de la raison de penser un fond ultime, le sans-fond de l'Etre. C'est le silence d'un secret dont la vérité "n'a plus besoin de sortir de soi et d'être pour soi, lorsqu'elle est soi en restant en soi" (ibid.).

Pour finir, je voudrais signaler une autre différence cruciale entre la pensée de Heidegger et celle de Laruelle qui concerne leur approche à la science. Nous avons abordé plus haut l'anti-scientisme de Heidegger, pour qui la ramification de la philosophie en sciences, leur émancipation de la philosophie et leur autosuffisance constitue un des traits essentiels de la "fin de la philosophie". Par contre, la non-philosophie laruellienne se pose la tâche ambitieuse de réévaluer le rapport entre philosophie et science et de proposer une "science de la philosophie" et, plus largement, une "théorie unifiée de la pensée" qui vaut autant pour la philosophie que pour la science. Annoncée déjà dans "La vérité selon Hermès" (1987) sous le nom "science rigoureuse de la vérité", elle est élaborée d'abord dans *Théorie des identités* (1992). La proposition de départ de Laruelle est que la science est une expérience de pensée autonome par rapport à celle de la philosophie, qu'elle peut déterminer par elle-même son rapport au réel et mettre ainsi en cause l'autorité de la philosophie. Cela dit, le projet d'une science unifiée de la pensée est conçu comme critique radicale du principe de philosophie suffisante (Laruelle 1992, 238). De ce fait, la science rigoureuse de la pensée suppose d'abord une nouvelle description, non-épistémologique du pouvoir de vérité propre à la science qui est à la fois *science transcendantale* par son objet réel et par son rapport aux autres sciences et *science empirique* par la nécessité où elle est de trouver son objet-phénomène hors d'elle-même (ibid., 247). Cette idée est précisée dans *Principes de la non-philosophie* (1996), où la théorie unifie de la pensée est conçue comme science première:

> Tenant de l'Un son être-déterminé-en-dernière-instance, elle [la science première] se présente sous la forme d'une discipline *théorique* qui doit autant à la science qu'à la philosophie sans être ni l'une ni l'autre, ni leurs divers mélanges (philosophie-comme-science, philosophie-de-la-science, philosophie-à-science, science-de-la-philosophie); et d'une *pragmatique* qui ne les considère que par le côté où elles sont transcendantalement déterminables par l'Un. De là son objet, une identité que l'on appellera 'essence (de) science' et qui est à la fois l'objet et l'essence de la science première. (Laruelle 1996, 45-46)

Laruelle note que la science première abolit sans reste l'autorité de l'ontologie philosophique supposée première – on pense ici évidemment à Heidegger –, mais nullement toute ontologie: cette identité-sans-synthèse de la science et de la philosophie équivaudra à une nouvelle ontologie mais seconde, ordonnée absolument au réel-Un. Il explique de même qu'il s'agit d'une primauté mais pas de priorité:

> 'Premier' désigne ici en réalité la primauté-sans-priorité de l'Un sur l'Etre ou la pensée, le fait que l'Un soit radicalement autonome et l'Etre relativement autonome. 'L'Un détermine-en-dernière-instance l'Être ou la pensée en général' signifie 1) qu'étant absolument immanent à lui-même ou en-Un, 2) il précède, non pas dans le Réel mais comme le Réel même, l'Être irréel ou la pensée, la transcendance en général, qui est elle aussi en-Un mais qui ne l'est plus qu'en-dernière-instance (c'est l'organon de la force (de) pensée), 3) sans du tout s'aliéner en elle ou s'identifier à elle, 4) mais en étant donné encore tel qu'il est (en-Un) jusque dans l'expérience la plus lointaine de l'Être. (ibid., 49)

Ainsi l'Être et ses modes – Sujet, Dasein, Donation, etc. – sont unilatéralisés par l'Un et forcés d'abandonner leur prétention à être premiers, dominants dans une hiérarchie circulaire. En rejetant l'autorité de la philosophie, la science première n'établit pas un nouveau rapport de domination par rapport à la philosophie ou aux autres sciences mais cherche, au contraire, d'établir la démocratie dans les rapports entre elles. C'est pour quoi Laruelle a révisé certaines positions développées dans sa "Philosophie II", p.ex. dans sa *Théorie des identités* (1992)[16], reposant sur l'affinité privilégiée de l'immanence radicale et de la science

---

[16] Rappelons que le programme de la *Théorie des identités* consistait dans la "réforme scientifique de l'entendement philosophique" (Laruelle 1992, 9).

d'où la philosophie se trouvait en quelque sorte "sous la science". Dès la *Théorie des étrangers* (1995), avec laquelle commence "Philosophie III", il s'agit de faire rentrer la philosophie, avec la science et à part égale, dans l'ordre transcendantal qui ne connaît plus de hiérarchie et donc d'établir une égalité démocratique de la pensée.

> La non-philosophie comme science première est la manifestation de l'essence (de) philosophie de la philosophie et identiquement de l'essence (de) science de la science, c'est-à-dire de l'identité apriorico-transcendantale de chacun des opposés, par quoi ils sont véritablement égaux et se libèrent de l'antinomie ou de la guerre à laquelle ils étaient en commun asservis. (…) Du point de vue terminologique, 'théorie unifiée' désigne donc le régime nouveau de la philosophie arrachée à sa domination 'fondamentale' sur le régional; sa 'régionalisation' ou sa 'localisation' par son identification (aux) régions de l'étant, sa spécification, pour ainsi dire sa matérialisation quasi intuitive. (Laruelle 1996, 60).

Le projet laruellien d'une théorie unifiée de la pensée va donc à l'opposé de la "tâche de la pensée" de Heidegger, qui se plaint:

> Ce que la philosophie, au cours de son histoire, avait tenté ça et là (…), à savoir d'exposer les ontologies des diverses régions de l'étant (nature, histoire, droit, art), ce sont maintenant les sciences qui le prennent en charge comme la tâche qui leur incombe en propre (…) Le caractère opérationnel et la référence au modèle de la pensée représentative et calculante en sont venu à régner en maitres (Heidegger 1990a, 285-286)

Laruelle se rend bien compte que la diagnose de Heidegger est correcte, mais il va prendre un autre chemin pour s'opposer autant au scientisme qu'à l'anti-scientisme de type heideggérien.

Dans la *Théorie des identités* il note que notre époque se définit par l'émergence irrécusable et l'extension d'une expérience techno-calculante de la pensée sous la forme des usages extra-gestionnaires et "intelligents" de l'informatique (Laruelle 1992, 235). Cela pose la question: dans quelle mesure la montée en puissance des technologies informatiques de l'intelligence et de la raison est-elle encore interprétable par la philosophie, qui avait toujours réduit l'autonomie des mathématiques et du calcul en les rejetant dans une phénoménalité inessentielle? Aussi problématique, selon Laruelle, est la réduction inverse – celle de la pensée au raisonnement et du raisonnement au calcul, lui-même recevant des moyens technologiques inouïs. D'où son hypothèse que "la pulsion techno-calculante a peut-être une origine que n'épuise pas son sens 'métaphysique'" (ibid.), c'est-à-dire que la cause de cette pulsion et "le triomphe de l'équipement d'un monde en tant que soumis aux commandes d'une science technicisée" (Heidegger 1990a, 286) n'indiquent pas simplement l'oubli de l'Etre ou du sens de l'Etre. L'émergence de la raison techno-calculante est pour

Laruelle plutôt une indication que la science, plutôt que la technologie, cherche à faire reconnaître sa spécificité contre l'ordre philosophique qui lui est régulièrement imposé et qu'il faut la laisser se manifester et faire conjoncture (Laruelle 1992, 236). C'est pourquoi la première tâche de la théorie unifiée de la pense est de partir des sciences elles-mêmes.

> La 'non-philosophie' est la tentative d'élaborer une *pensée* répondant aux critères scientifiques les plus généraux (détermination interne ou 'transcendantale', cohérence rigoureuse, exclusion de la circularité pour la déductibilité et l'expérimentation, etc.) adéquate par conséquent à la théorie et à la pratique immanente des sciences. (ibid., 31)

Mais "cohérence rigoureuse" ne veut pas dire logique ou système. Si la philosophie est un système linéaire (ibid., 303), la non-philosophie est, au contraire, une science de la philosophie procédant par synthèse 'fractale', non philosophique, d'énoncés (ibid., 43).

> La non-philosophie ne consiste plus à tirer des lignes, mais à fractaliser les lignes, même lorsqu'elles sont déjà affectées de plis ou de points de rebroussement, de dispersion, points critiques ou ruptures catastrophiques. La philosophie n'est pas elle-même (de son propre point de vue) fractale, mais il s'agit de la voir ainsi dans l'élément d'un autre discours qui use d'elle sans plus lui obéir. Car la théorie est 'vision-en-science' et ne se remplit du matériau philosophique qu'à lui imposer une nouvelle distribution, de type 'chaotique, qui n'est pas sans règles (...), mais qui est la fractalisation des règles philosophiques par des règles d'un type tout autre. Il y a une intuition a priori (de) la fractalité qui dépasse l'"imagination transcendantale' – le fonds de la philosophie – qui ne la dépasse pas métaphysiquement mais 'chaotiquement'. (ibid., 302)

Le chaos généralisé de Laruelle représente une statique et une dynamique linéarisées, absolument fractales de part en part, la fractalité n'étant plus soutenue par le support ou l'objet mais par l'identité-en-dernière-instance. Le but qu'il vise est de libérer d'une part la science et la pensée des contraintes de la Transcendance supposée première et du "désordre ontico-ontologique" (ibid., 310), et d'effectuer d'autre part une modélisation fractale de la philosophie par sa mise-en-chaos.

Ces idées sont partiellement révisées et redéveloppées plus loin dans *Philosophie non-standard* (2010), l'*opus magnum* de la "Philosophie V" qui offre la conception la plus élaborée d'une "science de la philosophie" conçue comme générique et quantique. Il est impossible de reconstruire ici cette conception même partiellement, c'est pourquoi je ne vais indiquer qu'un moment qui a de rapport direct à la question heideggérienne sur la "chose" ou l'affaire de la pensée.

Si Heidegger suggérait qu'il y a quelque chose d'*impensé* que la philosophie a omis et qui constitue la véritable tâche de la pensée non-métaphysique, Laruelle voit le problème de la philosophie ailleurs: "*Le problème de la philosophie est celui de sa gravitation conceptuelle encore inexpliquée, de sa force de gravitation qui assemble les astres des Idées dans un monde ou un logos. Ce n'est plus un problème d'autocritique ou de déconstruction mais de gravitation universelle dans la pensée*" (Laruelle 2010, 12). Il indique que la philosophie transcendantale est un pas vers le principe de cette gravitation qui peut aider à comprendre l'interaction entre concepts séparés de cet univers en expansion et en rétraction. Le champ transcendantal peut servir d'invention continue d'une nouvelle ontologie ondulatoire qui aide à ne plus déplacer selon une trajectoire de points conceptuels isolés. Mais selon Laruelle on ne sortira pas de la représentation standard avec une "micro-philosophie" des petites forces, pas plus qu'en mélangeant le devenir à l'être ou la différence à l'identité. C'est pourquoi il entreprend la constitution d'une matrice générique "qui fait travailler ensemble à titre de variables conjugables une structure philosophique traditionnelle comme la structure transcendantale et un noyau rationnel de pensée tiré de la physique quantique" (Mullarkey/Schmid 2014). Cela permettrait de faire travailler ensemble la philosophie et la science au lieu de les opposer ou d'en faire un mélange où l'une domine sur l'autre.

> Comprise à partir de la Matrice générique, comme collisionneur de pensées, la philosophie est la fusion du corpuscule et de l'onde sous le corpuscule, pas encore leur fusion 'sous l'onde'. C'est la corporalité et la granularité de la pensée qu'il faut remettre en cause, cesser de considérer qu'elle est laite exclusivement de corps conceptuels dotés de qualités à la fois globales et singulières, qu'elle relève de généralités catégorielles ou transcendantales et en même temps d'un événement toujours singulier. De ce point de vue la dualité champ transcendantal/événement singulier représente un achèvement possible de la pensée standard. Mais il est nécessaire de passer à une quantification de la pensée qui soit de style ondulatoire et générique plutôt que corpusculaire si l'on veut comprendre la gravitation philosophique. Et l'on sait combien la gravitation, sans doute physique, est une force difficile à expliquer. Nous cherchons le collisionneur des concepts. (Laruelle 2010, 23)

La matrice générique est ce collisionneur, producteur et détecteur de particules élémentaires de savoir, une technologie qui est l'équivalent d'un ordinateur mais non pas son double puisqu'elle n'est pas vouée à un calcul formel. Comme l'ordinateur elle a deux côtés, hard et soft:

> La matrice générique a des aspects d'ordinateur, un côté hard, matériel ou visible par ses matériaux de construction (les trois apports) et son câblage, tandis que son côté soft est fait de logiciels de deux types, les algébriques, soit comme nombre imaginaire soit comme idempotence et linéarité, les philosophiques, soit comme transcendantaux

(transcendantal kantien généralisé ou formalisé), soit comme métaphysiques (Un, Etre, Autre, Multiple). (ibid.)

Ainsi, le collisionneur asservit la réciprocité de la reproduction à l'unilatéralité de la production et "met dans une dualité ou complémentarité unilatérales le hard et le soft (et autres dualités comme l'axiomatique et l'herméneutique) qui interagissent et forment une machine non pas transcendantale mais immanentale" (ibid, 24).

La non-philosophie comme théorie unifiée exige donc des transformations réglées de l'apport scientifique et de l'apport philosophique. Laruelle avoue qu'au début de son projet (Philosophie I-II) il utilisait la critique afin de délivrer la philosophie de sa suffisance et que cette critique parait semblable à l'effort de Heidegger, à savoir – faire pour l'Un ce que Heidegger avait fait pour l'Etre, c'est-à-dire une forme de déconstruction.

> Le déplacement majeur opéré par la non-philosophie était la découverte du caractère non-commutatif de l'Un comme immanence et de l'Etre comme transcendance, mais le procédé était encore partiellement une extension aux rapports de l'Un et île l'Etre de l'opération sur les rapports de l'Etre et de l'étant. Cet effort ultra-heideggérien anime encore parfois le refus de l'axiome de la convertibilité de l'Un et de l'Etre (Aristote et Leibniz) qui organise toute l'histoire de la philosophie. L'utopie ou la futuralité de l'Un avant l'Etre, du flux de l'immanence avant la transcendance ne pouvait résulter d'un renversement et d'une décision, mais d'une pratique dite d'"avant-priorité' ou de 'forçage' générique de la priorité philosophique. Avant-priorité de l'Un et priorité de l'Etre forment un ordre mais unilatéral auquel l'Un n'est pas lui-même soumis, l'ordre n'étant pas réel mais effet dérivant du Réel. (…) L'unilatéralité ou la non-réversibilité est maintenant effectuée et motivée plus clairement par la quantique qui achève d'invalider ou de stériliser la suffisance de la représentation philosophique. (ibid., 27)

La forme renouvelée de la non-philosophie vient ainsi de sa rencontre avec une science précise qui actualise ses principes premiers comme avant-premièrs. Par la fondation quantique et générique de la science de la philosophie, Laruelle pense avoir annulé une partie de ce qu'il y avait d'aventureux et d'arbitraire dans la première invention intuitive de la non-philosophie.

3. Les faces différentes de l'identité

Quels sont les résultats essentiels de la présente confrontation entre la pensée du dernier Heidegger et la non-philosophie de Laruelle?

Comme nous l'avons vu, selon Laruelle Heidegger et Derrida sont les deux philosophes qui sont allé au plus loin dans la critique de la philosophie – Heidegger jusqu'à la proclamation de "la fin de la philosophie" et Derrida jusqu'à concevoir la Différance avant toute différence –, sans pouvoir pour autant dépasser la matrice philosophique. Or, la lecture close du dernier Heidegger, que j'ai proposé dans la première partie de cet article, montre qu'on ne peut pas réduire sa pensée à une "philosophie de la différence" comme le font beaucoup de ses interprétateurs, y compris Laruelle, puisque la nécessité de penser la différence comme telle exige pareillement de penser l'identité et que l'on trouve chez Heidegger quatre conceptions différentes de l'identité:

1) *L'identité de la métaphysique* pour laquelle deux choses sont appréhendés comme le même (A = A) et à partir du même et pour laquelle l'identité fait partie de l'Etre

2) *L'identité de Parménide* pour qui l'Etre est défini par une identité dans laquelle il a sa place

3) *L'identité de Schelling* qui est "l'indifférence absolue" de Dieu

4) *l'identité élaborée par Heidegger lui-même* qui procède de l'*Ereignis* comme un "laisser-coappartenir" et qui est la contrepartie de l'identité de la pensée et de l'être chez Hegel.

La critique laruellienne de Heidegger vise surtout l'identité métaphysique A = A, réfutée auparavant par le philosophe allemand lui-même. Donc la question qui se pose par-là est de savoir si cette critique arrive aussi à remettre en cause les autres concepts d'identité discutés par le philosophe allemand.

Si Heidegger laisse le Même de Parménide dans une ombre énigmatique, Laruelle affirme au contraire que pour Parménide "Le Même est Etre et Penser" et que cette formule structure toute philosophie et même pour moitié ses déconstructions (Laruelle 1992, 113). Or, l'identité n'est ni le Même, ni l'Etre-Un – il faut la penser, souligne Laruelle, comme l'Un sans-l'Etre ou hors-Etre, ce qui a pour conséquence que réel et pensée sont identiques seulement en-dernière-instance:

> L'Un est l'instance dernière – ou première, mais absolument première –, l'instance transcendantale aussi qui 'tient' en son propre sein, mais sans être affectée par elle, la pensée qui la représentera, qui sera même sa représentation adéquate bien que tardive, plus que tardive: de droit 'postérieure' ou décalée par rapport à elle. Plus profondément: uni-latéralisée par elle" (ibid., 114).

L'identité laruellienne en tant qu'"immanence radicale de l'Un "sans-Etre" est dirigée donc autant contre le Même, l'Un-Tout de Parménide, que contre le Un-ontologique de Heidegger (ibid., 108). Comme nous avons souligné plus haut, une des grandes différences entre la philosophie heideggérienne et la non-philosophie de Laruelle est que pour Heidegger l'identité et l'évènement sont convertibles tandis que pour Laruelle elles sont inconvertibles et forment une dualité unilatérale. Sous cet aspect, la contestation de l'identité heideggérienne est tout à fait légitime. Mais on peut se demander si chez Heidegger l'identité est seulement ontologique, c'est-à-dire si l'*Ereignis* a le dernier mot. Ne renvoie-t-il pas à la dimension du sans-fond et qu'est-ce que le sans-fond, sinon ce *Ungrund* qui est l'*indifférence absolue* ? A mon avis – et je partage ici le point de vue d'Otto Pöggeler – il ne faut pas réduire la pensée heideggérienne à une ontologie et "faire passer la question de l'Etre comme sa seule question" (cf. Pöggeler 1959, 598). Même si Heidegger tourne autour de la question de l'Etre, il évoque explicitement l'Un (*das Eine*) en tant que cet inconnu qui est l'autre à-venir[17]. Or, ce qui importe ici, c'est que son approche est tournée *en arrière*, puisque cet "autre avenir" est au fait "le premier début" (*ersten Anfang*): "On ne connait pas et on n'ose pas (approcher) l'Autre, qui sera le Un-(là) à l'avenir, puisqu'il est déjà présent au début de l'histoire, bien que sans fondement"[18] (GA 6.2, 29; trad. YR). Le Un sans-fond et sans fondement n'est pas à confondre avec l'Etre; on pourrait le penser à la rigueur comme "le dernier Dieu" ou "Dieu à venir", pour utiliser le vocabulaire heideggérien. En ce sens, la critique de Laruelle taxant l'Un de Heidegger d'amphibologie du Réel (Un-Étant, Un-Être, Un-Autre), me semble au moins discutable. Néanmoins, il existe une différence capitale entre les deux penseurs sur ce point, à laquelle je souhaite ici attirer l'attention, à savoir que le Un de Laruelle, contrairement à celui de Heidegger, n'est ni au début, ni à la fin de l'histoire comme son destin, mais toujours actuel dans son autonomie absolue.

La réflexion sur l'identité et la différence a des conséquences quant à la façon dont Heidegger et Laruelle conçoivent la chose et la tâche de la pensée. Comme nous l'avons vu, pour Heidegger *die Sache des Denkens* n'est plus la subjectivité de la conscience, respectivement l'identité du sujet et de l'objet, mais la clairière (*Lichtung*) en tant qu'ouverture à la présence de l'Etre ou à son retrait. Il s'agit donc d'une élaboration non-traditionnelle de cette question classique du domaine gnoséologique. Mais l'approche de Laruelle est plus radicale. Bien qu'il rejette, comme Heidegger, l'identité du sujet et de l'objet, de l'être et de la pensée, il s'oppose en même temps à la notion de clairière qui n'est pour lui qu'une forme singulière de l'Autre absolu, de son autoposition et auto-affirmation (1992, 17). Pour le non-philosophe la chose de la pensée, c'est le Un et, corrélativement, la-détermination-en-dernière-instance, où le clone et le réel Un ne sont identiques qu'en vision-en-Un. En d'autres mots, la matrice philosophique que Heidegger n'arrive pas à dépasser (selon Laruelle), est abrogée par la matrice générique où le Sujet transcendantal est sous-déterminé en-dernière-instance par un réel d'immanence absolue.

---

[17] Je me rends compte que Laruelle objecterait en ce point que le Un de Heidegger, c'est en fait une autre notion pour l'Etre ou l'Autre (Un=Etre=Autre), mais je tiens à accentuer les nuances de sens entre ces termes.

[18] "Man weiß und wagt nicht das Andere, was künftig da-s Eine sein wird, weil es im ersten Anfang unserer Geschichte, wenngleich ungegründet, schon west".

Le point sur lequel Heidegger est plus radical que Laruelle, c'est la position quant au rôle de la science et la relation entre science et philosophie. Comme nous l'avons indiqué plus haut, il existe sur ce point une différence cruciale entre la pensée de Heidegger et celle de Laruelle. Bien que l'attitude de Heidegger à l'égard de la science est ambigüe et qu'il essaye de ne pas articuler uniquement ses aspects négatifs, mais aussi ce qu'il y a de positif[19], ce qui prévale en fin de compte, c'est la mise en garde contre l'autosuffisance de la science et son l'instrumentalisation technique. Du fait qu'il relie l'émergence de la raison scientifique et technique à l'histoire de la métaphysique, Heidegger décrit le stade de la fin de la philosophie comme étant marqué par la ramification des sciences et "le triomphe de l'équipement d'un monde en tant que soumis aux commandes d'une science technisée et de l'ordre social qui répond à ce monde" (Heidegger 1990a, 286). Le mot célèbre de Heidegger que "la science ne pense pas" (Heidegger 1973, 26-27), suggère que la science ne s'occupe que du fonctionnement de l'étant qu'elle recherche, enquête, calcule, explique et prouve sans penser l'Etre. La science est axée sur la théorie des concepts structuraux, "auxquelles n'est accordée qu'une fonction cybernétique, toute signification ontologique leur étant déniée. Le caractère opérationnel et la référence au modèle de la pensée représentative et calculante en sont tous venus à régner en maitres" (Heidegger 1990a, 286).

La dégradation de la philosophie en recherche, à la manière des sciences, est pour Heidegger un autre signe de la "fin" de la philosophie:

> Le développement décisif du caractère d'entreprise de la science moderne forge également un humain d'une autre stature. Le savant disparaît. Il est remplacé par le chercheur qui travaille dans des entreprises de recherche. Ceci, et non le soin d'un apprentissage, donne à son travail l'air vif. Le chercheur n'a plus besoin chez soi d'une bibliothèque. Il est aussi constamment en mouvement. Il négocie lors de réunions et enseigne lors de congrès. Il est lié à des contrats avec les éditeurs. Ceux-ci déterminent maintenant quels livres doivent être écrits. (Heidegger GA 5, 85; trad. YR)[20]

Laruelle, pour sa part, n'ignore pas l'émergence de la raison techno-calculante, mais elle est pour lui un phénomène positif indiquant que la science cherche à se libérer de l'ordre philosophique qui lui est imposé afin de se manifester dans sa spécificité. La philo-

---

[19] Par exemple, Heidegger souligne que le fait que la science ne pense pas soit sa chance, car cela "assure sa démarche propre et bien définie" (Heidegger 1973, 26).
[20] "Die entscheidende Entfaltung des neuzeitlichen Betriebcharakters der Wissenschaft prägt daher auch einen anderen Schlag von Menschen. Der Gelehrte verschwindet. Er wird abgelöst durch den Forscher, der in Forschungsunternehmungen steht. Diese und nicht die Pflege einer Gelehrsamkeit geben seiner Arbeit die scharfe Luft. Der Forscher braucht zu Hause keine Bibliothek mehr. Er ist überdies ständig unterwegs. Er verhandelt auf Tagungen und unterrichtet sich auf Kongressen. Er bindet sich an Aufträge von Verlegern. Diese bestimmen jetzt mit, welche Bücher geschrieben werden müssen."

sophie tend, selon lui, toujours à s'imposer comme un savoir supérieur, voir ultime, et "ne se compte à égalité avec la science que pour s'excepter aussi de leur rapport et pour se poser en législatrice ou en fondatrice de l'autre terme et de son supposé rapport au Réel, rapport dont elle se prétend titulaire" (Laruelle 1996, 59). A la différence de l'anti-scientisme de Heidegger, pour Laruelle III-V il s'agit – comme nous l'avons indiqué – de faire rentrer la philosophie, avec la science et à part égale, dans un ordre transcendantal sans hiérarchie et d'établir une discipline liée autant à la science qu'à la philosophie, sans être ni l'une ni l'autre, mais une théorie unifie de la pensée comme science première.

Or, si différentes et incompatibles que soient les approches de Heidegger et de Laruelle, elles ont au moins deux choses en commun: la tentative hérétique de réexaminer le statut de la philosophie en se posant hors d'elle comme non-philosophie et le désinvestissement de l'entreprise de la philosophie "académique", conçue soit comme dégradation de la pensée en "recherche" (Heidegger), soit comme geste autoritaire d'autoposition législatrice (Laruelle).

Prof. Dr. Yvanka B. Raynova, Institute for the Study of Societies and Knowledge – Bulgarian Academy of Sciences, Sofia / Institut für Axiologische Forschungen, Wien,
raynova[at]iaf.ac.at

Références

Beaufret, Jean. "La fin de la philosophie et la tache de la pensée", dans Martin Heidegger. *Questions III et IV*. Paris: Gallimard, 1990, 279-280.
Dastur, Françoise. "Heidegger, penseur de la modernité, de la technique et de l'éthique", *Po&sie*, vol. 115, no. 1, 2006: 34-41, DOI: 10.3917/poesi.115.0034.
Derrida, Jacques. *L'écriture et la différence*. Paris: Seuil, 1967a.
Derrida, Jacques. *De la grammatologie*. Paris: Minuit, 1967b.
Derrida, Jacques. *La Dissémination*. Paris: Seuil, 1972.
Derrida, Jacques. *Politiques de l'amitié*. Paris: Galilée, 1994.
Gasché, Rodolphe. *Inventions of Difference: On Jacques Derrida*. Cambridge, MA/London: Harvard University Press, 1994.
Hegel, Georg Wilhelm Friedrich. *Enzyklopädie der philosophischen Wissenschaften im Grundrisse 1830. Dritter Teil: Die Philosophie des Geistes (Werke 10)*. Frankfurt am Main: Suhrkamp, 1986.
Heidegger, Martin. "Identité et différence", in idem. *Questions I*. Paris: Gallimard, 1968a, 253-308.
Heidegger, Martin. "Qu'est-ce que la philosophie?", in idem. *Questions II*. Paris: Gallimard, 1968b, 7-40.
Heidegger, Martin. *Qu'appelle-t-on penser?* Paris: PUF, 1973.
Heidegger, Martin. "L'expérience de la pensée", in idem. *Questions III et IV*. Paris: Gallimard, 1990, 19-41.
Heidegger, Martin. "La fin de la philosophie et la tâche de la pensée", in idem. *Questions III et IV*. Paris: Gallimard, 1990a, 281-306.

Heidegger, Martin. "Le tournant", in idem. *Questions III et IV*. Paris: Gallimard, 1990b, 307-322.
Heidegger, Martin. *Gesamtausgabe* (GA). Frankfurt am Main: Vittorio Klostermann, 1970ff.
Janicaud, Dominique. "Heidegger – Hegel: un 'dialogue' impossible?", in Franco Volpi et al. *Heidegger et l'idée de la phénoménologie*. Dordrecht: Kluwer Academic Publishers, 1988, 145-164.
Kant, Emmanuel. *Critique de la raison pure*. Paris: Félix Alcan, 1905.
Laruelle, François. "La vérité selon Hermès", *Analecta Husserliana*, Vol. XXII, 1987:97-401.
Laruelle, François. *Théorie des identités*. Paris: PUF, 1992.
Laruelle, François. *Les philosophes de la différence*. Paris: PUF, (1986), édition numérique 2015.
Laruelle, François. *Principes de la non-philosophie*. Paris: PUF, 1996.
Laruelle, François. "Identity and event", *Pli* 9, 2000: 174-189.
Laruelle, François. "Enfin le fondement générique d'une science de la philosophie", *Organisation Non-Philosophique Internationale*, 9 février, 2008a. Web. <http://www.onphi.net/letters/21/enfin-le-fondement-generique-d-une-science-de-la-philosophie>.
Laruelle, François. *Philosophie non-standard. Générique, quantique, philo-fiction*. Paris: Kimé, 2010.
Laruelle, François. "What can non-philosophy do?" *Angelaki: Journal of the Theoretical Humanities*, Vol. 8, No. 2, 2013:69-189, DOI: http://dx.doi.org/10.1080/0969725032000162648
Laruelle, François. "Deconstruction and Non-Philosophy," *Chiasma: A Site For Thought*, Vol. 1, Issue 1, 2014:54-63, <https://ir.lib.uwo.ca/chiasmaasiteforthought/vol1/iss1/4>
Laruelle, François et Florian Forestier. "Entretien avec François Laruelle : Autour de Christo-fiction", *Actu-Philosophia*, 17 janvier, 2015. Web. <http://www.actu-philosophia.com/Entretien-avec-Francois-Laruelle-Autour-de>.
Ledic, Juraj-D. *Heideggers "Sach-Verhalt" und Sachverhalte an sich: Studien zur Grundlegung einer kritischen Auseinandersetzung mit Heideggers Seinsbegriff*. Frankfurt a.M.: Ontos Verlag, 2009.
Liddell, Henry George and Robert Scott. *A Greek-English Lexicon*. New York/ Chicago/ Chicinnati: Amercian Book Company, 1897.
Marion, Jean-Luc. "La fin de la fin de la métaphysique", Laval théologique et philosophique, Vol. 42, No. 1, février 1986: 23–33, DOI : 10.7202/400214ar
Marx, Karl et Friedrich Engels. L'ideologie allemande. Preface. 1845, texte en ligne <https://www.marxists.org/francais/marx/works/1845/00/kmfe18450000a.htm>
Merleau-Ponty, Maurice. *Résumés de cours. Collège de France 1952-1960*. Paris : Gallimard, 1968.
Mullarkey, John et Anne-Françoise Schmid. "Argument", in Programme du Colloque "La Philosophie non-standard de Francois Laruelle", Centre Culturel de Cerisy, 2014 <http://www.ccic-cerisy.asso.fr/laruelle14.html>
Raynova, Yvanka B. *Être et être libre: Deux "passions" des philosophies phénoménologiques. Études d'herméneutique comparative*. Frankfurt am Main: Peter Lang, 2010.
Raynova, Yvanka B. Sein, *Sinn und Werte: Phänomenologische und hermeneutische Perspektiven des europäischen Denkens*. Frankfurt am Main: Peter Lang, 2017.
Raynova, Yvanka B. "La 'fête mobile' de la non-philosophie", *Labyrinth: An International Journal for Philosophy, Value Theory and Sociocultural Hermeneutics*, Vol. 19, No. 2. Winter 2017a: 5-13.
Trawny, Peter. *Martin Heidegger*. Frankfurt am Main: Campus, 2003.
Vattimo, Gianni. *Les aventures de la différence*. Paris: Minuit, 1985.
Vattimo, Gianni. "'Verwindung': Nihilism and the Postmodern in Philosophy," *SubStance*, Vol. 16, No. 2, Issue 53, 1987:7-17.

DISCUSSION

KAREL HLAVÁČEK (Prag)

Adorno und Habermas im Vergleich:
Vom Säkularismus zum Postsäkularismus?

Abstract

Adorno and Habermas: From Secularism to Post-Secularim?

The article analyses the 'post-secular turn' in critical theory by comparing Jürgen Habermas' late philosophy with the philosophy of his predecessor Theodor W. Adorno. It poses the question to what extent can Habermas be seen as a post-secular theorist when setting his work against that of Adorno? Following Birgitte Schepelern Johansen, the author develop a concept of post-secularism as a move beyond the strict division between religion and non-religion, and apply the concept to the work of the two critical theorists in question. Finally, Adorno's work is identified as a 'religious secularism' and Habermas' work as a 'post-secular secularism'. Thus, the author points out the ambivalence, which the alleged 'post-secular turn' breeds, and suggest a reconsideration of the religious motives discovered in Adorno's work.

Keywords: Theodor W. Adorno, Jürgen Habermas, religion, post-secularism, critical theory.

Einleitung

Einer der wichtigen Akteure in der seit ungefähr der Jahrtausendwende geführten Debatte über "Postsäkularismus" ist Jürgen Habermas. Er selbst hat einen Begriff des Postsäkularen vorgelegt, welcher zwei Aspekte, Faktum und Programm, beinhaltet: eine fortdauernde Präsenz von religiösen Gemeinschaften in europäischen Gesellschaften und das Programm des Dialoges mit Religion. Habermas will Religion nicht mehr für irrational erklären, sondern vielmehr einen Dialog mit ihr führen.

Das stellt einen wesentlichen Unterschied zu seinem Vorgänger Theodor W. Adorno dar. Adorno zählt noch zu den Philosophen, die starke rationalistische Kritik an Religion ausübten. So denkt Adorno, Religion sei ein "Opfer des Intellekts" (Adorno 1969, 22) und, wenn er Tendenzen zur Belebung von Religion sieht, kritisiert er diese stark. Da er das Programm der rationalistischen Religionskritik verfolgt, ist Adorno ist noch unter die säkularistischen Philosophen einzuordnen.

In diesem Sinne kann im Rahmen der kritischen Theorie der Frankfurter Schule über eine postsäkulare Wende gesprochen werden. So versteht auch Habermas selbst seine Bemühung – diese Selbstinterpretation ist schon im Rahmen seines Begriffes des Postsäkularen beinhaltet: Früher war Philosophie säkularistisch, heute will sie postsäkular werden. Trotzdem kann die These, die die Enwicklung vom Säkularismus (Adorno) zum Postsäkularismus (Habermas) gleichsetzt, problematisiert werden. Wohl mögen Adorno und Habermas selbst mit dieser These einverstanden gewesen sein, doch scheint diese zu einfach. War das nicht Adorno, der sich viele religiöse Konzepte – wie etwa die Auferstehung des Fleisches, Erlösung, Versöhnung oder Bilderverbot – angeeignet hat und Philosophie nur aus der Perspektive von Erlösung betreiben wollte? Und war das nicht Habermas, der gerade diese Perspektive abgelehnt hat?

In diesem Artikel stelle ich also folgende Fragen: Inwieweit kann man Adorno als Vertreter des Säkularismus und Habermas, hingegen, als Vertreter des Postsäkularismus betrachten? Inwieweit kann man die Entwicklung der kritischen Theorie von der Philosophie des früher massiv populären Direktors des Instituts für Sozialforschung Theodor W. Adorno zur Philosophie eines der einflussreichsten Philosophen der heutigen Zeit Jürgen Habermas als postsäkulare Wende interpretieren?

Um dieses Problem zu lösen, muss zunächst die Frage beantwortet werden, was (Post)Säkularismus[1] eigentlich ist. Es ist eine zentrale Frage, denn von der Auffassung dieses Konzeptes hängt auch das Ergebnis der Analyse ab. Um den Begriff des (Post)Säkularismus zu bestimmen, entwickle ich das Konzept weiter, das Birgitte Schepelern Johansen vorgestellt hat und das den Postäkularismus mit einer Bewegung jenseits der strikten säkularen Trennung von Religion und Nicht-Religion identifiziert.[2]

(Post)Säkularismus geht durch mehrere Segmente der Gesellschaft hindurch: Es gibt ihn in unserer Weltanschauung, in der Philosophie, in den Wissenschaften, in der

---

[1] Ich benutze die Verkürzung (Post)Säkularismus, um beide Konzepte zugleich einzubeziehen.
[2] Die Fragestellung des Textes setzt voraus, dass mit idealen Typen (Max Weber) gearbeitet wird, so wird z.B. Säkularismus idealtypisch definiert. Auch die Werke von Adorno und Habermas werden dann unter bestimmte Typen eingeordnet. Das stellt auch die Schwäche dieses Textes dar: solch eine Einordnung erfordert immer eine gewisse Vereinfachung.

öffentlichen Debatte und dem öffentlichen Raum, in den staatlichen Institutionen usw. Es wurde zu einer Gewohnheit, dass die Rolle der Religion primär im Bezug auf Politik betrachtet und untersucht wird.[3] Ich konzentriere mich in erster Linie auf das Zusammenbestehen von Religion und Vernunft, sowie Glaube und Wissen in der Philosophie selbst, denn genau dieser Blickwinkel kann den oben spezifizierten Eindruck der grossen Rolle der Religion bei Adorno am klarsten beleuchten.

Der vorliegende Artikel besteht aus drei Teilen. Im ersten Teil wird das Konzept des Postsäkularismus entwickelt. In den darauf folgenden zwei Teilen führe ich dann eine Analyse des (Post)Säkularismus durch, zunächst bei Adorno und anschließend bei Habermas.

(Post)Säkularismus als eine Form des Bewusstseins und seiner Manifestation

Es war Habermas, der die Diskussion über Postsäkularismus in Deutschland maßgeblich beeinflusst hat. Für ihn ist als postsäkular eine Gesellschaft zu bezeichnen, die "sich auf das Fortbestehen religiöser Gemeinschaften in einer fortwährend säkularisierenden Umgebung einstellt" (Habermas 2001, 10). Aus dieser Auffasung ist viel über mögliche Struktur des Postsäkularismus zu lernen.

Postsäkularismus – wie von Habermas spezifiziert – beinhaltet bei näherem Blick zwei Facetten: Die Erste ist das Vorhandensein eines postsäkularen Bewusstseins, die Zweite ist dessen konkrete Manifestation. Wenn eine Gesellschaft postsäkular werden will, muss sie sich reflexiv und bewusst mit der Frage nach dem Fortbestand der Religion befassen: sie muss ein postsäkulares Bewusstsein zeigen. Aber ein solches Bewusstsein genügt nicht: es muss eine konkrete Manifestation dessen stattfinden. Als Grundstruktur des Postsäkularismus kann also im losen Bezug auf Habermas die Kombination von postsäkularen Bewusstsein (subjektive Facette) und seiner Manifestation (objektive Facette) identifiziert werden.

Das gilt nicht nur für Gesellschaften als Ganzheiten, sondern auch für individuelle Menschen. Bei Habermas z.B. besteht sein postsäkulares Bewusstsein – vereinfacht ausgedrückt – darin, dass er das Fortbestehen der religiösen Gemeinschaften sieht, das nicht mehr als bloßes Überleben der archaischen Lebensformen zu interpretieren ist. Die Manifesta-

---

[3] Siehe Calhoun, Jürgensmeyer, VanAntverpen (2011, 5). So ist es letztendlich auch bei Habermas: der Schwerpunkt seiner Aufmerksamkeit liegt im politischen Zusammenleben der säkularen und religiösen Bürger im Rahmen eines säkularen, liberalen und demokratischen Staates.

tion dieses Bewusstseins finden wir letztendlich in seiner Konzeption des nachmetaphysischen Denkens.[4] Es mag aber mehrere konkrete Formen des Postsäkularismus geben.

(Post)Säkularismus als eine Grenzsetzung und Grenzüberschreitung

Mit dem, was Habermas für postsäkulares Bewusstsein und dessen konkrete Manifestation hält, können wir uns nicht abfinden. Um ein allgemeines Konzept des Postsäkularismus zu finden, müssen wir von diesem konkreten Konzept absehen, und eine allgemeinere Charakterisierung finden. Die Frage lautet, welche Kriterien das Bewusstsein und seine Manifestation erfüllen müssen, um als "postsäkular" bezeichnet werden zu können.

Ein Konzept, dass eine mögliche Antwort auf diese Frage biete, hat Birgitte Schepelern Johansen vorgestellt. Sie behauptet, "[...] das Postsäkulare bezieht sich immer auf eine Situation, in der wir uns jenseits des Säkularen befinden, und [...] das Säkulare in seinem Kern beruht auf der Teilung zwischen Religion und Nicht-Religion" (Johansen 2013, 10). Es handelt sich also um ein Konzept des Säkularismus als Grenzsetzung, als eine strikte Unterscheidung zwischen Religion und Nicht-Religion. Postsäkularismus wäre dann als Überschreitung dieser Grenzsetzung zu verstehen.

Säkularismus bestimmt eine Grenze zwischen dem, was nicht-religiös und was religiös ist, und trennt beide Bereiche voneinander ab. Das Nicht-Religiöse stellt im Rahmen der europäischen Aufklärung immer die Vernunft dar: die Trennung, die durch den Säkularismus hergestellt wird, ist also die zwischen Vernunft und Religion, zwischen Wissen und Glaube; im Hintergrund gibt es dann zudem die zusammenhängenden Entgegensetzungen von objektiv und subjektiv, von öffentlich und privat.

Dazu muss noch angemerkt werden – und das tut Johansen nicht –, dass Säkularismus die religiöse Seite der oben genannten binaren Trennung negativ sieht: als kognitiv oder intellektuell minderwertig, irrational, als politisch gefährlich, als heteronom und autoritär, als ideologisch, neurotisch, überwunden, überflüssig usw. Die säkularistische Opposition ist also durch eine Bewertung gekennzeichnet, die die irreligiöse Domäne bevorzugt. Säkularismus konstruiert eine Grenze zwischen Religion und Nicht-Religion, um sich selbst als die irreligiöse Seite zu bezeichnen, und um die religiöse Seite für minderwertig zu erklären.

---

[4] Habermas schreibt: "Das säkulare Bewusstsein, in einer postsäkularen Gesellschaft zu leben, spiegelt sich philosophisch in Gestalt eines postmetaphysischen Denkens wider." (Habermas 2005, 146-147).

Postsäkularismus bedeutet dann, dass die säkulare Grenze zwischen Religion und Nicht-Religion bzw. der Charakter der abgegrenzten Bereiche in Frage gestellt werden.[5] Das kann auf verschiedene Weise passieren: es könnte beispielsweise gefragt werden, ob im Rahmen des Säkularismus religiöse Elemente überleben (und dabei die Grenze zwischen Religion und Nicht-Religion bezweifelt werden), es könnte gefragt werden, ob Religion wirklich irrational ist, es mögen Überlegungen kommen, ob einige Elemente der Religion ihren Wert haben (und dabei der überlegene Status des säkularen Bereichs in Frage gestellt werden). Es mögen Vorschläge kommen, man solle die religiösen Inhalte in die säkulare Sprache übersetzen (und bei der Übersetzung die Grenze zwischen dem Religiösen und dem Nicht-Religiösen überschreiten) oder es mögen Versuche kommen, die Grenze zwischen Religion und Säkularität total zu destruieren. Allgemein kann also behauptet werden, dass die postsäkulare Hinterfragung der säkularen Grenze den absoluten Charakter der Grenzen, und/oder den übergeordneten Status des säkularen Bereichs bezweifelt.

Ein idealtypisches Modell des Säkularismus kann als eine Gedankenströmung[6] begriffen werden, die die Grenze zwischen Religion und Nicht-Religion als absolut und undurchlässig postuliert, die Religion als absolut minderwertig ansieht (sie enthält also keine Wahrheiten und Inspirationen), die keine Möglichkeiten des Dialoges zwischen Religion und Nicht-Religion sieht (und auch keine andere Möglichkeiten der Übergänge zwischen beiden) und die die religiöse Irrationalität durch Vernunft ersetzen will.

Dagegen ist ein idealtypisches Modell des Postsäkularismus schwer zu entwickeln, da es mehrere Möglichkeiten gibt, den Säkularismus zu bezweifeln. Darüber hinaus ist die Trennung des idealtypischen Säkularismus eigentlich kein Postsäkularismus, sondern eher eine Art Religion, die die Trennung von Vernunft und Glaube anerkennt, Vernunft negiert und Glaube als absolut setzt. Postsäkularismus ist keine einfache Opposition des Säkularismus, es ist vielmehr der breite Raum, in dem einige der idealtypischen Voraussetzungen des Säkularismus bezweifelt werden, da sie als unhaltbar betrachtet werden.[7]

---

[5] Der Begriff des Postsäkularismus als Bezweiflung des unreflektierten Säkularismus stimmt mit Casanova überein. Casanova analysiert verschiedene Typen der Säkularität und den ihnen entsprechenden der Postsäkularität. Er kommt zu dem Schluss, dass wir nicht postsäkular in dem Sinne sind, dass wir wieder religiös würden oder die Kirche wieder mächtig würde. Eher bezweifelt er den unreflektierten oder naturalisierten Säkularismus. Casanova, *Die Erschließung des Postsäkularen*. In: Lutz-Bachmann (2015, 9-40

[6] Dagegen verstehe ich den Begriff "(Post)Säkularität" vor allem in Bezug auf eine zeitliche Periode und "das (Post)Säkulare" als einen allgemeinen Begriff.

[7] Dabei geht es immer um eine Verbreiterung des reflexiven Zugangs, nicht um eine Zerstörung der Reflexivität. Vom Postsäkularismus sollte man präsäkulare Neigungen unterscheiden, die die Reflexivität in religiöser Quasinatürlichkeit aufgehen lassen wollen, wie es bei einigen Fundamentalismen unserer Zeit zu beobachten ist.

Postsäkularismus, wie ich ihn verstehe, besteht also aus zwei Facetten: dem postsäkularen Bewusstsein (subjektive Facette) und der Manifestation des Bewusstseins (objektive Facette), wobei die Manifestation in der Bezweiflung der Grenze zwischen der Religion und der Vernunft besteht. Ob es sich um Postsäkularismus handelt, erkennen wir also primär an der Weise, wie die Grenze zwischen Religion und Nicht-Religion bestimmt wird, welchen Status beide Bereiche eigentlich besitzen und welche Übergänge es zwischen beiden Bereichen gibt.[8]

(Post)Säkularismus bei Adorno

Bei Adorno ist die Frage nach der Präsenz des postsäkularen Bewusstseins sicherlich viel strittiger als bei Habermas. Er ist der Meinung, Religion solle durch Vernunft ersetzt werden, wenn er sagt: "Nichts an theologischem Gehalt wird unverwandelt fortbestehen; ein jeglicher wird sich der Probe stellen müssen, ins Säkulare, Profane einzuwandern." (Adorno 1969, 20). Adorno will sich Religion also mithilfe der Vernunft aneignen, indem er sie säkularisiert. Diese Tendenz zur Übernahme der Religion durch die Vernunft zeigt, dass ein postsäkulares Bewusstsein bei Adorno nicht zu finden ist. Adorno war – was die subjektive Facette des Postsäkularismus angeht – also ein Vertreter des Säkularismus.

Wie steht es aber bei Adorno um die objektiven Facette des Postsäkularismus? Auch hier finden wir einen klaren Säkularismus: Religion wird als verschieden von der Vernunft verstanden, und zwar als eine in hohem Maße minderwertige Domäne. Im Einklang mit der Intention, religiöse Inhalte zu säkularisieren, steht bei Adorno auch das Programm der starken rationalistischen Kritik der Religion. Obwohl er authentische Religion nicht ausschließt,[9] denkt er, dass sie außerhalb der Bedingungen der modernen Gesellschaft liegt und somit nicht mehr rational vertretbar ist. Er schreibt:

> Im besten Fall – also wo es sich nicht bloß um Nachahmung und Konformismus handelt – ist der Wunsch der Vater solcher Haltung [Offenbarungsglauben]: nicht die Wahrheit und Authentizität der Offenbarung entscheidet, sondern das Bedürfnis nach Orientierung, der Rückhalt am festen Vorgegebenen; auch die Hoffnung, man könne durch den Entschluß der entzauberten Welt jenen Sinn einhauchen, unter dessen Ab-

---

[8] Zum Bewusstsein der Autoren haben wir nur einen mittelbaren Zugang – durch das, was sie geschrieben haben, also durch eine Manifestation ihres Bewusstseins. Trotzdem glaube ich, dass die subjektive Facette und ihre Einbeziehung in die Analyse sinnvoll ist, denn gerade bei Adorno und Habermas erfasst sie einen wichtigen Unterschied.

[9] Motive dieser Art bei Adorno hat Schiller gesammelt – Adorno erkennt ein nonkonformistisches Potenzial der Religion an und hält individuelle religiöse Erfahrungen für nicht ausgeschlossen. Transzendenz aber zergehe im "Fortschritt von Aufklärung und Entmythologisierung" (Schiller 1997, 69).

wesenheit man so lange leidet, wie man als bloßer Zuschauer aufs Sinnlose hinstarrt. (Adorno 1969, 22)

Adorno sieht Religion auf typisch säkularistische Weise: als eine problematische Option, die Vernunft negiert und die selbst negiert werden muss, womit der Bereich der Religion bei Adorno also einen deutlich minderwertigen Status gegenüber dem Bereich der Vernunft hat.

Dieser minderwertige Status besteht demzufolge darin, dass Glaube Authentizität vermissen lässt. Darüber hinaus stellt der Glaube für Adorno ein irrationales "Opfer des Intellekts" (Adorno 1969, 22) dar, welches Autonomie ausschließt, denn "damit ich den Offenbarungsglauben annehmen könnte, müßte ihm meiner Vernunft gegenüber eine Autorität zukommen, die bereits voraussetzte, dass ich ihn angenommen habe – ein unausweichlicher Zirkel" (Adorno 1969, 25). Adorno denkt also, dass Religion irrational und nicht authentisch ist und Autonomie ausschliesst.

Die Grenze zwischen Religion und Nicht-Religion, also zwischen Religion und Vernunft, findet man bei Adorno zwischen Offenbarung und persönlicher Erfahrung,[10] die, wie Martin Seel (2004) bemerkt hat, Kontemplation genannt werden kann.[11] Diese Auffassung von Religion setzt sie mit traditionellen Formen der Religion – Judentum und Christentum – gleich, und identifiziert ihren Kern mit der Offenbarung, der man ohne Rücksicht auf die Vernunft glauben muss. Dieses Konzept ist eigentlich eine konkrete Variante der säkularistischen Konstruktion des Unterschiedes zwischen Religion und Nicht-Religion. Die Trennlinie zwischen Religion und Vernunft, Glaube an Offenbarung und an Vernunft, wird nicht nur als Grenze zwischen Irrationalität und Rationalität wahrgenommen, sondern Vernunft soll Glaube monologisch ersetzen. In diesem Sinne wäre Adorno also als ein typischer Anhänger des Säkularismus zu verstehen.[12]

Trotz dieser scheinbaren Klarheit ist aber die Frage nach dem Säkularismus bei Adorno doch kompliziert. Die Frage nach der objektiven Facette des Postsäkularismus setzt nämlich nicht nur die Analyse der Trennlinie zwischen Vernunft und Religion und des

---

[10] Adorno spricht von ungeschmälerter oder auch unreglementierter Erfahrung. Er schreibt beispielsweise: "Das Objekt ungeschmälerter Erfahrung, zum Unterschied vom bestimmungslosen Substrat des Reduktionismus, ist objektiver als jenes Substrat. Die von traditionellen Erkenntniskritik am Objekt ausgemerzten und dem Subjekt zugeschriebenen Qualitäten verdanken in der subjektiven Erfahrung sich dem Vorrang des Objekts". Adorno (2010, 82).
[11] Das Konzept der Kontemplation analysiere ich unten ausführlicher.
[12] Es muss nachgetragen werden, dass sich Adorno in seinem Essay *Vernunft und Offenbarung*, auf den ich mich berufe, vor allem von Karl Barth abgrenzt, obwohl seine abwertenden Worte allgemeiner formuliert sind. Es ist fraglich, ob Adorno sich auf die gleiche Weise gegen alle Formen der Offenbarungsreligionen abgrenzen würde.

Status' der beiden Bereiche voraus, sondern auch die der Möglichkeiten der Grenzüberschreitung. Und Adorno, der Religion durch seine Philosophie ersetzten will, wollte die religiösen Inhalte, die er für notwendig hielt, in seine eigene Philosophie integrieren. Dies rückt seine Philosophie in unmittelbare Nachbarschaft zur Religion, in eine Zone, die ein Grenzgebiet zwischen Vernunft und Glaube darstellt.

Die Analyse der Grenzübergänge zwischen Religion und Vernunft zeigt uns ein ganz anderes Bild als die Analyse der Grenze und des Status' der beiden Domänen Vernunft und Religion. Adornos Arbeit mit Begriffen, die aus religiösen Traditionen stammen, hat sogar zu einer Diskussion geführt, ob seine Philosophie eigentlich eine Form von "Theologie" darstelle.[13] Diese Diskussion findet ihre Rechtfertigung in der Tatsache, dass einige Grundannahmen von Adornos Philosophie als "religiös" oder zumindest "quasireligiös" angesehen werden können.[14] Um welche Motive geht es hier?

Eines von diesen Motiven ist die Frage nach dem Tod und seiner Überwindung. Der Tod ist eine Grenzerfahrung des menschlichen Lebens, der als solcher von den traditionellen Religionen stark thematisiert wurde, und zwar in Hinsicht auf die Hoffnung auf die endgültige Überwindung des Todes. Bei Adorno finden wir dieses Motiv auch. Er schreibt: "Wäre der Tod jenes Absolute, das die Philosophie positiv vergebens beschwor, so ist alles überhaupt nichts, auch jeder Gedanke ins Leere gedacht, keiner läßt mit Wahrheit irgend sich denken. Denn es ist ein Moment von Wahrheit, daß sie samt ihrem Zeitkern dauere; ohne alle Dauer wäre keine, noch deren letzte Spur verschlänge der absolute Tod" (Adorno 1966, 362). Adorno fürchtet also nicht nur, dass der Tod für die Säkularität etwas Ungelöstes darstellt, sondern er geht drastisch und radikal davon aus, dass der Tod alles sinnlos macht. Doch der Tod ist aus der Sicht der säkularen materialistischen Philosophie eine Sicherheit, die nie überwunden werden kann. Durch die Ablehnung der absoluten Natur des Todes geht Adorno daher hinter die Grenzen einer säkularen materialistischen Philosophie zurück. Für diese Sehnsucht nach der Überwindung des Todes finde ich keinen besseren Ausdruck als "religiös".

Mit der Überwindung des Todes ist bei Adorno die Sehnsucht nach absoluter Gerechtigkeit verbunden: Adorno fürchtet, nur durch Überwindung des Todes könne Gerechtigkeit erreicht werden, denn es gäbe schon viele menschliche Leben, die vernichtet wurden

---

[13] Vgl. Brittain (2010), De Vries (2005), Hans Ernst Schiller, *Zergehende Transzendenz*, in: Lutz-Bachmann (1997, 69-85).

[14] Wie diese Motive zu bezeichnen sind, ist eine schwierige Frage. Nach ihrer Analyse wird klar, dass sie keinesfalls "säkular" oder "materialistisch" sind; zugleich sind sie aber auch nicht "postsäkular", denn Adorno wollte doch Religion durch Vernunft ersetzen. Letztendlich wähle ich den Begriff "religiös", der vielleicht am besten den Charakter von Adornos Philosophie beschreibt – es soll aber klar sein, dass es sich keinesfalls um eine traditionelle Religiosität handelt.

– und für die gibt es in dieser immanenten Welt keine Gerechtigkeit mehr. In diesem Zusammenhang schreibt Adorno über die Erfahrung, dass "der Gedanke, der sich nicht enthauptet, in Transzendenz mündet, bis zur Idee einer Verfassung der Welt, in der nicht nur bestehendes Leid abgeschafft, sondern noch das unwiderruflich vergangene widerrufen wäre" (Adorno 1969, 363). Auch diese Sehnsucht von Adorno scheint eher "religiös" als säkular zu sein, denn im Rahmen der säkularen Immanenz kann das unwiderruflich Vergangene nicht ungeschehen gemacht werden.

Die Welt, von der hier Adorno spricht, wäre die erlöste Welt: Adornos Utopie ist die der Erlösung. In *Minima Moralia* spricht Adorno von einer Philosophie der Erlösung sogar als von der einzig möglichen:

> Philosophie, wie sie im Angesicht der Verzweiflung einzig noch zu verantworten ist, wäre der Versuch, alle Dinge so zu betrachten, wie sie vom Standpunkt der Erlösung aus sich darstellten. (Adorno 1951, 362)

Nicht einmal Erlösung ist bei Adorno ein völlig säkularisierter Begriff, denn die erlöste Welt müsste auch durch die Überwindung des Todes und absolute Gerechtigkeit bestimmt sein.

Alle oben genannten religiösen Motive, die bei Adorno gefunden werden können, sind durch das Motiv der Hoffnung bedingt. Man muss auf sie hoffen, ohne Hoffnung gäben sie keinen Sinn. Adorno drückt es so aus: "ohne Hoffnung ist kein Gutes" (Adorno 1966, 370) und behauptet, seinem "unversöhnlichen Denken ist die Hoffnung auf Versöhnung gesellt". (Adono 1966, 29). Obwohl Hoffnung nicht "transzendent" ist in dem Sinne, in dem Überwindung des Todes oder absolute Gerechtigkeit notwendig transzendent sind, zählt sie doch zu den (quasi)religiösen Motiven bei Adorno: denn es ist immer noch Hoffnung auf Erlösung, von der bei Adorno letztendlich die Rede ist. Die Transzendenz, die wir in den Motiven der absoluten Gerechtigkeit und Überwindung des Todes identifiziert haben, breitet sich notwendig aus – andere Begriffe bei Adorno's "Materialismus" werden durch sie notwendig "angesteckt".

Bei Adorno geht das ganze Streben nach Gerechtigkeit davon aus, dass etwas Ungerechtes passiert ist – und dieses Ungerechte stellt Schuld dar. In der *Negative(n) Dialektik* schreibt Adorno:

> Die Schuld des Lebens, das als pures Faktum bereits anderem Leben den Atem raubt (…), ist mit dem Leben nicht mehr zu versöhnen. Jene Schuld reproduziert sich unablässig, weil sie dem Bewußtsein in keinem Augenblick ganz gegenwärtig sein kann. Das, nichts anderes zwingt zur Philosophie. (Adorno 1966, 355)

Es ist also die Schuld, die die eigentliche Quelle von Adornos Philosophie darstellt: seine Philosophie ist ein Versuch mit Hilfe von Hoffnung von der Schuld hin zur Erlösung zu gelangen. Das ist nicht eine immanente, säkulare oder materialistische Struktur. Wenn man darüber nachdenkt, wie sie zu bezeichnen sei, dann scheint "religiös" eine relativ gute Bezeichnung zu sein.

Diese "religiösen" Motive können jedoch nicht als traditionell religiös verstanden werden, denn sie verlieren ihren direkten Kontakt mit der Offenbarung und sollen – Adorno zufolge – als säkularisiert angesehen werden. Das heisst, Erlösung und andere Begriffe sind nicht als etwas Transzendentes zu verstehen, sondern als etwas Immanentes. Wie sich aber aus den oben genannten Zitaten ergibt, ist es fraglich, ob Adorno sein Säkularisierungsprogramm vollendet hat: Z.B. gibt es die Überwindung des Todes oder die absolute Gerechtigkeit im Rahmen der Immanenz nicht.[15]

Die "religiösen" Motive, die ich oben aufgezählt habe, mögen schon früher in der Diskussion über Adornos "Theologie" bekannt gewesen sein.[16] Doch es gibt auch ein Motiv, das noch nicht entsprechend berücksichtigt wurde. Adornos "Religiosität" wäre – den existierenden Analysen zufolge – als eine Art weitestgehend negativ interpretierte "Erlösungstheologie" zu verstehen. Adorno war ein Anhänger eines an die jüdische Tradition anknüpfenden Bilderverbotes – und lehnte im Rahmen dieser Position strikt die positive Abbildung der Erlösung ab und sprach von einer negativen Dialektik. Im Bezug darauf tendieren seine Interpretatoren dazu, seine "Theologie" als vorwiegend negativ – als Negation der Negation – zu verstehen.[17]

Dieses Verstehen mag aber zu viel auf Adornos negative Selbstinterpretation vertrauen. Wie Martin Seel gezeigt hat, geht Adornos Werk auf ein Konzept der Kontemplation zurück, das sowohl die ethische als auch die erkenntnistheoretische Basis seiner Philosophie bildet. Kontemplation wäre bei Adorno ein langer gewaltloser Blick auf einen Gegenstand, der subjektive Willkür brechen kann und "objektive" Erkenntnis ermöglicht. Sie bildet, wie Seel behauptet, ein "positives Zentrum Adornos Philosophie" (Seel 2004, 2). Kontemplation – als Tugend der Erkenntnis und ihre ethische Voraussetzung zugleich –

---

[15] So spricht z.B. Hent De Vries über eine Spur des Anderen, die in Adornos Werk wirksam ist. Auf diese Weise wäre Adornos Philosophie als eine "minimale Theologie" zu verstehen (De Vries 2005).
[16] So analysiert die meisten Motive schon Hans-Ernst Schiller (Schiller 1997, 69-85).
[17] So spricht Schiller darüber, bei Adorno bliebe "nicht mehr als Verweigerung, die Leerstelle, die der Tod Gottes hinterließ, mit Idolen der heillosen Profanität zu füllen. Lutz-Bachmann (1997, 84). Brittain sagt, Adorno wollte theologische Momente nur negativ nutzen, "um das existierende Leben aufzusperren" (Brittain 2010, 8). Radikal ist Houseman, der in Adornos Philosophie "negative Eschatologie" sieht (Houseman 2013). Alle diese Interpretationen gehen allerdings davon aus, dass Adornos "Theologie" weitgehend negativ sei.

wird von Seel als der dominierende positive Gehalt Adornos vermutlich negativer Philosophie begriffen.

Seel versteht jedoch, obwohl er mit seiner These eine schwierige Herausforderung für alle Anhänger der negativen Interpretation von Adornos Werk vorlegt, Adornos Philosophie als eine säkulare Gedankenwelt – und verbindet sie nicht mit "Religiosität" oder "Theologie". Für ihn ist Kontemplation mit säkularer Ethik zu verbinden. Es ist aber gerade Adornos Ethik, die mithilfe säkularer Begriffe nicht adäquat verstanden werden kann. Kontemplation bildet bei Adorno nicht den Kern einer voll säkularisierten Ethik, sondern das positive Zentrum seiner "Theologie". Die gesellschaftlich realisierte Kontemplation wäre bei Adorno dem sehr nahe, was er als Erlösung bezeichnet. Adorno sehnt sich nach dem "nicht mehr feindseligen Vielen" (Adorno 1966, 16), und ein solcher Zustand wäre gerade die realisierte Kontemplation, die die Gewalt der subjektiven Willkür bricht: "Der lange, kontemplative Blick jedoch, dem Menschen und Dinge erst sich entfalten, ist immer der, in dem der Drang zum Objekt gebrochen, reflektiert ist." (Adorno 1951, 157). Adornos "Theologie" ist also nicht so weitgehend "negativ" wie üblicherweise geglaubt. Wenn also Adornos "Religiosität" näher analysiert werden soll, sollte man weiter in die angedeutete Richtung schreiten: zur Interpretation von Adornos Werkes als einer spezifischen Erlösungstheologie, die als zentrales Motiv die Kontemplation benutzt.[18]

Kontemplation scheint aber bei Adorno nicht nur den positiven Gehalt seiner nicht "auszupinselnden" Erlösung zu haben, sondern sie bildet auch die erkenntnistheoretische Basis seiner "Religiosität". Adorno lehnt zwar Offenbarung ab, aber in der Kontemplation, die stark mit der Aufmerksamkeit, die man dem Kunstwerk widmet – also mit einer ästhetischen Erfahrung –, verbunden werden soll (Seel 2004, 64-76), befindet er sich doch in unmittelbarer Nähe zum Religiösen. Denn, wie Charles Taylor bemerkte, öffnen einige Formen der Kunst eine "unsichere Grenzzone" (Taylor 2007, 545) zwischen Religion und säkularer Welt. Gerade in solch einer Zone hält sich Adorno auf: Er versucht zwar eine Grenze zwischen Glaube und Vernunft zu konstruieren, sie wird jedoch in seinem Werk vernebelt.

Aufgrund der oben genannten Ausgangspunkte von Adornos Philosophie dürfte deutlich sein, dass sie – obwohl sie radikal säkularistisch sein will – ihre Grundmotive in "religiösen" Hoffnungen auf eine so radikale Weise schöpft, dass es beträchtliche Schwierigkeiten gibt, sie als säkularistisch zu bezeichnen. Adornos Philosophie ist ebenso radikal "religiös" wie säkularistisch: Sie lehnt Offenbarung und Metaphysik ab, lebt aber aus derselben Hoffnung, die in Offenbarung und Metaphysik ihr ursprüngliches Zuhause hatten.

---

[18] Diese Aufgabe überschreitet jedoch den Rahmen dieses Textes.

Die Grenze zwischen Religion und Vernunft wird bei Adorno relativiert und überschritten. Seine Philosophie bewegt sich auf eine so paradoxe und aporetische Weise in den Grenzgebieten zwischen Religion und Vernunft, dass die Frage nach Adornos Säkularismus wahrscheinlich nicht klar beantwortet werden kann.

Wenn wir Religion im Prinzip mit dem heteronomen Offenbarungsglauben des traditionellen Judaismus und Christentums gleichsetzen, dann lässt sich sagen, dass Adornos Philosophie säkularistisch ist. Das ist jedoch eine einseitige Interpretation: hängt Religion nicht sehr eng mit den religiösen Gefühlen und Sehnsüchten zusammen, die Adorno zu den Grundlagen seiner Philosophie macht, dass sie vielleicht von Religion gar nicht getrennt werden können?

Aus der Perspektive, die Religion mit Offenbarung oder Ritual gleichsetzt, konstruiert Adorno eine klare Grenze zwischen Religion und Nicht-Religion, wobei er Religion als minderwertig und überwunden ansieht. Aus dieser Sicht wäre Adorno also radikal säkularistisch. Wenn aber Religion nicht mit Offenbarung, sondern eher mit religiösen Hoffnungen – auf die Negation des Todes, auf Erlösung oder absolute Gerechtigkeit – zu verbinden wäre, dann wäre Adornos Philosophie "religiös". Sie wäre als eine Erlösungstheologie anzusehen. "Religiös" scheint hier eine bessere Bezeichnung als "postsäkular" zu sein, denn bei Adorno fehlt das Bewusstsein davon, dass Religion nicht zu überwinden ist. Es fehlt die subjektive Facette des Postsäkularismus, ohne die es keinen Postsäkularismus gibt.

Aber das, was bei Adorno als "religiös" verstanden werden kann, mag leicht "postsäkular" werden: als eine Inspiration für postsäkulare Philosophie. Diese Inspiration besteht in der bewussten Ablehnung, darin, von den religiösen Hoffnungen abzulassen, die sie als unentbehrlich erkannt werden. Die postsäkulare Inspiration, die Adorno bringt, besteht also in einem "Bewusstsein von dem, was unentbehrlich ist". Das ist der Kern von Adornos "Religiosität". Adorno bestimmt die Grenze zwischen Religion und Vernunft auf eine säkularistische Weise, übersteigt diese Grenze aber auf eine "religiöse" Weise.

Wie ist also Adornos Philosophie zu nennen? "Religiöser Säkularismus" vermag sehr gut diese Aporie, die bei Adorno ausgemacht werden kann, zu erfassen. Denn Adorno ist einerseits radikal säkularistisch, anderseits ist er aber auch radikal religiös. Seine Philosophie kann deshalb meines Erachtens nach als "religiöser Säkularismus" bezeichnet werden.

(Post)Säkularismus bei Habermas

In welche Richtung wird dann Adornos "religiöser Säkularismus" von Habermas weiterentwickelt? Wie arbeitet Habermas mit den Motiven, die bei Adorno zu finden sind? Was bringt in dieser Hinsicht die "postsäkulare Wende"?

Wenn die Frage nach dem Vorhandensein der subjektiven Facette des Postsäkularismus – dem postsäkularen Bewusstsein – bei Habermas gestellt wird, dann ist die Antwort ziemlich klar: Er ist postsäkular. Habermas ist ein Philosoph, der zumindest seit der Jahrtausendwende einen postsäkularen Diskurs geführt hat; man kann wahrscheinlich sogar behaupten, dass Habermas das Konzept des Postsäkularismus durch seine *agenda setting power* in akademischen Zirkeln populär gemacht hat.

Wie manifestiert sich das postsäkulare Bewusstsein bei Habermas? Warum bezweifelt er die säkularistische Konstruktion der Grenze zwischen Religion und Nicht-Religion?

Wie schon oben erwähnt wurde, ist für Habermas eine Gesellschaft postsäkular, die "sich auf das Fortbestehen religiöser Gemeinschaften in einer fortwährend säkularisierenden Umgebung einstellt" (Habermas 2001, 10). Habermas selbst will diese Vorstellung realisieren, indem er Religion als einen Dialogpartner akzeptiert. Das ist ein wesentlicher Unterschied zu Adorno. Habermas ist an einem Dialog mit Religion interessiert, während Adornos Philosophie daran keine Interesse hat.

Das postsäkulare Hinterfragen beginnt bei Habermas damit, dass er – im Unterschied zu Adorno – Religion als eine potentiell rationale Größe anerkennt, denn nur dann kann es einen echten Dialog geben. Habermas spricht in diesem Sinne davon, dass Religion nicht mehr als irrational angesehen werden kann.[19] Er schreibt: "Ich verteidige in diesem Streit Hegels These, dass die großen Religionen zur Geschichte der Vernunft selbst gehören." (Habermas 2005, 12-13). Hier wird also der Status der Religion als etwas Minderwertiges – konkret Irrationales – in Frage gestellt.

Vielleicht am eindrucksvollsten ist bei Habermas aber die Analyse der Schwächen der säkularen Vernunft: Habermas sagt nicht nur, dass Religion nicht mehr als irrational angesehen werden kann, sondern er zeigt auch Aspekte auf, die er für wichtig hält und die dem Glauben im Gegensatz zur Vernunft zur Verfügung stehen. Hier spricht er von "einem Bewusstsein von dem, was fehlt". (Habermas 2009, 408). Das heißt, Habermas erhöht nicht nur den Status von Religion (er sagt, Religion sei nicht irrational), sondern erniedrigt auch den Status der Vernunft (er meint, dass der Vernunft bewusst ist, dass ihr etwas fehlt). Dadurch will er den Dialog zwischen Religion und Vernunft ermöglichen.

---

[19] Ab und zu scheint Habermas ein wirklicher Verteidiger der Religion zu sein – z. B. wenn er sie gegen die Beschuldigung zu befreien versucht, dass eine Beziehung zu Gott masochistisch sei. (Vgl. Calhoun, Mendieta, Van Antverpen 2013, 640-644).

Was fehlt also dem "Bewusstsein von dem, was fehlt"? Das Erste, das Habermas bei der Vernunft vermisst, sind die Quellen der bürgerlichen Solidarität. Habermas spricht davon, dass die Vernunft ein Defizit bezüglich der Motivation, solidarisch zu sein, aufweist (Calhoun, Mendieta, Van Antverpen 2013, 619-621). Auch betont er, dass seine Philosophie, die die ethischen Fragen des guten Lebens *ad acta* gelegt hat, Solidarität keinesfalls erzwingen kann. Sie ist vielmehr an die Bereitschaft der Lebensformen zur Solidarität angewiesen.

Das ist aber nicht alles, obwohl fehlende Solidarität bei Habermas der stärkste Grund für eine Zusammenarbeit mit der Religion zu sein scheint.[20] Habermas ist sich auch bewusst, dass seine Philosophie im Vergleich zur Religion keine Erlösung verheißen und keinen Trost bringen kann. Das ist zwar in seinen Augen eine gut begründete Bescheidenheit, trotzdem ist es zugleich aber auch eine Schwäche der säkularen Vernunft. Habermas spricht von der "prinzipiellen Trostlosigkeit des philosophischen Denkens" (Habermas 2009, 46). Es ist klar, dass für säkulare Vernunft, wenn sie in Verbindung mit Lebensformen bleiben soll – und für Habermas ist säkulare Vernunft sicherlich nicht nur ein abstraktes, vom Leben getrenntes Denken, sondern sie entspringt einer agnostischen Lebensform, die also genauso trostlos ist wie ihre Philosophie –, muss die Trostlosigkeit ein tiefes Problem darstellen.[21]

Das Problem der Trostlosigkeit zeigt sich bei Habermas – und hier knüpft er an Adorno an – vor allem bei existenziellen Grundfragen wie bei der Forderung nach einer absoluten Gerechtigkeit und beim Protest gegen Tod. Das erwähnt Habermas schon in seiner Friedenspreisrede aus dem Jahre 2001, wo er in Anknüpfung an die Diskussion der ersten Generation der Frankfurter Schule über die Irreversibilität vergangenen Leidens sagt, "die verlorene Hoffnung auf Resurrektion hinterlässt eine spürbare Leere", und nicht einmal die Skepsis gegenüber dem Glauben "dementiert […] nicht den ohnmächtigen Impuls, am Unabänderlichen doch noch etwas zu ändern". Und er fügt hinzu: "Die ungläubigen Söhne und Töchter der Moderne scheinen in solchen Augenblicken zu glauben, einander mehr

---

[20] In der Tat scheint es manchmal, als ob Habermas am Dialog mit Religion nur interessiert sei, weil er in ihr eine wichtige Quelle der Solidarität sieht und einen potentiellen Helfer bei der Sorge, die ihn niederdrückt. Dieser Eindruck wurde in der Kritik der Funktionalisierung der Religion ausgedrückt. "Funktionalisierung" ist in diesem Sinne negativ, als eine Reduktion, angesehen (vgl. Habermas 2010, 79).

[21] Adorno fühlt sicher auch, dass Vernunft im Vergleich zum Glauben etwas verloren hat: bei ihm finden wir ja auch "ein Bewusstsein davon, was fehlt". Das folgt schon aus dem ersten oben genanten Zitat – Vernunft kann dem irdischen Geschehen keinen metaphysischen "Sinn einhauchen" und muss deswegen aufs "Sinnlose hinstarren". Bei Adorno ist Philosophie also in gewissem Sinne trostlos, jedoch glaubt er, dass er diese Trostlosigkeit im Rahmen des säkularen Denkens kompensieren kann (vgl. unten).

schuldig zu sein und selbst mehr nötig zu haben, als ihnen von der religiösen Tradition in Übersetzung zugänglich ist – so, als seien deren semantische Potenziale noch nicht ausgeschöpft (Habermas 2001, 13-14).

Vom Tod spricht Habermas auch im Zusammenhang mit dem Wunsch des Agnostikers Max Frisch, der den Wunsch äußerte, dass seine Totenfeier in der Kirche stattfindet. Habermas denkt, Frisch "hat offenbar die Peinlichkeit nichtreligiöser Bestattungsformen empfunden und durch die Wahl des Ortes öffentlich die Tatsache dokumentiert, dass die aufgeklärte Moderne kein angemessenes Äquivalent für eine religiöse Bewältigung des letzten, eine Lebensgeschichte abschließenden *rite de passage* gefunden hat" (Habermas 2009: 408).

Bei Habermas können bezüglich dessen, was der säkularen Vernunft fehlt, mindestens drei Bereiche genannt werden: fehlende Quellen der Solidarität, Trostlosigkeit im Bezug auf Grundfragen wie absolute Gerechtigkeit oder Hoffnung auf Auferstehung, sowie das Fehlen eines würdigen Übergangsritus.[22]

Das postsäkulare Hinterfragen bei Habermas geht also so weit, dass er Religion als etwas, was anders ist als Vernunft und was zugleich nicht irrational ist, ansieht und, dass sie dadurch, dass sie Zugriff zu einigen wichtigen Potenzialen wie Hoffnung, Trost, Quellen der Solidarität usw. hat, potenziell sehr wertvoll ist. Dadurch wird nicht nur der Status der Religion aufgewertet, sie wird auch als eigenständig erkannt. So gesehen, erscheint Glaube bei Habermas nicht als etwas, was das säkularistische Bewusstsein für minderwertig und irrational halten würde, sondern als eine vollwertige Lebensform, die sogar etwas bieten kann, was säkulare Vernunft nur mit Nostalgie aus ihrer eigenen Distanz heraus betrachten kann.[23]

Um von der Religion lernen zu können, will Habermas einen Dialog zwischen Religion und Vernunft beginnen. Wie schon oben erwähnt, denkt er, dass Religion inspirierend für die Vernunft sein kann, indem ihre Inhalte in die säkulare (oder – wie Habermas sagt – "allgemein zugängliche") Sprache übersetzt werden. Die religiösen Inhalte mögen von säkularer Vernunft angenommen werden, wenn sie von ihrem opaken Kern (siehe unten) befreit werden und in die allgemein zugängliche Sprache übersetzt werden. So

---

[22] Das, was fehlt, analysiert auch Brieskorn, der zu gewissermaßen unterschiedlichen Ergebnissen kommt: es fehlen Übergangsritus, Solidarität und Motivation zur Solidarität, Sicherheit über die Fundamente der Legitimität und religiös begründete Meinungen in der Öffentlichkeit (Brieskorn, 2010, 30-31). Brieskorn konzentriert sich mehr auf die politischen Schwerpunkte bei Habermas; es gibt jedoch auch die "religiösen".

[23] Bei Habermas war das nicht immer so. Junker-Kenny oder auch Harrington unterscheiden beispielsweise drei Phasen seiner Beziehung zur Religion, wobei nur die dritte so entgegenkommend ist (Junker-Kenny 2011, 4; Harrington 2007, 543-544).

kann z.B. die religiöse Vorstellung, dass der Mensch ein Bild Gottes sei, in die Kategorie der menschlichen Würde übersetzt werden. Es gibt also auch die Möglichkeit, durch den Dialog die Grenzen zwischen Religion und Nicht-Religion zu überschreiten.

Auf dem Weg zum Postsäkularismus bezweifelt Habermas also die überlegene Rolle der Vernunft gegenüber der Religion (Religion ist nicht irrational, Vernunft vermisst einige wichtige Elemente wie Hoffnung), und konstruiert ein Modell der Grenzübergänge zwischen Religion und Nicht-Religion (Dialog und Übersetzung).

Doch hat das postsäkulare Hinterfragen bei Habermas auch seine Grenzen; es gibt auch wichtige Anteile des Säkularismus bei ihm. Habermas hält seine Philosophie für einen Hüter der Grenzen zwischen Nicht-Religion und Religion: die öffentliche Rolle der Philosophie sei es, "Hüterin der Rationalität, die sich ihrer eigenen Fehlbarkeit bewusst bleibt," (Habermas 2009, 16) zu sein. Für Habermas ist Philosophie strikt mit Vernunft und Wissen zu verbinden, Glaube gehört nicht zur Philosophie. So hören wir bei Habermas wiederholte Warnungen vor solchen Philosophien, die sich in Religion verwickeln. Habermas spricht z.B. von "schwärmerischer Philosophie, die sich verheißungsvolle Konnotationen eines erlösungsreligiösen Wortschatzes nur ausleiht und zunutze macht, um sich von der Strenge diskursiven Denkens zu dispensieren" (Habermas 2005, 257). Von diesem Blickwinkel aus betrachtet ist es also für Habermas sehr wichtig, Wissen vom Glauben und Vernunft von Religion klar zu unterscheiden, und die Vernunft vor potenziellen (auch religiösen) Irrationalität zu schützen.

Wie bestimmt Habermas die Grenze zwischen Nicht-Religion und Religion, Wissen und Glauben? Hier muss gesagt werden, dass es eine ganz klare Trennung – trotz des großen Gewichts, das Habermas dieser Trennung beimisst – nicht gibt. So spricht Habermas nicht von einer Linie, die Wissen und Glauben teilen würde, sondern von einem Grenzbereich.[24] Außerdem schreibt er an einer anderen Stelle, die Beziehung von Wissen und Glauben sei unklar: "[Die säkulare Vernunft] ist über das Opake ihres nur scheinbar geklärten Verhältnisses zur Religion beunruhigt" (Habermas 2009, 408).

Trotzdem kann bei Habermas eine Grenze zwischen Wissen und Glauben gefunden werden. So spricht er z.B. über Offenbarungsglauben und rituelle Praktiken als wichtige Teilungskriterien: "Rituelle Praktiken bezeugen ein frühes Stadium in der Entwickelungsgeschichte des Geistes…. Dieser Umstand ist es, der die Religion – unerbittlicher noch als die Autorität der Offenbarung – von allen säkularen Gestalten des Geistes trennt" (Habermas 2009, 32). Die Elemente der Religion, welche die säkulare

---

[24] Habermas sagt: "Der Grenzbereich zwischen Philosophie und Religion ist (…) vermintes Gelände" (Habermas 2001, 14).

Vernunft nicht annehmen kann, wären also die Autorität der Offenbarung sowie rituelle Praktiken. In dieser Hinsicht unterscheidet sich Habermas' Auffassung von Religion nicht viel von der Adorno's: die Vernunft denkt, Religion sei unvernünftig, weil sie einer Autorität glauben "muss" und weil sie Rituale durchführt, die der Vernunft irrational zu sein scheinen.[25]

Das hat wichtige Konsequenzen. Wenn Habermas Wissen vom Glauben abgrenzt, zeigt sich deutlich, dass der Glaube bei ihm – trotz seiner Bemühung Religion als Dialogpartner wahrzunehmen – noch immer als minderwertig wahrgenommen wird, und zwar in einem ähnlichem Sinn wie bei Adorno. Habermas scheint – wie sich aus dem oben genannten Zitat ergibt – Offenbarungsglauben noch im säkularistischen Sinne mit autoritativer Heteronomie zu verbinden und rituelle Praktiken mit einer irrationalen kollektiven Ebene, die die diskursive Ebene zu vermeiden sucht.

Spuren von dieser Auffassung von Religion findet man auch an anderen Stellen im späten Werk Habermas', vor allem dort, wo er sein postmetaphysisches Denken von Religion abgrenzt. So besteht das postmetaphysische Denken in "der Differenz zwischen Glaubensgewissheiten und öffentlich kritisierbaren Geltungsansprüchen" (Habermas 2005, 149) Religionen haben Habermas zufolge einen "opaken Kern" (Habermas 2005, 150), er schreibt ihnen "diskursive Exterritorialität" (Habermas 2005, 135) zu, und die Berufung auf "die dogmatische Autorität eines unantastbaren Kerns von infalliblen Offenbarungswahrheiten" (Habermas 2005, 135), wodurch sie sich "*vorbehaltsloser diskursiver Erörterung entziehen*" (Habermas 2005, 135). Der religiöse Kern bleibt daher "dem diskursiven Denken [...] abgründig fremd" (Habermas 2005, 150).

Aus den oben genannten Zitaten folgt, dass Habermas der Auffassung ist, dass Wissen klar oder verständlich sei, Glaube dagegen opak. Wissen sei fallibel, kritisierbar und dadurch unsicher, Glaube dagegen eher dogmatisch und dadurch sicher. Wissen sei eher autonom, Glaube eher autoritativ. Die Unterscheidung des Wissens vom Glauben ist also mit Andeutungen eines Mangels an kognitiver Fähigkeit und Autonomie verbunden.[26] Inwieweit unterscheiden sich diese Einwände von denen, die Adorno für relevant hält? Die

---

[25] Ohne hier eine komplexe Analyse der Benutzung des Begriffes "Ritual" bei Adorno durchzuführen, kann behauptet werden, dass sich bei Adorno viele Stellen finden, an denen Adorno den Begriff eindeutig pejorativ benutzt: vor allem im Zusammenhang mit Irrationalität, die auch in Aufklärung eingeschlichen ist. Z.B.: "Der Antisemitismus ist ein eingeschliffenes Schema, ja ein Ritual der Zivilisation, und die Pogrome sind die wahren Ritualmorde." (Adorno (966, 207-208).

[26] Habermas drückt hier aber nicht nur seine falschen Vorurteile aus, dass das Problem in der Undurchdringlichkeit der religiösen Überzeugungen besteht. Das Problem liegt eher darin, dass auch die Ablehnung dieser Undurchdringlichkeit selbst undurchdringlich ist – dahinter steckt "der opake Kern" eines Entschlusses, agnostisch zu sein. Die Ausgangspunkte der agnostischen Philosophie bleiben in der gleichen Dunkelheit wie bei religiös orientierten Philosophien.

Argumente sind ähnlich, nämlich säkularistisch: beide Autoren vermissen Autonomie und halten Abstand von dem, was sie für den autoritativen Charakter des Glaubens halten.[27]

Ähnlich sind aber nicht nur diese Einwände, sondern auch die zugrunde liegende Vorstellung, dass die Religion mit ihren traditionellen Formen (Christentum, Judentum) zu identifizieren ist.[28] Habermas denkt – im Unterschied zu Adorno – sicher auch an den Islam, das ist aber ein eher unerheblicher Unterschied. Denn grundsätzlich bleibt der Bereich der Religion gleich, und der Charakter der Grenze zwischen Vernunft und Religion ändert sich nur teilweise: er bleibt im Kern säkularistisch.

Gerade hier mag der schwächste Punkt seines Versuchs, einen Dialog mit der Religion zu beginnen, gefunden werden, da Adornos Auffassung von Religion einen Inbegriff des Säkularismus darstellt. Die "postsäkulare Wende" vermag, wenn sie mit diesem Konzept weiterarbeitet, den Säkularismus zwar schwächen, aber nicht beseitigen.[29]

Der Versuch, Religion als Partner anzunehmen, wird also durch Überreste des Säkularismus gestört. Im Hintergrund bleibt die säkularistische Überzeugung, dass klare Grenzen zwischen Religion und Nicht-Religion gezogen werden müssen. Philosophie versteht ihre eigene Rolle als Rolle der "Hüterin" dieser Grenze. Diese Überzeugung erwächst aus dem tiefen säkularistischen Eindruck, Religion sei auf irgendeine Weise gefährlich und minderwertig. Gefährlich sei sie vor allem politisch gesehen – wenn irrationale Gehalte die politische Diskussion durchdringen, bestehe die Gefahr, dass Argumente in Gottes Willen verwandelt würden. Minderwertig sei Religion auch in kognitivem Sinne – sie dispensiere sich von der Strenge der diskursiven, argumentativen Rede.

Adornos Säkularismus wird also geschwächt, aber nicht beseitigt. Wie geht dann Habermas mit Adornos "Bewusstsein von dem, was unentbehrlich ist", also mit seiner Religiosität, um?

Adornos "religiöses" Projekt wird von Habermas im Namen des nachmetaphysischen Denkens abgelehnt. Das Konzept der Religion bleibt ähnlich, aber das Konzept der Vernunft hat sich geändert: das nachmetaphysische Denken kann nicht mehr

---

[27] Eine ausführlichere Analyse mag auch Unterschiede zeigen (wozu auch der veränderte Status der Religion gezählt werden könne) – an dieser Stelle werden aber die Ähnlichkeiten betont.

[28] Die Diskussion über das Konzept der Religion sollte viel differenzierter sein. Das Konzept der Religion muss auf die Feststellungen, die religiöse Elemente in säkularen Gesellschaftsformen suchen und finden, Rücksicht nehmen (siehe z.B. Luckmann 2014).

[29] Casanova spricht in diesem Sinne davon, dass bei Habermas das "Stadialbewusstsein", also die Vorstellung, dass nach einer Phase der Entwicklung des Geistes eine andere, ihr übergeordnete Phase, folgt. In diesem Zusammenhang bleiben dann Offenbarungsglaube oder Ritual für Habermas überwunden (Lutz-Bachmann 2015, 28). Pritchard fürchtet sogar, dass es bei Habermas mehr um Konfliktprävention gehe, als darum, Religion ernst zu nehmen (Pritchard 2010).

das Projekt der Erlösung verfolgen. Habermas schreibt, dass "sich die Vernunft mit einem solchen Projekt überfordert" (Habermas 2001, 14). An einer anderen Stelle – wie schon oben erwähnt – warnt er vor religiöser Philosophie, "die schwärmerisch die methodische Grenze zwischen Glauben und Wissen zu überschreiten versucht" (Habermas 2009, 32). Obwohl Habermas solche Sorte von Warnung meistens auf Heidegger bezieht, kann der Leser sich des Eindrucks nicht erwehren, dass sich diese Worte auch auf Adornos Thesen beziehen ließen.[30] Die nachmetaphysische Vernunft weist einen wesentlichen Unterschied zu Adornos kontemplativer Vernunft auf, die *solidarisch mit Metaphysik im Augenblick ihres Sturzes* sein will.

Dort, wo bei Adorno "Religiosität" identifiziert werden kann, die ihren Ausdruck in einer Art kontemplativen Erlösungstheologie findet, kommt es bei Habermas zu einer starken Säkularisierung: die geradezu mystische, nicht auszumalende und unrealisierbare Erlösung wird zur formal ausgedrückten idealisierenden Bedingungen der kommunikativen Verständigung im Milieu der universal realisierten Menschenrechte.[31] Diese Entwicklung wird durch eine erkenntnistheoretische "Intersubjektivierung" gekennzeichnet: die "prophetische" Qualität, die in der individuellen und intersubjektiv schwer fassbaren kontemplativen Erfahrung Adornos zu Hause ist, wird zu den "allgemein zugänglichen" Formulierungen der kommunikativen Vernunft.

Es ist keine Überraschung, dass Habermas nicht nur Adornos Religiosität ablehnt, sondern auch seine ästhetische Erfahrung, in der diese Religiosität wurzelt. Er sagt, Kunst bleibe "in einer symbolischen, aber nichtsprachlichen Kommunikation verwurzelt", und lasse sich dann "begrifflich einkreisen und erläutern, aber nicht restlos in expliziten Urteilen einholen" (Habermas 2012, 75). Philosophie aber soll – Habermas zufolge – vorbehaltlos dem sprachlichen Umgang geöffnet bleiben. Daraus folgt, dass ästhetische Erfahrung nicht mehr die Grundlage der Philosophie bilden darf.

Habermas ist "religiös unmusikalisch", das mag aber darin die Ursache haben, dass er verglichen mit Adorno "unmusikalisch" ist. Wenn Adorno die Mühe das sprachlich auszudrücken, was er in ästhetischer Kontemplation erfahren hat, aufgeben müsste, hätte er es als "Opfer des Intellekts" interpretiert, ähnlich wie im Falle des unproblematischen Offen-

---

[30] Adorno sieht eigentlich alles als "vernünftig" an, was er in persönlicher Erfahrung (geistige Erfahrung, ungeschmälerte Erfahrung, unreglementierte Erfahrung) finden und dann konzeptualisieren kann. So schöpft er sehr viel aus seiner ästhetischen Erfahrung. Das postmetaphysische Denken lehnt aber nicht nur religiöse Wahrheiten ab, sondern gerade auch die ästhetische Erfahrung (Habermas 2005, 150).

[31] Die universal realisierten Menschenrechte bezeichnet Habermas im Essay *Zur Verfassung Europas* als seine "realistische Utopie" (Habermas 2011). Kommunikative Vernunft als Habermas'sche Utopie wird z. B. von Münz-Koenen analysiert (1997, 141-201).

barungsglaubens. Indem er dieses Opfer ablehnt, stützt er sich auf die Grenzen dessen, was sprachlich ausgedrückt werden kann. Anders ist es bei Habermas, für den eine Erfahrung, die nicht mehr begrifflich gefasst werden kann, nicht mehr zur Philosophie gehört. Für Adorno war Erfahrung wichtiger als Sprache, für Habermas ist Philosophie mit Sprache zu identifizieren.

Adornos aporetische Grenzüberschreitung zwischen Vernunft und Religion wird von Habermas als unhaltbar begriffen und zurückgewiesen: in der Zukunft sollen die Grenzübergänge zwischen Vernunft und Religion von Übersetzung gehütet, die Habermas als verlässlicher sieht. Das adornosche "Unentbehrliche" wird bei Habermas zum Fehlenden; das Bewusstsein von dem, was unentbehrlich ist, wird zum Bewusstsein von dem, was fehlt.[32]

Das ist eine reduktionistische Entwicklung: Habermas ist im Vergleich zu Adorno reduktionistich in dem Sinne, dass seine Philosophie einige Bereiche des Denkens verlässt. Es ist eine Art weicher Reduktionismus: Habermas begrenzt unsere Welt nicht auf Philosophie; die religiösen oder ästhetischen Wahrheiten mögen außerhalb der Philosophie weiterleben. Wenn also vom Reduktionismus gesprochen werden soll, dann nur vom "philosophischen" Reduktionismus, der darin besteht, dass religiöse Philosophie *de facto* verboten wird.[33] Es könnte von einer "Demokratisierung" der Philosophie gesprochen werden: die religiösen Hoffnungen, die nur auf eine individuelle, "kontemplative" Weise erfahren und nicht von allen geteilt werden können, werden zu Gute einer allgemeinen Zugänglichkeit von den zu diskutierenden Gehalten ausgeschlossen.

Die Analyse der Grenzkonstruktion zwischen Religion und Nicht-Religion bei Habermas zeigt also ambivalente Ergebnisse. Einerseits bezweifelt Habermas das säkularistische Vorurteil, dass die Irrationalität von Religion postuliert, erkennt Schwächen der Vernunft und schafft Übergänge zwischen Religion und Vernunft. Anderseits beharrt Habermas mit Nachdruck auf der säkularistischen Trennung zwischen Religion und Nicht-Religion, wobei bei dieser Trennung im Kern Merkmale der religiösen Minderwertigkeit im Vergleich zur Vernunft erhalten bleiben. Darüber hinaus lehnt er Adornos Religiosität ab, geht also von Adorno in gewissem Sinne in Richtung Säkularisierung und Reduktionismus.

---

[32] Sicher finden wir ein Bewusstsein davon, was fehlt, auch bei Adorno. So können wir Adorno zufolge z.B. dem Geschehen nicht mehr den metaphysischen Sinn einhauchen. Dieses Bewusstsein des Fehlenden wurde aber bei Habermas radikalisiert: Adorno besteht darauf, dass einige religiöse Motive bewahrt werden sollen und müssen, Habermas denkt aber, dass Philosophie diese Motive nicht weiter bewahren kann. Sie werden zum Fehlenden.

[33] Der Grund dafür, warum es sich um Reduktionismus (also um etwas negativ zu Bewertendes) handelt, besteht darin, dass das, was aus unserer Sprache verschwindet, zum totalen Verschwinden tendiert.

Es kann gesagt werden, dass Adornos "religiöser Säkularismus" bei Habermas zu einem "postsäkularen Säkularismus" wurde.

Obwohl also Habermas das postsäkulare Bewusstsein zeigt – er will Religion als Gesprächspartner annehmen und ist sich der Schwächen der Vernunft bewusst –, ist fraglich, ob Habermas als "postsäkular" zu bezeichnen ist, was die Arbeit mit der Grenze zwischen Religion und Nicht-Religion angeht. Dies hängt von der Position des Menschen, der es beurteilein soll – für einen verbissenen Säkularisten mag Habermas unnötige und potenziell gefährliche "dialogische Sentimente"[34] erwecken, während einige Theologen Habermas stark kritisieren;[35] der Mittelweg nimmt nüchterne Stellung ein.[36] Jedenfalls geht es aber im Vergleich zu Adorno um eine sowohl erkenntnistheoretische als auch inhaltliche Säkularisierung.

Fazit

Wie ist also die postsäkulare Wende in der kritischen Theorie – als die Entwicklung von Adorno zu Habermas – zu bewerten?

Adornos Philosophie ist nicht als "postsäkular" zu bezeichnen, da sie eine rationalistische Kritik an der Religion übt und ein starkes Säkularisierungsprogramm verfolgt. Vielmehr entwickelt Adorno einen "religiösen Säkularismus", der in der strikten Trennung von Vernunft und Religion besteht. Er ist zudem der Meinung, dass Offenbarungsglaube irrational sei. Eine solche Vorgehensweise ist typisch säkularistisch: es gibt eine klare Unterscheidung zwischen Religion und Nicht-Religion, wobei Religion als minderwertig wahrgenommen wird. Dieser Säkularismus ist aber bei Adorno ein religiöser: Er ist sich dessen bewusst, was an der Religion unentbehrlich ist.

Wenn postsäkulare Inspirationen bei Adorno gesucht werden sollen, die durch die Hinterfragung der säkularistischen Linie zwischen Religion und Nicht-Religion gekennzeichnet sind, dann findet man sie in Adornos "Religiosität": er geht vom Bewusstsein der Schuld aus, und beharrt, um sie zu überwinden, auf religiösen Hoffnungen, die sich vor allem auf die Negation des absoluten Todes, der Erlösung und der absoluten

---

[34] So bewertet McLennan die dialogischen Bemühungen von Habermas (McLennan 2007, 857).
[35] Sehr kritisch stellt sich zu Habermas z.B. Adams (2006, 3). Habermas sei "zu positiv im Hinblick auf Religion und zu ignorant im Hinblick auf Theologie". Es gibt jedoch mehrere kritische, theologische Reaktionen: Norbert Brieskorn warnt beispielsweise vor gegenseitigem Betrug, der bei gelegentlichen Allianzen drohe. Elisabeth Pritchard macht auf ein ähnliches Element aufmerksam und denkt, es gehe mehr um Prävention der Konflikte als um Dialog (cf. Habermas 2010, 24; Pritchard 2010).
[36] So hält Lutz-Bachmann Habermas' öffentliche Vernunft für "eine postsäkulare Antwort auf die szientistische Rationalität" (Lutz-Bachmann, 2015, 82).

Gerechtigkeit beziehen. Diese Motive wären als "ein Bewusstsein von dem, was unentbehrlich ist", zu bezeichnen. Adorno weiß, dass einige religiöse Motive viel mehr als bloße Irrationalität sind, und er erkennt sie als unabdingbar an. Dieses Bewusstsein bewegt ihn dazu, dass er nicht nur den Theismus, sondern auch den Atheismus kritisiert, und sich gegen reduktionistische Philosophien wendet, die das, was unentbehrlich ist, abschaffen wollen.

Adornos aporetische Philosophie kann wahrscheinlich nicht festgehalten werden, denn ihre inneren Spannungen und Kontradiktionen sind zu groß: Adorno wollte eigentlich eine materialistische Philosophie entwickeln. Habermas wählt nun einen Weg, der sowohl Adornos Säkularismus als auch Religiosität ablehnen will. Den Säkularismus leht er ab, indem er seine "postsäkulare Wende" durchführt. Er schwächt das säkularistische Vorurteil, dass Religion irrational sei, identifiziert die Schwächen der Vernunft und will mit der Religion einen Dialog führen, um diese Schwächen kompensieren zu können. Religiosität lehnt er ab, indem er sie für eine Überlastung der Vernunft hält, und sich von den Grenzgebieten zwischen Religion und Vernunft, zurückzieht. Habermas macht Adornos "religiösen Säkularismus" zu einem "postsäkularen Säkularismus".

Diese Entwicklung weist aber zwei wesentliche Probleme auf. Das erste Problem ist das Verständnis von Religion, das ähnlich ist wie bei Adorno: die Trennung zwischen Religion und Nicht-Religion, die Habermas vertritt, sein Konzept der Religion, ist im Kern säkularistisch. Dieses Konzept geht nämlich ursprünglich gerade davon aus, dass Religion irrational und gefährlich ist. Obwohl Habermas sich sehr bemüht, dieses Vorurteil zu beseitigen, vertritt er es doch in einer abgeschwächten Form. Wieder und wieder schleichen sich stille Vorurteile gegen Religion in seine postsäkulare Philosophie ein. So seien Rituale ein Zeichen für ein "frühes Stadium in der Entwicklungsgeschichte des Geistes", religiöse Überzeugungen versuchten "sich dogmatisch der Strenge des diskursiven Denkens zu entziehen" usw. Ist Wissen und Glauben wirklich auf diese Weise zu trennen? Hat Wissen wirklich keine unreflektierten Vorurteile, die sich auch der Strenge der diskursiven Argumentation entziehen?

Das zweite Problem besteht darin, dass die Wende zwar "postsäkular" zu sein scheint, aber faktisch, von Adorno ausgehend, auf gewisse Weise in Richtung Säkularismus verläuft, da sie Adornos Religiosität ablehnt: das, was man bei Adorno "Bewusstsein von dem, was unentbehrlich ist" nennen kann, wird bei Habermas zu einem "Bewusstsein von dem, was fehlt". Adornos Philosophie ist eine "religiöse" Philosophie der Religion, Habermas' Philosophie ist eine irreligiöse Philosophie neben der Religion. Das stellt eine wesentliche Säkularisierung einer *de facto* religiösen Philosophie dar. Kann diese Säkularisierung wirklich als eine postsäkulare Wende verstanden werden? Ist der Verlust der Möglichkeit, eine religiöse Philosophie zu entwickeln, nicht ein zu hoher Preis, den das nachmetaphysische Denken bezahlen muss?

Im Bezug auf diese Probleme gibt es für die postsäkulare Wende zwei große Fragen. Die erste Frage lautet, ob an einem Verständnis von Religion, das diese mit einem irrationalen oder zumindest dogmatischen Offenbarungsglauben gleichsetzt, weiterhin festgehalten werden kann. Geht es hier nicht um eine wesentliche Unterschätzung der Rationalität der Religion, um eine veraltete Abgrenzung gegen die mächtige Kirche und deren Unterdrückung von menschlichen Überzeugungen und autonomer Vernunft? Die mächtige Institution Kirche ist im Prinzip eine Sache der Vergangenheit: sie existiert nicht mehr. Ist Religion nicht ganz anders zu verstehen? Ist es nicht gerade das adorno'sche und Habermas'sche Konzept von Religion, das den Grundstein des Säkularismus darstellt und das – um postsäkular zu werden – abgebaut werden muss?

Die zweite Frage lautet, ob das, was Adorno als unentbehrlich identifiziert hat, aufgegeben werden kann. Darf das, was unentbehrlich ist, zum Fehlenden werden? Soll Adornos "Religiosität" durch postsäkulare Wende säkularisiert werden?

Habermas will religiöse Gehalte nicht leugnen: er lässt sie neben der Philosophie weiter leben. Ist es aber nicht gerade die Philosophie, die – neben der Theologie – als der einzige Ort für die Reflexion dieser Gehalte verstanden werden soll? Stellt das *de facto* Verbot der religiösen Philosophie der Religion nicht ein stilles Vertreiben der Religion von einer der letzten Domänen, wo sie sich in der säkularen Zeit noch aufhalten durfte dar? Die Säkularisierung der Philosophie in der Entwicklung von Adorno zu Habermas führt zu einem spürbaren Verlust: die Gehalte, die so wichtig wie unentbehrlich sein mögen, dürfen in einem traditionellen Bereich nicht mehr auftauchen.

Diese säkularisierende Entwicklung kann nicht nur als inhaltliche, sondern auch als eine erkenntnistheoretische Wende angesehen werden: Adornos Ansichten sind in seiner subjektivistisch verfärbten "Kontemplation" entstanden, die eine unsichere Grenzzone zwischen säkularer Welt und Religion bildet, während die Habermas'sche Philosophie im Rahmen der wesentlich intersubjektiven kommunikativen Vernunft entsteht. Habermas sieht diese Entwicklung als eine nötige: "prophetische" Untertöne, die mehr monologisch als dialogisch entstehen,[37] mögen Irrationales und Gefährliches tragen – deswegen auch Warnungen vor religiösen Philosophie. In der "normalisierenden" Intersubjektivisierung, die Adornos Kontemplation auf dem Wege zur Habermas'schen kommunikativen Vernunft

---

[37] Adornos Philosophie ist monologisch in dem Sinne, dass sie nicht einfach mit anderen Menschen geteilt werden kann; es rühren Behauptungen und Inhalte, die wohl nicht argumentativ gerechtfertigt werden können. Als Beispiel kann hier die Hoffnung auf absolute Gerechtigkeit benutzt werden. Warum soll sie unentbehrlich sein? Da mag Vernunft stehen bleiben.

durchläuft, geht die religiöse Qualität verloren. Der Habermas'sche Säkularismus ist also ein erkenntnistheoretischer.

Die Frage, die der dialogischen Philosophie in Anknüpfung an Adorno gestellt werden sollte, lautet, ob diese Dimension wirklich geopfert werden darf – ob gerade sie nicht den richtigen Ausgangspunkt zur Diskussion mit Religion darstellt.[38] Ist die epistemologische Wende, die die Gefahr ablehnt, nicht durch eine Begrenzung der Reichweite des Denkens gekennzeichnet, die eine Selbstrestriktion des Denkens darstellt und selbst gefährlich sein mag? Die religiösen Hoffnungen scheinen zu bleiben, ob Philosophie sie behandelt oder nicht – und wenn sie nicht philosophisch (also rational) behandelt werden dürfen, mögen sie dann erst recht irrational werden. Die Gefahr kann vielleicht besser dadurch eliminiert werden, dass Denken im gefährlichen Raum zu bleiben wagt, wobei es aber nicht mehr die richtige Erkenntnis der potenziell gefährlichen Gehalte vortäuscht. Philosophisches Denken soll keine Selbstrestriktionen aufbürden – es wäre genug, wenn es bescheiden wäre und keine Sicherheit mehr vorspielte. Adorno hat noch davon gesprochen, subjektive Erfahrung könne objektive Erkenntnis bringen (Adorno 2010, 74-93).[39] Ist es nicht diese gefährliche Behauptung, die abgebaut werden, wobei die kontemplative Erfahrung gerettet werden sollte?

Habermas macht Adornos "religiösen" Säkularismus zu einem postsäkularen Säkularismus. Ein anderer Weg von Adornos aporetischen "religiösen" Säkularismus zum Postsäkularismus hin wäre, die säkularistische Teilung zwischen Religion und Nicht-Religion zu verlassen, und das Bewusstsein davon, was unentbehrlich ist – und ihre erkenntnistheoretische Grundlage –, zu bewahren. Auf diese Weise würde man in den breiten postsäkularen Raum vorstoßen, der nicht mehr auf dem säkularistischen Kern beruht.[40]

Dr. Karel Hlaváček, Ostrava University / Charles University,
hlavacekarel[at]gmail.com

---

[38] Benedikt XVI beispielsweise hält Adorno für einen großen Philosophen, gerade wegen dessen offener Stellung zur religiösen Hoffnungen.

[39] Bei Adorno sind sicher auch Motive zu finden, die seinen Objektivismus stillen, wie etwa das Nicht-identische der Objekte, das respektiert werden muss, oder die Behauptung, Philosophie sei zwar ernst, "aber so ernst wieder auch nicht", weswegen sie der "Clownerie" ähnlich sei. (Adorno 1966, 24).

[40] Im Sinne von Barbieri wäre dieser Vorschlag als Bemühung um einen Übergang von der "öffentlichen Postsäkularität" zur "philosophischen Postsäkularität" zu verstehen (Barbieri 2015, 41-78).

Literaturverzeichnis

Adams, Nicholas. *Habermas and Theology*. Cambridge, New York: Cambridge University Press, 2006.

Adorno, Theodor und Max Horkheimer. *Dialektik der Aufklärung. Philosophische Fragmente*, Frankfurt am Main: Suhrkamp, 2000.

Adorno, Theodor W. *Minima Moralia. Reflexionen aus dem beschädigten Leben*. Frankfurt am Main: Suhrkamp, 1951.

Adorno, Theodor W. *Negative Dialektik*. Frankfurt am Main: Suhrkamp, 1966.

Adorno, Theodor W. *Philosophie und Gesellschaft. Fünf Essays*. Stuttgart: Reclam, 2010.

Adorno, Theodor. W. *Stichworte, Kritische Modelle II,* Frankfurt am Main: Suhrkamp 1969.

Barbieri, William. "Sechs Facetten der Postsäkularität", in Lutz-Bachmann, Matthias. (ed.). *Postsäkularismus. Zur Definition eines umstrittennen Begriffs*. Frankfurt am Main: Campus Verlag 2015, 41-78.

Brittain, Craig C. *Adorno and Theology*, London, New York: T&T Clark International, 2010.

Brieskorn, Norbert. "On the Attempt to Recall a Relationship", in Habermas, Jürgen et al. (ed.). *An Awareness of What is Missing. Faith and reason in a Post-Secular Age*. Cambridge, Malden: Polity, 2010, 24-35.

Calhoun, Craig. Mendieta, Eduardo. Van Antverpen, Jonathan (eds.). *Habermas and Religion*. Cambridge, Malden: Polity, 2013.

Calhoun, Craig. Jürgensmeyer, Mark. VanAntverpen, Jonathan. (eds.) 2011. *Rethinking Secularism*, Oxford, New York: Oxford University Press, 2011.

De Vries, Hent. *Minimal Theologies, Critiques of Secular Reason in Adorno&Lévinas*, Baltimore, London: The John Hopkins University Press, 2005.

Habermas, Jürgen et al. (ed.). *An Awareness of What is Missing. Faith and reason in a Post-Secular Age*. Cambridge, Malden: Polity, 2010.

Habermas, Jürgen. *Glauben und Wissen. Friedenspreis des deutschen Buchhandels*. 2001. Web. 20. Oktober 2017 < http://www.friedenspreis-des-deutschen-buchhandels.de/445722/>

Habermas, Jürgen. *Die Zukunft der menschlichen Natur. Auf dem Weg zu einer liberalen Eugenik?* Frankfurt am Main: Suhrkamp, 2002.

Habermas, Jürgen. *Zwischen Naturalismus und Religion*, Frankfurt am Main: Suhrkamp, 2005.

Habermas, Jürgen. *Kritik der Vernunft. Philosophische Texte, Band 5*. Frankfurt a. M.: Suhrkamp, 2009.

Habermas, Jürgen. *Nachmetaphysisches Denken II. Aufsätze und Repliken*. Berlin: Suhrkamp, 2012.

Habermas, Jürgen. *Zur Verfassung Europas. Ein Essay*. Frankfurt am Main: Suhrkamp, 2011.

Harrington, Austin. *Habermas and the Post-Secular Society*. In: *European Journal of Social Theory*, vol. 10, Nr. 4 (2007): 543-560.

Houseman, Tom. Auschwitz as Eschaton: Adorno's Negative Rewriting oft he Messianic in Critical Theory. *Millenium: Journal of International Studies* Vol 42, Nr. 1(2013): 155-176.

Johansen, Birgitte. "Post-secular Sociology. Modes, Possibilities, Challenges." In: *Approaching Religion* Vol 3, Nr. 1 (2013): 4-15.

Junker-Kenny, Maureen. *Habermas and Theology*. New York, London: T&T Clark International, 2011.

Luckmann, Thomas. *Die unsichtbare Religion*. Frankfurt am Main: Suhrkamp, 2014.

Lutz-Bachmann, Matthias. (Hrsg.). *Kritische Theorie und Religion*. Würzburg: Echter, 1997.

Lutz-Bachmann, Matthias. (Hrsg.). *Postsäkularismus. Zur Definition eines umstrittennen Begriffs*. Frankfurt am Main: Campus Verlag 2015.

McLennan, Gregor. "Towards Postsecular Sociology?" *Sociology* Vol. 41, Nr. 5, (2007): 857-870.

Münz-Koenen, Inge. *Konstruktion des Nirgendwo. Die Diskursivität utopischen Denkens bei Bloch, Adorno, Habermas*. Berlin: Akademie Verlag, 1997.

Pritchard, Elisabeth. A. Seriously, What Does "Taking Religion Seriously" Mean? *Journal of the American Academy of Religion* Vol 78, Nr. 4 (2010): 1087-1111.

Schiller, Hans Ernst. "Zergehende Transzendenz", in Lutz-Bachmann, Matthias. (Hrsg.). *Kritische Theorie und Religion*. Würzburg: Echter, 1997, 69-85.

Seel, Martin. *Adornos Philosophie der Kontemplation*. Frankfurt am Main: Suhrkamp, 2004.

Taylor, Charles. *A Secular Age*. Cambridge / London: Belknap Press of the Harvard University Press, 2007.

SUSANNE MOSER (Vienna)

A personalist versus a rationalist theory of virtues

Abstract

The purpose of this article is to make visible Max Scheler's great contribution to philosophical research on virtues and values, and to re-integrate it into the current discourse. Christoph Halbig's marginal reference to Scheler provides a good opportunity for this. Since both authors pursue completely different objectives, the question arises as to how much of Halbig's approach to a theory of action can be reconciled with Scheler's personalist understanding of virtue. While Halbig seeks criteria for assessing the actions of others, Scheler points to the empowerment supplied by virtue itself. The author argues that Scheler already anticipated some ideas, which has led to a new awareness of virtues in contemporary psychology.

Keywords: Max Scheler, Christoph Halbig, ethics, action theory, virtues, values, feelings

Introduction

In recent years, one can observe a revival of the concept of virtue, taking place not only in philosophical discussions, but also in moral psychology, theories of action, and economics. In increasingly complex situations, it becomes more and more important for people to have qualities of character that help them act appropriately. The ability and power to act well was originally defined under the concept of virtue. It was only later that virtue was reduced to morality, which led to its becoming increasingly obscure, if not disparaged. Max Scheler makes this clear when he speaks of virtue as an "old maid" – an analogy which was not entirely groundless, especially considering that, during the Victorian Age, the concept of virtue was reduced to chastity alone.

> And yet, in other times, for instance, in the heyday of the Middle Ages, as well as among the Hellenes and Romans before the Imperial Period, this old, rambling, toothless maid had been a most graceful, attractive and charming character. (Scheler, 1919, 13)

One often thinks of the term "virtue" as referring to a troublesome effort, and forgets that it originally meant a "blissful knowledge of the power of the good", something that goes far beyond fitness and capability (ibid. 14).

In today's public debates, virtue is not unlikely to provoke controversy. While some praise it as a major factor of *Authentic Happiness* (Seligmann 2002), others warn of the danger of virtue-terror (Sarazin 2014). Thus, the question arises as to what value virtue has at all, and where the limits of a virtue ethics lie.

In his book *Der Begriff der Tugend und die Grenzen der Tugendethik* (*The Notion of Virtue and the Limits of the Virtue Ethics*), published in 2013, Christoph Halbig argues that the full meaning of virtue for ethics can be understood only through an axiology of virtue. It is necessary to clarify "what virtues are, and what their value is" (Halbig 2013, 17). Hence, Halbig refers to Max Scheler, whose main concern had been the rehabilitation of virtues as values: "Undoubtedly, the focus of Scheler's argument is the effort to rehabilitate virtue as a central intrinsic value" (ibid, 66).

In the following, I aim to make visible Scheler's great contribution to philosophical research on virtues and values, and to re-integrate it into the current discourse. Halbig's marginal reference to Scheler provides a good opportunity for this. I shall point out that both authors pursue completely different objectives, which raises the question as to how much of Halbig's approach to a theory of action can be reconciled with Scheler's personalist understanding of virtue. While Halbig seeks criteria for assessing the actions of others, Scheler points to the empowerment supplied by virtue itself. In this context, I would like to show that Scheler already anticipated some ideas, which has led to a new awareness of virtues in contemporary psychology. Based on the comparison between Halbig and Scheler, the tension present in current discussions can be clarified: If virtue is not understood as a joyous self-empowerment, but as a possibility to judge others, it can become a kind of terror virtue. My reflections will be embedded in constant reference to Aristotle and his understanding of virtue.

Halbig's Rationalist approach to Virtues

Halbig's research on virtue is action-based. He is intent on determining whether an action is praiseworthy or not. Firstly, he finds a criterion for the assessment of actions: an action is virtuous when it is an appropriate response to an intrinsic value. For Halbig, virtues are "intrinsically valuable attitudes to other intrinsic values" (Halbig 2013, 18). To argue this, he approaches virtues from their opposite, from the perspective of vices. For Halbig, an appropriate answer on the issue of values cannot be obtained in this perspective. Because in the instances of vice, either the value is lacking, as in the case of indifference or recklessness, or the response rejects the value character of its objects, as in the case of malice. For example, someone was delighted by an evil deed, a sadistic or cruel man enjoyed the suffering of others, a cynic distorted the good he found in his environment, making it appear ridiculous and trying to unmask it as a subtle form of evil (ibid., 193).

The examples Halbig gives point to the need for emotional responsiveness. The virtuous person must have the needed sensitivity in order to at all be able to grasp certain values. However, the author leaves us in the dark as to how this is will come about. He also indicates that a demand or an appeal comes from the values we have grasped, resulting in the need for a particular reaction or response. The appropriateness of this reaction, Halbig believes, is the why the virtuous are admired and praised. The exercise of virtues deserves appreciation, in the sense that it represents "the appropriate answer to a real value" (ibid., 46), which, for its part, represents the "standard for the correctness of this reaction" (ibid., 44).

Halbig assumes that virtues are responses to values. For him, these values are touchstones and standards by which we orient our actions. Moreover, the virtuous person must respond in the correct way, which means he must respond appropriately to the given values. Halbig assumes that we do not invent values, but find them. Virtues are a kind of telescope with which we grasp these values.

We do not consider virtues as a headlamp that penetrates a world that would otherwise have no moral qualities at all; we consider them as a telescope and a source of energy that traces and strives, and is admirable for these reasons. (Copp/Sobel 2004, 552, cited after Halbig 2013, 361)

Halbig is a value realist. He sees virtues in terms of their ability to grasp values that are given – not invented or created by men. How exactly this is to be understood, he does not clarify. He is somewhat clearer as to his intentions: he wants to go beyond the scope of duties and into the area of value. He is looking for evaluation criteria for moral action, which cannot be comprehended in terms of the concept of duty (Halbig, 2013, 362). He believes that in virtue, he has found a concept that can criticize omission, "even if the law is not violated and duty is not unfulfilled" (ibid., 363). He elucidates this by the following example: whoever has decided to donate to a particular charity can fulfill the imperfect duty of charity. If he does not recognize the need of the neighbor, he cannot be accused for this lack as representing a violation of duty. He deserves criticism, however, because he has fallen short of the ideal of charity (ibid., 362).

A further criterion of whether or not an action is praiseworthy is its being guided by reasons based on values[1]: the "reasons for grand and for generous actions are both based on the value of the well-being of others" (Halbig 2013, 170). The honest man is characterized by orientation towards the value of truth. He will act in accordance with reasons such as, "this is simply wrong", "it is a pity that he has pretended to consent to the decision of the boss", "the truth must come to light" or "he should encourage his children to express their opinions openly" (ibid., 151). The examples that Halbig gives us are statements about something or someone, requests and appeals to do something. In all cases, an external assessment is made – in one case guided by an ideal; in the other, by certain reasons. The double meaning of virtues – as qualities of a person and as orientation points in the sense of an ideal, does not come into view at all.

In addition, Halbig underestimates the connection between emotions and values when he assumes that values provide reasons for virtuous praxis (Halbig 2013, 151). Here we are left with the impression that a person considers situations purely rationally in the light of values from which he derives reasons leading him to virtuous actions. This impression is strengthened by the fact that Halbig emphasizes the conceptual connection between the ethical virtues and the intellectual truths: an honest man must at the same time make sure that his convictions are really justified. In addition, if called on to do so, he must be able to defend his convictions against objections (ibid., 81).

But this is not always the case with values. Oftentimes, we are not aware of values, they lie like the hidden part of an iceberg, under the threshold of consciousness, and are only visible when they are violated. It that case, we react mostly emotionally. And even if we are aware of our values, we often fail to justify or explain them. When asked why truthfulness is good and lying is bad, an interviewee replied to this large-scale question, "I don't know. It just is. It's just so basic. I do not want to be bothered with challenging that. It's part of me. I don't know where it came from, but it's very important." (Bellah 1987, 27)

Halbig is convinced that Scheler would share his assumption that virtues are intrinsic values (Halbig 2013, 66). However, Halbig does not go further into Scheler's philosophy, but uses it to criticize certain philosophical positions, especially Thomas Hurka's assumption that there is an axiological subordination of the virtues to values.[2] For Halbig,

---

[1] Halbig's approach to virtues is based on investigations published in his book *Praktische Gründe und die Realität der Moral* (Practical Reasons and the Reality of Moral). There he comes to the conclusion that "practical reasons are generally based on values" (Halbig 2013, 170).

[2] "Hurka formulates this subordination by the so-called axiological principle of comperativity: 'The value of a virtuous attitude towards a good or an evil is always less than the 'positive or negative' value of this object itself.'"(Halbig 2013, 65)

Scheler attributes to the virtues an axiological superposition over their objects, as the experienced power has a higher value than that to which it empowers. The example of the cowardly soldier who is yet able to throw a hand grenade at the last moment, thereby saving his comrades, is revealing in this respect. The soldier, according to Halbig, has done the right thing, but is not virtuous, because he was not aware that he had the ability to risk his life for someone else (ibid., 61). Thomas Hurka, by contrast, sees this soldier as courageous, even if the act occurred "out of character". While Halbig points out that "the cowardly soldier who rescues his comrade has, indeed, acted out of character - and therefore cannot prove himself brave in the act. With Max Scheler it must be remembered that virtues are personal values, in so far as they represent directions of the (moral) person's 'moral' ability. The cowardly soldier lacks such a skill, and he cannot manifest it in the individual act." (ibid., 61) Halbig likewise seek a connection between the virtues and the person, but it does not become clear what he means by saying that virtues are "the perfections of a person" (ibid. 359). In fact, he is not interested in "the being of the person, but in her probation in action" (ibid., 361). The way of acting, he points out, is orientated to ideals, which open up a dimension of evaluation that goes beyond what is purely compulsory.

Scheler's personalist approach

In *Zur Rehabilitierung der Tugend,* Scheler regards virtue as a "*quality of the person himself*" (Scheler, 1919, p. 15).[3] Scheler argues that we very often consider virtue with regard to its usefulness for others: one calculates the advantage of the skills and abilities of a person, mostly depending on the context in which they are used, whether it be the family or the nation. Virtue, however, is not there for the "enjoyment of others, but [is] a free ornament of its bearer"[4] (ibid., 15). For Scheler, virtue is "a lively consciousness *of power for the good*, completely personal and individual" (ibid., 16)[5]. This self-empowerment, this "experienced power", is a greater good than that "to which" it empowers. As virtue grows, it always becomes easier to achieve for the virtuous person. "Goodness becomes beautiful by becoming easy."[6] (ibid., 17) Scheler accuses Kant of reducing virtue "to a mere effect of

---

[3] *The Rehabilitation of Virtue* has not yet been translated into English. All the translations in this article are mine. In the footnote, I give the respective German text.
[4] Die Tugend sei je doch nicht da für die "Nutznießung anderer, sondern ein freier Schmuck ihres Trägers."
[5] "Tugend hingegen ist als ein lebendiges *Machtbewusstsein zum Guten* ganz persönlich und individuell."
[6] "Das Gute wird schön, indem es leicht wird."

obliging willingness" (ibid., 16). In the moral law and duty, Kant sees only "non-personal surrogates for lacking virtues"[7] (ibid., 17).

It is no coincidence that Scheler published his essay *Zur Rehabilitierung der Tugend* together with his essay *Ressentiment* in the volume *Der Umsturz der Werte*.[8] Scheler's reference to Nietzsche is unmistakable. Like Nietzsche, Scheler is concerned with overcoming *ressentiment* and enabling self-empowerment. In contrast to Nietzsche, however, he sees in Christianity not a cause of *ressentiment* but a possibility for overcoming it. Virtue, which he understands in a Christian way as "the free gift of grace" (ibid., 15), is for Scheler the key to self-empowerment, and not, as in Nietzsche, an instrument of manipulation used to weaken others.

In *Formalism in Ethics and Non-Formal Ethics of Values,* Scheler develops his concept of virtue, which is in contrast to the formal ethics of Kant. Scheler argues that Kant understands virtue only as "the *sediment* of individual dutiful acts" (Scheler 1973, p. 28). But we cannot speak of duty unless we are able to do what we should do. "The to-be-able-to concerned *precedes* any idea of duty." (ibid., p. 28) For Scheler, virtue is a foundation of the moral value of *all* moral actions. The theory of virtue precedes the theory of duty (Scheler, 1973, p. 28). The Kantian moral law and duty are only imperfect surrogates for missing virtues. Scheler rejects Kant's view that one can speak of virtues only when they are connected with sacrifices: "Kant makes the moral value of an action dependent on its *cost*, on the *sacrifices* made by the one who acts." (ibid., 228) For Scheler, Kant is the victim of a kind of value-illusion based on *ressentiment*, i.e., to hold that something is more valuable because it requires more effort, and more labour to achieve (ibid., 228). The morally superior person is, in any case, the one who achieves these contents with the least trouble, and who has the least resistance to do good. "He who has the least resistance against the good is the best." (ibid., 230)

For Scheler, however, an additional aspect of virtue, besides the to-be-able-to, is the ought. One can speak of virtue only if there is an ought, otherwise "there would be no virtue but solely 'proficiency'" (ibid., 206). Virtue is not the "aptitude for anything, but willing and doing something that is given and experienced as ideally obligatory" (ibid., 238). Scheler distinguishes between the ideal ought and the ought that contains a claim or an order. "Whenever we speak of 'duty' or 'norms', we are concerned not with an 'ideal' ought, but with a specification of it as something that is *imperative*." (ibid., p. 203) This may be the inner command of self-obligation, or external acts such as "command", "advice", or

---

[7] "Das sogenannte Sittengesetz und die Pflicht sind hingegen nur unpersönliche Surrogate für mangelnde Tugenden."
[8] The overthrow of values

"recommendation" (ibid., 205). Thus, speaking about virtues, we must be aware of both their sides, the "to-be-able-to" and the oughtness:

> It is from the situation in which something is given as an (ideal) ought and, at the same time, as something that 'can' be done, that the concept of '*virtue*' springs. Virtue is the immediately experienced *power* to do something that ought to be done. (ibid., 205)

For Scheler all oughtness must have a foundation in values (ibid., 82). The ought, on the one hand, can be based on the "insight into objective values" (ibid., 490), but also on the "evidential insight" into the "individual value-essence" of the person (ibid., 489). For Scheler, the "person-value is higher than all values of things, organizations and community." (ibid., XXIV) The human person is the bearer of the values of virtues as well as of the values of the person himself (ibid., 100). The peculiar individual value-content of the person is the basis on which a consciousness of an individual "ought" is built, "the evidential knowledge of a 'good-in-itself' but precisely in the sense of a "good-in-itself-for-*me*" (ibid., 490). The ought comes to this person as a "'call', no matter if this 'call' is addressed to others or not" (ibid., 490). Scheler emphasizes that there is in no case a neglect of universal values, for "interpenetration of universally valid moral values with those of individual validity can yield complete evidence of the good-in-itself" (ibid., 493). According to Scheler, all false individualism is excluded by the fact that there is an original co-responsibility of each person for the whole (the solidarity principle). Scheler thus places the concern for the community "at the living *center of the individual person*" (Scheler, 1916, XII).

For Scheler, virtue is necessarily connected with an appeal directed towards the person, and which contains a certain ought. The essential point is that the person concerned must be able to comply with this requirement. Virtue is the guarantee that the person can actually realize what he/she is called upon to do. Scheler's approach is personalist inasmuch as the person is the highest authority as to what is good for him/her; yet he/she does not fall into subjectivism. Rather, Scheler is concerned with the mediation between universally valid and individual values, which leads him to the conclusion that I have to realize the "good-in-itself- for-me" (Scheler, 1973, p. 534). In this sense, virtue is the ability to fulfill what is given to me as a personal "ought". Thus, virtues empower us to respond to the individual call we receive.

Emotions

Halbig mentions that the virtue of compassion is an emotion, but he is not further interested in the connection between virtues, emotions and values (Halbig 2013, 32). In contrast, Scheler stresses the importance of feelings and emotions; for him, the being of feelings and emotions is the "'sign' 'of the *being* and the *non-being* of values'" (Scheler, 1973, 355). Emotional life differs for Scheler according to the different levels of values: feelings and sensations are at the level of the pleasant, vital emotions at the level of the vital, and emotions, as responses to values, are at the cultural level. We are happy or sad about something, touched by or excited about something. If we are happy, angry or sad about something, this "about" indicates that the objects here are not simply comprehended, but are in front of me "charged with value-predicates, which are given in feeling" (ibid., 258). Importantly, for Scheler these value-qualities are given in a special way by intentional feeling, which is totally different from mere feeling-states. This kind of "feeling originally intends its own kind of objects, namely values." (ibid., 258) Value-qualities demand certain qualities in the emotional reactions of response. If these demands are not fulfilled, then we suffer: for example, we are sad when we cannot look forward to a worthy event, or cannot mourn as required by the death of a loved one. In order to understand the life of the psyche, one has to study this interconnection of meaning between value-complexes and emotional reactions. Scheler speaks here of the appropriateness of emotions. Both "too much" and "too little" may be out of place. For Scheler, the appropriate reaction depends on the concrete situation, which has to be studied through empirical research. For him, the understanding of the life of the psyche life belongs to the realm of psychology, not philosophy. In contrast to the Aristotelian understanding of virtue, Scheler does not speak of virtues at this level of emotions. At this point, it seems to me important to refer both to contemporary research on emotions and to the Aristotelian point of view.

In contemporary philosophical research, there are many discussions on the connection between emotions and values (Moser 2014). In *The Rationality of Emotion*, Ronald de Sousa shows that emotions are rational inasmuch as they are appropriate responses to axiological qualities. In my comparison between De Sousa and Max Scheler, I point out that Scheler understands emotions as appropriate responses to value-qualities, given by intentional feeling, whereas De Sousa assumes that the emotions are direct answers to value-qualities. Kevin Mulligan has recently supported Scheler's viewpoint (Moser 2015, 234).

Halbig's understanding of virtues as appropriate responses to values seems to me to belong to philosophical research on emotions, since he often connects virtues with emotions. I would like to quote one of his examples.

> "The fact that someone deliberately expresses an untruth is undoubtedly a suitable object of certain attitudes (anger, willingness to disclose the lie, etc.) of an honest man. (ibid., 54)

He gives us here the example of anger as a response to the felt violation of the value of honesty.

Aristotle supposes a fundamental connection to exist between virtues and emotions. He emphasizes that the virtue of a human character is in many ways bound to emotions (1178a15). One has to deal appropriately with the existing emotions. Aristotle does not reject them; on the contrary, he points out that it is very important to have emotions, i.e., to have fear in case of danger or to be angry when we are disregarded. Fearlessness would lead to foolhardiness, and the lack of anger would indicate weakness. The emotion shows us something important, it serves as a warning signal. Someone who has no fear would react foolhardily and would not long survive. For Aristotle it is very important to be emotionally sensitive. We are responsible for developing our emotional life by developing the appropriate sensitivity and responsiveness need for proper reaction. This is what Aristotle points out when he says,

> Speaking generally, it is not the case, as the rest of the world think, that reason is the principle and guide to virtue, but rather the feelings. (Aristotle 2015, 1206b17-19)

In *Magnia Moralia*, Aristotle points out that the impulses must come from affectivity. That is why it is so important that the feelings be in the right condition. The rational element, that is, reason or logos, is then the instance, which gives the consent. If, on the other hand, the impulses originate only from reason, feelings do not necessarily follow, but often oppose.

> Wherefore a right disposition of the feelings seems to be the principle that leads to virtue rather than the reason. (ibid., 1206b25-27)

Thus, Aristotle does not see a general struggle going on between reason and feeling, as does Kant, but embraces emotionality, which for him is oriented towards the good. He emphasizes that it is very important to cultivate the right feelings, not to reject them. To have feelings at the right times, with reference to the right objects, towards the right people, with the right motive, and in the right way, is what is both intermediate and best, and this is a characteristic of virtue.

While Aristotle assumes that virtues - at least to a certain extent – can be achieved through education and habit, Scheler understands virtue as a kind of reversal and transformation of the whole person. The transformation of the person, which takes place through virtue, is regarded by Scheler as "the extreme opposite of all habit" (1919, 14). In this sense, Wolfhart Henckmann points out that Scheler has a "trans-ethical understanding of virtue" (Henckmann 1998, 128).

Scheler assumes that a person's constitution is decisive for the way the person experiences the world. At the value-level of the person, Scheler refers to spiritual feelings that are no longer conditioned by value-complexes exterior to the person. "Bliss and despair appear to be the correlates of the moral value of our personal being." (Scheler 1973, 343) It is the being and the self-value of the person himself that is the foundation of bliss and despair. In despair, there lies at the core of our personal existence an emotional "No!"; in bliss, an emotional "Yes!" These spiritual feelings, which Scheler distinguishes from purely psychic feelings, take possession of the whole of our being. The problem is that these spiritual feelings cannot be produced or merited by our conduct. Thus, they are trans-ethical, in the same way as the virtues. In *Zur Rehabilitierung der Tugend,* Scheler speaks similarly of virtues. These are the inner wealth and abundance of a person, from whom they emanate like light. They cannot be produced but are "the free gift of grace". We can only be open to them (Scheler, 1919, 16).

At this point, I would like to refer to a recent study in positive psychology that involves an exploration of positive emotions, as well as positive character traits; the latter include the virtues and everything that strengthens human virtues, which in turn stimulate positive emotions (Seligman 2002). In his book *Authentic Happiness. Using the New Positive Psychology to Realize Your Potential for Lasting Fulfillment,* Seligman complains that the focus in literature has always been on negative emotions. He sees one of the reasons for this in the culture of suspicion, which goes back to Freud, among others, and involves the widespread assumption that behind a person's every good deed there must be some hidden negative motivation. However, in research data, there is not the slightest indication that human strength and virtue stem from negative motives. Rather, the strengthening of the virtues not only involves positive emotions, such as confidence, hope, or trust, but leads to permanent fulfillment. Seligman assumes something like a transformative force in virtues, which is not only situated at the level of action, but on the level of the person. Believing that happiness and joy can be achieved at the level of action, without developing virtues, leads people to starve in the midst of abundance.

In a sense, Scheler's approach is similar to Seligman's. Both locate virtue at the level of the person, no matter how great their differences may be. Both emphasize the power that emanates from virtue and its great importance for a life in abundance. Both are for the strengthening of the positive emotions and both are convinced that only in this way is a sustainable overcoming of pathological phenomena possible. Scheler could thus easily be regarded as the precursor of a positive psychology

Orientation towards the Good

For Halbig, the virtuous person is in a continuous maturing process in his orientation towards the good (Halbig 2013, 362). Through education and exemplary behaviour, we learn to assign appropriate values to certain good things. Thus, the reference to the good comes into being through our relation to things that are good. The appropriate appraisal of basic good things is not due to a reflection on them, but rather to the experience of exemplary and virtuous ways of dealing with them (ibid., 365). The moral development of children does not depend on the practice of abstract duties, but on living models, by which they can orient themselves. Here, Halbig is very close to Aristotle, for whom the role model of the good man plays a central role in capturing the good: for those things are valuable and pleasant, that are such to the good man (*spoudaios*) (Aristotle 1176b25). Aristotle points out that it is important to be virtuous even in order to be wise, because only the virtuous person choses the right things, which wisdom helps him to realize (ibid., 1145a5). Thus, only the good man can be wise, for it is impossible to be practically wise without moral virtue (Aristotle, 1144a35). Just as different things seem valuable to boys and to men, so too should they be different for bad men and good men.

Halbig, like Aristotle, emphasizes the connection between good things and the good. The example adduced by Halbig suggests that children get their orientation towards the good by learning how to deal with good things, which are presented to them as good and desirable by their parents. Aristotle also points out that only the role model and the virtuous can show us what we should strive for. There is, however, a great difference between the Aristotelian ethics of good things and Scheler's ethics of values. Scheler rejects, similarly to Kant, any ethics of good things and purposes, and any ethics based on inductive experience, whether this experience be historical, psychological, or biological (Scheler 1973, 45). Whether someone acts in a morally righteous way or not depends, according to Scheler, on that person's values. The moral differences between individuals lie not in the purposes they intend or in the goods they choose, but in the value-contents and their relations, which "form the possible field for the positing of purposes" (Scheler 1973, 42). The person of high moral standing follows in his/her inner conations an order of preference oriented towards the objective order of non-formal value-ranks. "This order of preference becomes (...) the inner rule of automatism of conation itself." (ibid., 43) From what has been said so far, it is clear that Scheler sees the morally good and virtuous in the realization of the higher – if possible, the highest – value of the objective order (Schleissheimer 2003, 127).

In order to actually realize this moral good, one must have the ability to do so. Here Scheler refers to Martin Luther, who was convinced, that "man can will the good and can do good (...) only if he possesses the consciousness of the power and the ability for the good" (Scheler 1973, 236). On the other hand, we have the peculiar consciousness of an obligation to do something when we become aware of an ability and a power. Scheler points out that through every singly moral act of positive value, the ability for the good increases:

> In other words, there is an increase in what we designated as the virtue of the person (which is very different from the habituation and practice of actions related to the virtue in question), which is the experienced power to realize the good that ought to be." (ibid., 537)

The peculiarity of this ability is for Scheler manifest in the special kinds of contentment, joy, and pleasure that we take in the mere to-be-able-to-do-something (ibid. 232). "Every preferring of a higher value to a lower one is accompanied by an increase in the depth of the positive feeling." (ibid., 356) Every preferring of a higher value to a lower one makes a subsequent similar preferring easier.

Virtue and Happiness

Halbig assumes it is very difficult to be both virtuous and happy. He emphasizes that Nietzsche held "not without reason, the thesis that we are actually the victims of our virtues" (Halbig 2013, 242). It is true that virtues can lead to happiness; however, the sacrifices often required of the virtuous can make it impossible for them to lead a life of happiness (ibid., 358).

For Scheler, on the contrary, happiness is the root and the source of virtue. "Happiness is therefore in no way a 'reward for virtue', nor is virtue the means to reach blissfulness" (ibid. 359). Spinoza had already seen this connection, when he asserted, "Blissfulness is not the reward of virtue; it is virtue itself." (ibid., 235)

In my opinion, we can understand Scheler's concept of virtue only by referring to his concept of love and happiness, which he developed in *Ressentiment*. In this work, he points out the large difference in the "directions of its movement" between the Ancient and Christian views of love (Scheler 2010, 30). While love in Antiquity was understood as a striving from the lower to the higher, from the imperfect to the more perfect, love in Christianity is conceived of as a gift of God and thus as "a source of power" (Moser 2014, 25). Here there is a "reversal in the movement of love" (Scheler 2010, 31). The criterion of love is that the noble stoops to the vulgar, the healthy to the sick, the rich to the poor, the Messiah to the sinner. There is no longer any "highest good" independent of, or beyond, the act and movement of love. In my opinion, Scheler equates virtue with this power we obtain from

God's love, which enables us to act in a way that makes us, and the people around us, happy. For Scheler, virtue is not a bulwark against negative emotions, but the enabling power towards the good. Thus, it is no accident that Scheler mentions Spinoza, who assumes that the more the soul rejoices in divine love, the more power it has over its affects, and the less it will suffer from bad affects.

Thus, because it enjoys this divine love, the soul has the power to inhibit bad desires (Spinoza 1994, 296). Scheler concludes that one should live a life of joy and not prohibition. Instead of "you shall not," it would be better to point out, "you can." Hence, we should not try to reform a drunkard by means of admonitions and prohibitions:

> We can accomplish the reform by encouraging him to develop new interests as well as his latent faculties, by pointing to the positive aims of life in whose pursuance a drunkard's vice disappears and is, as it were, covered up. (Scheler 1973, 235)

In this respect too, Scheler can be considered a pioneer of positive psychology.

Conclusions

Both Halbig and Scheler regard virtue as an intrinsic value, as a value appreciated for its own sake, and not because of its usefulness for some other purpose. While Halbig mostly argues in terms of action, Scheler pursues a personalist approach. For Scheler, the virtues are values of the person and occupy the highest place in the person's value order. Halbig understands virtues as appropriate attitudes with regard to other, intrinsic values. The answer to the questions as to what values are and whether there is such a thing as a value order, he leaves open, to be given through a general theory of values. Although Halbig is convinced that Scheler would agree with Halbig's own approach to values, we are confronted with two completely different approaches here. Scheler's considerations of virtue are embedded in a comprehensive theory of value, while Halbig does not really attempt to clarify the concept of value. This is evident particularly in the problem as to how we can grasp values, how they are given to us.

Both Halbig and Scheler are value realists. They assume that values are not constituted or invented by the subject, but are detected and found. But while Scheler develops a subtle value-acquisition theory in which he assumes that we have a certain kind of feeling that opens up values to us, this topic remains completely unclear in Halbig. The latter offers grounds for the assumption that virtues make us grasp values when he uses the metaphor of the telescope helping us to discover values. Virtue, however, is not merely a means of grasping values, but a special constitution of the person comprising the person's whole striving power. While Scheler develops a differentiated theory of emotional life, in which the connection between feelings and values becomes visible, Halbig does not really bring into discussion the role of emotions for the acquisition of values. Although he often refers to emotional responses in his examples, the connection between emotions and values is not further investigated, the way it is in current philosophical research on emotions.

Halbig explicitly argues that Scheler shared the basic assumptions of his theory, understanding virtues as attitudes intrinsically valuable with regard to other intrinsic values. But even Halbig's choice of conceptuality indicates that he wants something different than Scheler. While Scheler wants to point out that virtue is a source of power to realize the values that are important for the person, Halbig wants to develop assessment criteria for human attitudes. In virtues, he believes to have found the criteria for judging behaviour beyond moral duty. However, since the criteria of an objective hierarchy of values are lacking here, there is a risk this will lead to moralization and virtue terror. Going through the world with the disposition of criticizing the behaviour of others, but without having a clear value-order, can lead to a diffuse moral overload.

For Scheler virtues are qualities of the person, while in Halbig's understanding, virtues are attitudes of the person towards other values. He is not particularly interested in the person per se. Therefore, it is difficult for him to explain the relationship between person and virtue, and to understand the perfection of the person, to which he refers at the end of his book. The understanding of virtue as attitude, and the metaphor of the telescope, suggest that Halbig understands virtue as an ability to orient oneself towards an ideal, and not as a particular quality of the person him/herself. In my view, the greatest difference between Halbig on the one hand, and Scheler and Aristotle on the other, lies in the understanding of the latter two that the virtues are, in a way, transformers that encompass the entire human being and change it sustainably. For Scheler, the essence of virtue lies in the development of the whole person, in the realization of his/her individual calling.

While Halbig understands the virtues as a telescope serving to discern ideals or values far removed from us, for Scheler, they are an expression of the inner abundance of the person. Here Scheler is close to Aristotle, who equates virtue and goodness in a person. What we do depends on our goodness. This is why Aristotle gives so much weight to education and role models. Virtue is anchored in the person, and not in an ideal. Whereas Aristotle posits virtues at all levels of striving, Scheler locates them only in the person. While Aristotle, in a perspective "from below", understands the virtues as the right way of dealing with emotions, Scheler aims to change the entire person "from above". Both emphasize the great importance of emotionality for the virtues.

Aristotle sees the irrational part of the soul as the leader of the virtues and therefore points out the importance of the right kind of emotional constitution. Scheler, by contrast, assumes there is a special way of grasping the values, which is through intentional feeling. A person's virtue is, for Scheler, a kind of gift, a bestowed grace that empowers the virtuous person to accomplish the good. Scheler's approach to virtues is embedded in his comprehensive metaphysics, in which an inner connection exists between the divine, bliss, and the virtues. Halbig, on the other hand, proceeds from a rational theory of action, in which values are the sources of reasons.

For Scheler, as for Aristotle, virtue is connected with a joyous feeling, i.e., a blissful awareness of one's consciousness and power to do what is good. Both Aristotle and Scheler are interested in the person's reaching the highest possible level of values, connected with the highest kind of happiness. For Scheler, this form of life is totally personal and individual, and can vary widely from person to person. His interest is not so much in the case of a well-functioning polis; on the contrary, he desires a form of society in which the individual good can co-exist with the good of society and with the in-itself good.

While Aristotle assumes that virtue is acquired through habituation and education, divine grace plays a role here, according to Scheler. Halbig follows Aristotle in also assuming virtues are acquired through education and role models. By contrast, he regards the connection between virtue and happiness as problematic. He sees the joy associated with the exercise of virtues as connected with the sacrifices they demand. Thus, he follows Nietzsche's view that virtues are more useful to the others than to their bearer. However, Aristotle and Scheler, quite independently of their metaphysical conceptions, can be seen as precursors of positive psychology in their assertion that virtues promote positive emotions, which help us not only to lead a happy and long life, but also to have a protective shield against fate in difficult times.

Dr. Susanne Moser, Institut für Axiologische Forschungen, Wien /
Karl Franzens-Universität Graz, susanne.moser[at]univie.ac.at

References

Aristotle. *Magna Moralia*. Trans. by R.W. Ross, Oxford: Clarendon Press, 1915.

Bellah, Robert, Richard Madsen, and William Sullivan. *Gewohnheiten des Herzens. Individualismus und Gemeinsinn in der amerikanischen Gesellschaft*. Köln: Bund-Verlag 1987.

Copp, David, and David Sobel. "Morality and virtue: An assessment of some recent work in virtue ethics," Ethics, vol. 114, no. 3, 2004, pp. 514–554.

Halbig, Christoph. *Der Begriff der Tugend und die Grenzen der Tugendethik*. Berlin: Suhrkamp 2013.

Henckmann, Wolfhart. *Max Scheler*. München: Beck 1998.

Moser, Susanne. "Vom Wert der Liebe", *Labyrinth*, Vol.16, Nr.2 (2014): 20-47.

Moser, Susanne. "Werte und Gefühle: Max Scheler und Ronald der Sousa im Vergleich", in Brigitte Buchhammer (Hrsg.). *Neuere Aspekte in der Philosophie: aktuelle Projekte von Philosophinnen am Forschungsstandort Österreich*. Wien: Axia Academic Publishers 2015, 213-246.

Sarazin, Thilo. *Der neue Tugendterror. Über die Grenzen der Meinungsfreiheit in Deutschland*. München: Deutsche Verlags-Anstalt, 2014.

Scheler, Max. "Zur Rehabilitierung der Tugend", in ders. *Vom Umsturz der Werte*. Leipzig: Der neue Geist Verlag, 1919, 12 - 42.

Scheler, Max. *Formalism in Ethics and Non-Formal Ethics of Values*. Translated by Manfred S. Frings and Roger L. Funk. Evanston: North Western University Press, 1973.

Scheler, Max. *Ressentiment*. Translated by Louis A. Coser. Marquette Studies in Philosophy, 5th printing, 2010.

Schleissheimer, Bernhard. *Ethik heute. Die Frage nach dem guten Leben*. Würzburg: Königshausen & Neumann, 2003.

Seligman, Martin. *Authentic Happiness: Using the New Positive Psychology to Realize Your Potential for Lasting Fulfillment*. New York: The Free Press, 2002.

Spinoza, Baruch. *A Spinoza Reader: The Ethics and Other Works*. Ed. and trans. by Edwin Curley. Princenton, NJ: Princeton University Press, 1994.

www.ingramcontent.com/pod-product-compliance
Lightning Source LLC
Chambersburg PA
CBHW081331230426
43667CB00018B/2895